What readers are saying:

"A powerful book to find courage to live life intentionally and with meaning. Patrick's life story is inspiring and his learnings can be applied to everyone. Through humanity, vulnerability and charisma, Patrick helps us reflect and find ways to face challenges and reinvent oneself. Worth reading!"
Barbara Martin Coppola, CEO of Decathlon, INSEAD MBA

"An inspiring life story of making difficult professional and life changes. Patrick has assembled a worthy collection of life and career lessons, with plenty of humor, humility and vulnerability, and turned this into a practical set of insights and exercises that are really helpful for startups and larger company CEOs and executives alike."
Matthijs Glastra, CEO of Novanta (NASD: NOVT), INSEAD MBA

« Leap » by Patrick Mork is a must-read if you consider your next career move and wonder where to start! I truly enjoyed the combination of the author's inspiring life trajectory and the many tips and exercises you can apply to take a deep dive and start your own self-reflection.

A very authentic and meaningful story, with life's highs and lows and all the learnings that come with it. An inspiring introspection with resilience and courage to take a new career path. A motivating and positive book that will give you the boost you need to leap!
Magali Depras, Chief Strategy & Corporate Social Responsibility Officer at TC Transcontinental, INSEAD MBA

Patrick writes a detailed guide that will have you reexamining your career and how you conduct yourself, whether you are a C suite executive or reporting into one. He uses deeply personal life experiences (some very painful) to illustrate how you can take these experiences and apply them using the tools he provides. The book is well worth the time to read but more importantly, it is worth the effort to employ these tools into your own career.
Rob Dyer, Chief Operating Officer at Capcom

Part-autobiography, part self-help manual, "Step Back and Leap" is a captivating read from the get go. Patrick Mork has lived a rich, varied life and he's a strong storyteller, which might be why I found myself racing through this book in a single day. Mork is both open and unapologetic about his failures and successes alike, which makes the book refreshing and insightful. He articulates the classic problems of Marketing in Silicon Valley (and more broadly in tech), drives home the importance of purpose, and layers in a series of useful tips and exercises he's developed in his latest career as an executive/ corporate team coach. And when he takes you on the white knuckle ride of the Sequoia Century, you'll be hanging on the edge of your seat.

As a three-time CMO on the cusp of (exciting) career change, I found myself scribbling down some of the bolder pieces of advice to take on my next journey. In the end, you may not agree with every square inch of Mork's approaches and philosophy, but you will exit the book entertained and inspired to be bolder in seeking your own truth.

Leela Srinivasan, CEO at Parity, Board Member at Upwork

"The sustained narrative, of both your life and your career, moved me to tears on several occasions. If this book does not inspire others to live better, be better, lead better and just generally work harder on themselves, then nothing else will. You have created a treasure!

Claire Harbour, Executive coach, Former GM at LVMH, INSEAD MBA

I've known and worked closely with Patrick for over a decade and know that many would benefit from this book which is a result of his deep self reflections and focus on constant, transformational change.

Congratulations Patrick! Thank you for letting me be a small part of this amazing journey.

Brad Bao, Founder and Chairman at LIME

Step Back and LEAP

9 Keys to unlock your life and make change happen

BY

PATRICK MORK

with Richard Beynon

"To my parents, my ex wife, my amazing children Raphael and Natasha and my close friends for helping me become the man, father and leader I am today."
—Patrick Mork

TABLE OF CONTENTS

Introduction
EMBRACE CHANGE

Change is the only constant in life.

—HERACLITUS

It came like a punch out of nowhere straight into the solar plexus. "As of today," my boss said evenly, "you're no longer an employee at Course Hero."

The day had begun badly, and I can't say getting fired improved things. Of course, I fought back for a minute or two, but I knew it wasn't possible to change the mind of Andrew Grauer, my 30-something boss, and I could also hear the desperation in my voice, which I didn't like one bit. Desperation in Silicon Valley is not unusual – but it's not something you ever want to hang on the line.

Also, I'm not being entirely honest when I say the decision to give me the boot came out of nowhere. There'd been signs, there'd been omens. I'd screwed up in one or two instances, and hiring the right team of people had been challenging and gone slower than I'd expected.

The day, it was 6 March 2017, had, as I said, started badly.

As usual, I'd begun with a ride to work on my Cannondale Super Six. It's only five miles from my apartment in Redwood City to Course Hero's offices on Seaport Boulevard but, already, at 7.30 am, traffic was starting to build as thousands of commuters headed for their individual hives, like so many bees reporting for duty. Just as I was.

By the time I crossed the overpass over Highway 101, which cuts from north to south, connecting San Jose to the Bay Area and San Francisco to the north, and despite the chill of early spring, I was drenched in sweat. This was due not only to my furiously pumping legs. Deeper than that was my anxiety about the job, about my performance, and about my future.

I swooped down from the overpass and passed the local county jail beyond it.

My mind was on fire. These were the facts: I had been behind on some projects. I'd struggled to hire a team around me to scale up our efforts and I had said one or two things that were, frankly, not politically correct, given the delicate environment at tech companies at the time (think Uber and the ousting of Travis Kalanick and you get the picture). But I forced myself to think positively about the day. I was on the verge of solving the problem of assembling a great team. I just had to make final offers to some terrific candidates. Our marketing metrics were looking great and the re-branding, which I'd helped lead, had gone really well. I was highly unlikely to offend anyone again with foolish compliments on their appearance.

Fuck it, I could do this.

A few minutes later, I locked my bike outside the gym.

And then I was in the shower, letting the hot jets of water wash away, not just the grime and the sweat of my ride in, but also my fears and trepidation. All I needed were a couple more weeks and I'd be past the worst. My team would be fully staffed, I'd be completely up to speed, ahead of the curve, rarin' to go. I just needed two more weeks.

All day, I was infused with a strong sense of purpose. I set up meetings, reviewed resumes, interviewed job candidates and was really impressed with a couple of applicants fresh from Cornell, like our CEO, and Stanford. I checked progress on half a dozen projects. And I fired off a letter letting a really hot – in the professional sense – applicant know that she'd landed the job she'd applied for.

At around five that afternoon, I got a Slack message from Andrew telling me that, instead of meeting in our usual venue for our weekly update, I should join him in a conference room on the far side of the building. I acknowledged the change, grabbed my laptop, and headed off.

Andrew had been joined by Course Hero's CFO, Steve van Horne. On the table in front of him lay a plain manila envelope. As my eye fell on that, I felt like the air had, in an instant, been sucked from the room.

Because I knew what it meant.

"Have a seat," Andrew said evenly.

I sat and watched the freight train barrel down the track towards me, its headlight flaring so brightly I could barely focus on anything else.

And, then, that right jab sank into my gut.

"Let me get right to the point, Patrick. We've lost trust in your ability to lead the marketing team. We've found some of your decisions questionable. And, so, we regret to say that this will be your last day at Course Hero."

I stared at Andrew in utter disbelief. Then my mouth opened and the clichés tumbled out. "Come on, guys, this can't be possible."

"I'm sorry, Patrick, but—" Andrew began, but I hadn't finished.

"I realize things haven't been perfect, but we have an amazing pipeline of candidates for the team. Just this afternoon, we were going to extend an offer to this woman from Walmart.com who's going to—"

"Patrick," Steve interrupted.

"Our email numbers and open rates have been great," I pressed on, "and we've had a record number of scholarship applicants. I just need more time—"

But they would have none of it.

"The decision's been made, Patrick. We're not going to reverse it. You know that."

I switched tack. "Okay, okay, if you're going to let me go," fire me, kill me, "then at least tell me why. Give me the specifics. I need to make sense of it all." I realized I was burbling, but I couldn't stop myself.

They just sat there, impassive as two Easter Island moai. Eventually, when I ran out of steam, Steve said: "Patrick, in my experience, it's better, in these situations, to avoid questioning the past and look to the future."

"I invited Steve here to discuss the terms of your termination agreement." Andrew slid the envelope across the table. His hand was shaking. That was something, at least. Then he stood and walked out quickly and I was left to discuss the terms of my execution with Steve.

I took a longer route home that afternoon to give myself time to think. Look to the future, Steve had advised. How the fuck could I do that, confronted, as I was, with an unpalatable, undigestible truth: I'd been fired twice in just eighteen months. Yes, I hadn't mentioned that, had I?

Two years before, in the aftermath of my divorce, I'd joined a small startup as Chief Marketing Officer. The company provided technology to help advertisers measure their mobile advertising spend, calculate the return on investment of this spend and, so, help them make the most of their budgets. I'd taken the job because I needed the money and I liked working out of San Francisco – but I wasn't wild about it, or about the company, or about the micro-manager of a CEO who would occasionally sit at my desk and edit our blog posts before they went live. Four months into my time there, he'd fired me over the phone. The experience had left a bitter taste in my mouth, but it hadn't had much effect on my self-confidence.

Losing the Course Hero gig was different. When I started out, I loved the company and its products. Course Hero operates one of the world's largest platforms of study supplements for students in high school and college. Their aim is to help students ask and answer any question. The way they do this is by crowdsourcing study documents from students all over the world, across thousands of different classes.

It was the sort of product I had reckoned could make a real difference to the lives and the learning experience of literally millions of students around the world. I *believed* in it. It wasn't about helping companies increase their ROI by a couple of percentage points. It was about *helping* people.

And, so, being kicked off the team at a company that helped improve people's lives, sucked big time.

I was riding into a cold wind for much of the way home. I only realized, on a wide sweeping turn, that tears of shame and humiliation were streaming down my cheeks. I brushed ineffectually at them with the heel of one hand.

The streets in Redwood City were fairly empty at this time of the evening. The sun had set and the chill of early spring had set in. I was half-blinded by my tears and distracted by the thoughts of my situation. I gripped the handlebars even more tightly and put my head down, cycling maniacally from one cone of light, thrown by the overhead streetlights, to the next.

Waves of self-pity overwhelmed me. I'd been so close. A couple of weeks was all I'd needed to prove myself, my abilities, my worth.

Damn it to hell.

I was on the final straight along Alameda de las Pulgas to home, head down, legs pumping.

And then, I heard a furiously honking horn. I looked up. Oh, my god! A garbage truck had turned into the avenue ahead of me and I was heading straight for it at a million miles an hour. Savagely, I wrenched the handlebars to one side and careened, half skidding, into the side road that led to my house, missing the rear end of the monstrous truck by inches.

I brought the bike to a stop. I was shaking. Every part of me was shaking. I closed my eyes and took a series of deep breaths. If I'd hit the vehicle, I'd have been wiped out: certainly crippled, probably killed.

My heartrate slowed. So close. Jesus Christ.

And then a thought occurred to me. Perhaps it wouldn't have been that bad. If I hadn't heard the garbage truck's frantic honking, if I hadn't looked up at the last possible moment, if I'd smashed into the back of the truck, merging nerve and sinew, muscle and bone with unforgiving steel... Admittedly, there'd have been one brief spasm of pain, but then, in all probability, oblivion. Permanent and welcome oblivion.

No more agonizing over my career and its collapse.

No more alimony payments.

Not another day of feeling racked by confusion, anger, frustration, humiliation.

Just serene oblivion, the endless void...

And then something rose up in me in protest. This wasn't who I was, a loser, a quitter, ready to give up in the face of failure. Yes, things were bad, perhaps they'd never been worse – but change was always possible, wasn't it? For a moment, though, as I contemplated the sheer scale of the changes I'd have to make to claw my way out of this pit, my heart faltered.

Then a memory flashed through my mind. Was this the most mortifying experience I'd ever had? Nearly 40 years before, I'd walked a gauntlet that was just as harrowing.

To understand what happened in Mexico all those years ago, I have to introduce you to my father. He's Norwegian, hence Mork, which means "dark" in Norwegian, or "murky" in English, tall, jovial, impatient and – restless. After picking up an MBA from INSEAD in France, he began a life roving from continent to continent, working at senior management levels in companies all over the world.

I was born in Belgium – my mother is Belgian – and started my school career there. But it wasn't long before Dad landed a job in Singapore, and I was plucked from school and enrolled at SAS, the Singapore American School. Of course, I missed the friends I'd made in Belgium, but I was six or seven, and adaptable, as kids often are, so I settled down, made a new bunch of friends, and flourished.

But only two years later, a job offer with Pepsico in Mexico arrived and Dad snapped it up. It fed his voracious appetite for novelty and his ambition to rise through the ranks of a US corporation.

So, off to Mexico we went. It seemed only sensible to send me to the American School in Mexico City, where tuition was carried out in English, as it had been in Singapore. The trouble was, the school was crap. Not only did the place look like a prison, but the teachers behaved like jailhouse wardens, working without enthusiasm, plodding through the syllabus like zombies. Even I, an eight-year-old, realized staying in that school was a non-starter.

The problem was, there were no quality schools in the vast metropolis that offered tuition in English. My mother eventually settled on Instituto Irlandes, the Irish Institute, a top-ranking Jesuit private school catering to the elite kids of the Mexican aristocracy.

Tuition was in Spanish, except for classes in science and, naturally, English.

I didn't speak a word of Spanish.

But I had the summer available after I checked out of the American School and before I started a new year at Instituto Irlandes – known to locals as Padres, the Fathers. My parents serenely assumed I could pick up enough Spanish to navigate my way through fourth grade.

These were the days before Duolingo. There was no YouTube with handy Spanish lessons available, no Udemy. I learned the language the old-fashioned way. Every day, for three months, a private tutor coached me from nine in the morning to five in the afternoon, shepherding me through the Berlitz language grammar books. I ground my way through all five of them over a hot and sweaty summer, learning grammar all day – and spending the evenings committing a torrent of Spanish vocabulary to memory.

I can't say it was fun. But, by the time the school term began, I was as prepared as any nine-year-old could be for a plunge into a new school in a new language.

And the truth was, it was hell from day one. I had the vocab, I knew the grammar but, confronted with teachers who spoke in rapid-fire Spanish, I floundered. And, the more I fell behind, the more the other kids in my class mocked me for my gringo stupidity.

I was driven to school by a guard, a guy called Eduardo. Sitting beside him in our 1970 Chevy Impala, one day in October, slowly making our way in the stop-start traffic down the Avenida Fuente de los Leones, I could see the dull gleam of the pistol at his waist. Mexico City, in 1981, was a bit like the wild west.

It was raining heavily, one of those Mexican downpours that gusts of wind conjure out of an apparently cloudless sky in just minutes. Lightning flashed, thunder rolled. Rain drummed on the roof of the Chevy and I retreated into my own little fantasy-land.

I imagined what I might do with the gun in the classroom. Take a bead on Sra Lopez, our history teacher. Drill her through the head. Turn the gun on any kid who threatened to lay a hand on me. Then seek out all the bullies who'd tormented me during the first couple of months of the term. I'd go for Roberto "Macana" first. Macana, I'd learned, from experience and not Berlitz, meant "club" – and he'd earned this nickname thanks to his habit of beating the shit out of kids he didn't like. Kids like me. And then I'd head for…

My daydream was interrupted by Eduardo.

"Señor Patrick, we're here."

"I don't want to go."

"Sorry, Señor Patrick, but you must go."

He'd pulled up to the curb, right outside Instituto Irlandes. I looked out at the red brick wall, and the kids, umbrellas held high, rushing through the dark green gates into the school grounds. I hated it, and I hated the thought of yet another lesson with Sra Lopez, who spent the entire lesson dictating notes in what seemed like bullet-train-speed Spanish, a language quite different from the Spanish I'd learned with my tutor.

"It's 7.55, Señor Patrick. Time to go." His voice was kind and gentle – and firm. I knew he wouldn't let me miss school. "You don't want to be late."

Of course, I wanted to be late. But I got out and, without a word to him, headed for the gates.

The leather straps of my backpack, heavy with books – the English-Spanish dictionary the heaviest of them all – bore down on me. Rain clattered against the roofs and hoods of the cars lined up outside. I tried to feel nothing as I stepped toward the gates, emblazoned with their Latin motto, *Semper Altius*. We'd been told what it meant: Always higher. I wasn't sure that's what I wanted. I thought I might be scared of heights.

Señora Lopez took us for the first period. She was telling us about the Mexican Revolution of 1910 to 1920 – or, rather, she was dictating notes about the Mexican Revolution. Why eight- and nine-year-old kids needed to know about a revolution that'd happened 70 years before, I didn't know but, since we'd be tested on the facts she was dictating, there was no point in arguing.

Which was fine for native Spanish speakers but, to me, it sounded like she was speaking at a hundred miles an hour. Even when I left gaps for words I didn't understand, I fell behind.

"For nine months, the Americans under General Pershing … something … Panza Villa, but he and his … something… forces retreated into the hills and—"

I managed to write down "General Pershing" but, since I didn't know what he'd done to Panza Villa and his something forces, the sentence simply didn't make sense.

While I tried to figure out this puzzle, Sra rushed ahead with something about some guy called Emeliano Zapata. Cool name, but I couldn't figure out who the hell he was or what, if anything, he had to do with the revolution.

All this time, Sra Lopez was pacing up and down in front of the class, firing off volley after volley of facts. And then she paused and yelled out, "Red! Red! Red!" and, as one, everyone in the class grabbed hold of a red pen to take down the key facts she'd warned us were bound to come up in the mid-term exams scheduled for the following week.

I took my red pen from my pencil case and told myself that, this time, I'd manage, this time I'd understand everything she said, this time I wouldn't end up with a page full of half sentences.

The first sentence went well:

"There were three chief reasons that the people of Mexico rose up and revolted against the government of President Diaz."

Perfect. I got it, more or less neatly written in red ink, as required. Next?

Sra Lopez held up one finger. Check. "Firstly—"

I wrote down the word … but then the ink in my ballpoint ran dry. I couldn't believe it.

"— Porfirio Diaz had been president for thirty years."

I needed another red pen. I dived back into my pencil case. I was sure I had a second red pen stashed in there. I scrabbled through the crayons, the pencils – one an HB, another a soft 4B for art – and two spare ballpoint pens, one blue and one black. Where was my red pen? I was vaguely aware that Sra Lopez's voice was droning on.

"—more and more dictatorial—"

I tried to catch the eyes of any of my classmates, but they all had their heads down and were scrawling furiously.

Finally, I turned to my right and asked Alonso, a tall, chubby kid, in the lowest voice I could manage, "Hey, Alonso, hey man, do you have another red pen I can borrow?"

He answered without turning to me, his pen racing across his page. "Sorry."

Frantically, I spun to my left and asked Raphael, a shorter kid with sandy brown hair and piercing green eyes, "Rafa, Rafa, do you have an extra pen, man? Please, mine is dry. Please!"

Raphael stopped writing for a moment. He looked straight at me and gave me a toothy grin: "Aww, that's too bad, gringo. I guess no notes for you—"

I turned back, wondering what I could do and managed, somehow, to tip my pencil case off my desk. It fell to the floor with a report like a rifle shot, and, suddenly, I was the focus of everyone's attention.

I became aware that Sra Lopez had stopped. I looked up. She was gazing at me with a look that could've stopped a wild buffalo in its tracks.

"Sorry, Señora Lopez. I've run out of red ink," I said in a small voice.

"You've run out of red ink? Then find your spare red pen, Señor Mork." At the Irish Institute, all the boys, however young, were addressed as "Señor" by the teachers.

"I don't have one, Señora."

"*Pinche* gringo," the boy behind me hissed. Fucking gringo. I knew Sra Lopez had heard, but she ignored him.

"You came to class with a whole pencil case full of pens and pencils – but only one red pen? You have to do better than this, Señor Mork."

"Yes, Señora," I muttered.

She turned back to the board. I scrambled down to pick up the pencil case and the pencils and pens that had skittered across the floor.

"Ow." Something had stung me on the back of my neck. My first thought was that it was a hornet. I put my hand up to the spot and felt the spitball lodged there, hard as a grape pip.

"What is it now?" Sra Lopez asked.

"Nothing, Señora."

"Well, then," she said crisply, "sit down and take notes with your usual pen."

I did as she said, but not before another spitball hit me behind the ear, together with more invective from different corners of the class: "*Que lento y tonto eres,*" and "*Eres tan pendejo.*" I felt blood rush to my face. And then, out of nowhere, someone slapped me across the back of my head. I spun around to confront my tormentor. It was Mario, a kid with flaming red hair and a mean little mouth.

"*¿No tienen bolígrafos en Bégica gringo?*" Don't they have pens in Belgium? And then, with a sneer, in English, "Fucking asshole." This was greeted by shouts and laughter.

"That's enough! Settle down at once!"

A red haze washed over me, hot oil boiled in my veins, and I hardly heard Sra Lopez's words behind me. I launched myself at Mario, knocking my desk over as I did so, sending notebooks and pencil case, the lot, flying.

The class was yelling, "Go, gringo, go," and "Hit him, Mario!" We were eight- and nine-year-olds, but we might as well have been fighters in a ring, and the bloodlust of the crowd was up.

"Sit down at once, both of you." A hand descended on my shoulder and I was yanked backwards. "Pick up your desk now, Señor Mork."

Sullenly, I did as I was told.

"The rest of you, be quiet or I'll send you to Father Patrick."

Before silence descended on the class, I decided I'd had enough: "You want to settle this," I hissed at Mario, "then let's take it outside."

I'd already learned that officialdom turned a blind eye to fights between boys that took place in a corner of the school property on the far side of the soccer field.

Mario met me during recess outside the canteen. I was now seriously regretting the decision I'd made. After all, I was small for my age, I'd never had a physical fight before, and I was not naturally combative.

There he was, fists clenched, a tight smile on that little mouth, waiting for me in front of a wedge of supporters.

"Come on, let's get it on, gringo."

We marched – or rather, he marched and I slunk along behind him, trying not to think of what lay ahead – to the soccer field. Throngs of boys accompanied us, shouting and waving their fists in gleeful anticipation of the battle to come. Word had spread of the challenge, and boys from other grades crowded around as well. I looked around desperately searching for a sight of a Jesuit father, a rescuer, but no one came.

The boys created a makeshift ring around us. I shucked off my sweater and eyed Mario uneasily. Did he really intend to *hurt* me? I tried to catch his eye, in the hope that he might change his mind, clap me on the shoulder and tell me it was all a prank. But, he'd already started weaving about, circling me, his fists held high, ready to lash out at me. I retreated. The crowd roared.

I put my hands up, and wondered what it would be like to try to hit someone deliberately. I prodded ineffectually at him, and the crowd went crazy.

"Hit him, gringo!"

"Hit him, Mario!"

He dodged aside and countered, hitting me glancingly on my jaw. It *hurt*. Furious, suddenly – how dare he! – I swung a fist at him, but he ducked. He threw a punch at my ribs, which connected. Recklessly, I pitched myself at him, ignoring a punch to my cheek, and another to my midsection. I connected once, I thought, although I couldn't be sure – and then it felt as if I'd run into a wall. A solid blow landed squarely on my nose, blood spurted, and the fight leaked from me.

My legs gave way and I found myself sitting on the grass. Somebody advised me to hold my head back but, when I did that, the blood ran down my throat and I choked on it. There were cheers for Mario, which I was only vaguely aware of.

My right cheek stung, and my upper lip seemed to have cracked. And then, without warning, the tone of the shouting changed, and the crowd started to melt away. A Jesuit father strode up, pushing his way between the hushed spectators. It was Father Patrick, like some kind of angry black angel, his beetle brows even bushier than usual.

"Enough!" he boomed, although he should have been able to tell it was all over. "You two, to my office, now. I'll see you first, Sr Mork. As for the rest of you, go back to your classrooms, on the double." He spun about, the black skirts of his cassock swirling out like the wings of a bat.

Father Patrick's office was a dimly lit cubby-hole, furnished as the Jesuits approved, with a plain, mustard-colored metal desk strewn with papers, books and registers. Photographs of him, in the company of other Jesuit crows, adorned the walls. Above his desk hung a plain wooden crucifix.

The priest was built like a rugby prop, with broad shoulders and powerful arms. I shivered and shifted my weight from one foot to the other. Briefly, I considered turning and making a run for it.

"Sit down," he said, without looking up.

I perched gingerly on the edge of the hard wooden chair facing his desk.

Father Patrick went on writing. I imagined that my punishment wouldn't end with just a few harsh words. Perhaps he'd suspend me as well. Perhaps Sra Lopez had reported on my behavior in class. Perhaps…

"Well, Señor Mork, what do you have to say for yourself?"

He fixed me with a penetrating stare. I knew he meant business.

"Nothing, Father," I whispered.

"Did you manage to get a blow in before Sr Garcia knocked you down?"

I squirmed, wondering what he was up to. I thought I had managed a couple, but should I confess to that now? Wouldn't that lead to even harsher punishment? Better the truth, though.

"Yes, sir – at least I think so."

"I think so, too. A fine bruise is already showing along Sr Garcia's jawline."

I couldn't help feeling a small glow of satisfaction. He might have bloodied my nose, but I'd given him something to remember, too. Whatever happened now, I'd at least have that.

"Now, listen carefully. I don't condone violence and neither does the school. That is not the way of the Church."

"No, Father."

"So, what I have to say might come as a surprise to you." He paused. I steeled myself. "The truth is that I'm proud of you, Patrick."

My confusion must have registered on my face. "You arrived here three months ago, one of the smallest boys in your class. Three months before that, I understand you couldn't speak a word of Spanish, is that true?"

"Yes, Father."

"And, yet, you came into a Spanish-speaking school and you've coped. You've struggled, I know that, I've spoken to your teachers. But, they speak highly of you. Sra Lopez, especially, has been impressed with the effort you've put into your work."

"Sra Lopez?"

Father Patrick smiled. Suddenly he looked like a kind uncle rather than a stern Prefect of Studies. "She can be frightening, I know, but she loves her students, believe me, even those who only bring one red pen to her classes."

He seemed to know everything.

"It won't happen again, Father."

"The teachers keep me informed of what goes on in their classrooms, so, I'm also aware that you have been the victim of bullying."

He waited for a response. What could I say? That I *had* been bullied? That I was this sad sack of a kid whom everyone teased? I sat in stone silence. Father Patrick nodded.

"I understand," he said. "It's been tough. And let me tell you a secret: it'll probably get tougher. What I want to know is, are you going to go on putting your fists up?"

"You want me to?" I blurted out. This whole conversation was going in a direction I had never imagined.

"It's not what I want that's important, it's what you want. And what you want is why you're here."

I tried to make sense of that in the silence that followed. I wanted to be accepted. I wanted to be friends with the kids who'd stood in the ring around Mario and me and cheered for him. I wanted to be able to speak Spanish as well as any one of them. I didn't want to have to lug that damn Spanish-English dictionary around with me.

He was waiting for me to say something.

"I just want to be normal," I managed at last.

"I understand," he said. "But, being normal takes hard work. You know something, though? I think you're up to it."

The phone on his desk rang at that moment.

"Excuse me," he said, and lifted the receiver. "Father Patrick." He listened for a few seconds, then said, "Of course. Ask her to step in." He put the phone down. "Your mother's arrived to take you home. I thought it better if both you and Sr Garcia took the rest of the day off."

Conventional wisdom has it that the Chinese ideogram that means "crisis" consists of two separate elements meaning "danger" and "opportunity". This is inaccurate. The first character does, in fact, mean "danger", but the second means, not opportunity, but "incipient moment" – a moment which signals the possibility of change.

I'm not sure my session with Father Patrick was the "incipient moment" that projected me in a new direction. All I know is that it marked the climax of a crisis, just as my near accident on Alameda de las Pulgas marked the climax of a different series of psychic and professional blows.

One thing leads to another. Mario bloodied my nose before what felt like the whole school and, certainly, most of my classmates. Was that the turning point? Just as importantly, did I *recognize* it as an "incipient moment"? Or, was it something Father Patrick said? The surprise revelation that I'd actually made a positive impression on Sra Lopez, was that it?

In all of life's small equations, who's to say which is the critical one, which event triggers the sequence that leads, ultimately, to the mountain top? Was it the fight, was it Father Patrick's sympathetic response? Or, was it structural? Less obvious? Perhaps my parents' decision to enroll me in the testing environment of Padres, for which I had to learn a new language, immerse myself in a new culture, and compete with kids who were, by and large, much more competent academically than I was – perhaps that was the real incipient moment. If I'd remained at the American school, where I'd effortlessly established myself at the top of the class, perhaps I'd never have been forced to grasp the real challenge with which Mexico confronted me?

As kids, things happen; then, other things happen. The causal chain isn't apparent to the kid with blood on his shirt, enveloped in a miasma of defeat.

But the adult who has just, by luck or by fate, avoided a fatal collision with, of all things, a garbage truck, has a real chance to use the incipient moment as a springboard to change. To emerge from a crisis renewed, ready to adapt to change, prepared to change ourselves, it helps to have a mentor. Although I didn't realize it at the time, Father Patrick served as my mentor back in Padres. In Redwood City nearly 40 years later, I was alone.

Being fired from a job that gives you purpose leaves psychic scars. In the aftermath of the explosion, you wake in the morning feeling numb. Your sense of self-worth, of self-confidence, has drained away. There seems no point to the day or, indeed, to your life. For men, at least, your identity is inextricably woven through the fabric of your job and your career, or so it seems to me. Remove that, and the cloth of your life unravels.

For a week after my near collision on Alameda de las Pulgas, I did nothing but feel sorry for myself. When I had the energy, I railed against fate and cursed the execs at Course Hero for their short-sightedness. But, for the most part, I did nothing at all.

Of course, I had obligations, and they weren't being served while I wallowed in a sea of self-pity. I'd separated from my wife in 2015. I had two children whom I loved and I supported. And, unless you're homeless, living in the Bay area takes serious moolah. I simply couldn't coast on my savings for long.

I got back on the phone, updated my resume, checked the web for job opportunities. I networked in all my old haunts, coffee shops like Big

Blue Bottle and Coupa Café in Palo Alto, Ciclismo in Redwood City, The Creamery in San Francisco. I let it be known that I was available, eager for a fresh challenge, ready to go. I fired off emails to founders, investors and recruiters, who might be looking for a marketing guru to help build their next unicorn.

But, even as I stepped up my campaign to land my next gig, even as I lashed myself to the mast, talked the talk and did everything I knew to whip myself up for the task at hand, I knew there was something missing. This time, something was different.

I felt as if I were trapped in some private hell, my own personal Groundhog Day, destined forever to repeat the mistakes of the past.

Take the generic conversation I seemed to be having every couple of days. It went something like this. My phone would ring. I'd answer it, ready with my assortment of tricks to dazzle and impress.

"Hi, Patrick," the caller might say. "My name is Ellen and I work in talent management for XYZ Capital. We came across your profile on LinkedIn and wanted to discuss a fabulous opportunity to be chief marketing officer at BillionDollar-Widgets. com. The company was started by…" And then she'd mention some MIT or Stanford graduate (or dropout) "… who has raised X-million dollars in the past twelve months. We're now looking for a seasoned marketing executive with a proven track record and clear product / market fit to help take the company to the next level. And…" dramatic pause, "… we think you're our guy."

Sigh.

The thought of returning to the treadmill, of doing yet another version of what I'd been doing for the past fifteen years, of waking up every morning for the rest of my life to the sound of Sonny and Cher singing *I Got You Babe* felt like … death by a thousand cuts. I needed something different. I needed something new. But I didn't know what and I didn't know how.

What I did know this time round was that I needed help.

So, I phoned Jim Donovan.

I belonged then, and now, to a group of alumni, graduates of INSEAD, the business school in France where I, like my father, did my MBA. We meet occasionally, catch up, share our troubles, both personal and professional, brainstorm solutions – and invite an external moderator or coach to help us challenge ourselves and our circumstances more productively.

Jim Donovan was one of these coaches. Smart, humble, with a mordant sense of humor and an eerie air of serenity, two of Jim's greatest gifts are his ability simply to listen, on the one hand, and to ask questions that pierce to the heart of the problem at hand.

We exchanged pleasantries for a minute but then, with characteristic acuity, he cut straight to the chase.

"What's going on, Patrick?"

"What makes you think there's a problem?"

"Your voice, man, it's about as tense as I've ever heard it."

I told you he was a good listener.

I explained what had happened. I told him I knew in my heart I could not continue applying the same solution over and over again and expect a different result – that there was a lot of wisdom in the assertion that doing so was a good, working definition of insanity.

"Well," he said, "what result do you expect? Or, rather, what result do you want?"

"That is exactly my problem. All I know at the moment is what I *don't* want. I don't want to continue doing what I'm doing. I hate clichés, but the cliché says it best: I feel like a rat on a treadmill and, Jim, I'm exhausted."

And, so, I began a nine-month journey with Jim, in search of the answers to that fundamental question: what did I want?

It was an arduous and structured program that involved looking really hard at my life. Each of our sessions bored down into some of my most fundamental beliefs and assumptions.

It was only towards the end of our work together that I recalled the question Father Patrick had asked all those years ago. Then, I'd answered that I wanted to be normal. Looking back, I now realized that, what I'd actually meant was: I want to be accepted, I want to be acknowledged, I want, in the end, as we all do, to be loved.

The nine months I spent with Jim led me to some simple but fundamental conclusions.

What did I want? I wanted to be filled with purpose. I wanted to feel that I was helping others and making a difference.

These are not, of course, unique goals. They're ambitions, I suspect, that are shared by most people on planet Earth.

The question that then confronted me was: what action was I going to take that would translate analysis into a lived reality?

Joseph Campbell's Hero is called to adventure. Initially reluctant to begin his journey, he hesitates on the cusp of change, waiting for a sign, a nudge, a *push* that sends him headlong into the special world of his quest for self-actualization.

I celebrated my tenth birthday in January of 1982. I wasn't looking forward to the party because, although I'd kept my head down, worked on my Spanish and, generally, tried to "fit in", things hadn't changed that much.

It was true, I avoided the worst of the bullying that had poisoned my first months at Padres. Perhaps the bullies had simply gotten bored with picking on me. Or, perhaps I'd successfully mastered the art of staying largely invisible. I wasn't accepted, though. I had no real friends. I was the shivering outsider, gazing with longing into the room in which people were warming themselves before a roaring fire, talking excitedly, enjoying each other's company.

"You should invite all your classmates, Patrick," my mother said, a week before the big day.

"I don't want to," I said. "And, anyway, they won't come."

"You'll be surprised. Besides, if you don't welcome them to your birthday, do you think there'll be any reason for them to welcome you?"

I shrugged but, in due course, handed out the invitations she'd written to all the kids in the class.

And then I was surprised when eighteen or twenty kids turned up. They must, I thought, have come for the goodies: the candy that filled the piñata, and the birthday cake that my mother had promised would be spectacular. I mumbled greetings and, acutely aware of my mother's eye, shook hands with each as they arrived, including my old nemeses, Macana and Mario. The biggest kid in the class, an ally of theirs, a boy called Torta, who towered over me, was also there.

The fifteenth was a cold and windy day, but not so cold, my mother said, that we couldn't start the festivities outside with the traditional piñata. My mother had fashioned a donkey from papier-mâché and hung it from a cable strung along the length of the courtyard.

As birthday boy, I had the honor of first strike. My mother tied the blindfold, and my classmates spun me around enthusiastically until I was completely mixed up. Finally, they let me loose. I had no idea where I was in relation to the piñata. I struck at the air, spun around, swung my stick repeatedly, missed repeatedly. My ears rang with the laughter and mockery of the kids watching my futile efforts.

"*Vamos flaco, gringo,*" Torta yelled, "we're starving."

It was all worse than I'd imagined. When, at last, I managed to hit the damn donkey, I only struck one of its legs, and a trickle of candies spilled out. Macana plucked the stick from me and, blindfolded, hit the piñata amidships with his first swing, and a cascade tumbled out.

I guess my mother was aware of my unhappiness and, no sooner had everyone scooped up the candies released from the piñata, than she clapped her hands. "Right," she said, "now for the birthday cake. Follow me."

She led the way past the stone fountain and into our living room. Our housekeeper, Encarna, was standing at the table. A cloth covered a mysterious shape. "Gather round, boys," my mother said cheerfully. "Ready, Encarna?" The housekeeper nodded. "Go!"

Encarna whipped off the cloth and revealed a life-sized replica, in full and authentic color, of the hero of that year's movie blockbuster, ET. I think every boy in Grade 4 had seen ET, and loved it. The sight of the little alien, with his super-long fingers and his cute shuffling feet, inspired at least three seconds of awe-struck silence, before shouts and yells broke out.

"And I promise you," Mom said, "it's just as delicious as it looks. Cut the cake up for your friends, Patrick." She handed me a knife.

I prepared to plunge the knife into the heart of ET when Torta said, "No, not like that, gringo."

I paused, wondering what I was doing wrong.

"In Mexico, we do it a different way. On your birthday, first taste goes to the birthday boy – but you've got to bite it right where it stands."

"I don't understand," I stuttered.

"Lean over the cake, take a bite out of the side. There, where his stomach sticks out."

Mario chuckled, and I caught a glimpse of Macana giving Torta a wink. They were up to something. My chest tightened. Another prank, designed to embarrass me.

"Go on, Patrick," said Raphael, a boy whose teasing had never been vicious. I scanned the boys around the table. I remembered the ring of spectators urging Mario to beat the shit out of me. "It's a tradition," he added. Yeah, it's probably also a tradition to beat the shit out of every gringo who has the balls to attend a Mexican school.

What was the worst that could happen? Besides, my mother was right there. She wouldn't allow things to get out of hand. Cautiously, still suspicious, I bent over until my face was just inches from the golden frosting over ET's tummy.

I opened my mouth to take a bite out of my birthday cake.

And a heavy hand – it must have been Torta's – descended on the back of my head and pushed my face firmly into the frosting, filling my mouth with it. Above and around me, everyone burst out laughing. I could even make out my mother's laugh among all the others.

Pause here for a second. This was a moment of crisis. Of danger – and of possibility. It was, looking back on it from the vantage point of time, an incipient moment.

Imagine a freeze-frame of that moment. I was bent over my fabulous birthday cake. My face was buried in frosting, my mouth full of a mixture of frosting and cake. I faced a fork in my path. Take one path and my world, already on shaky foundations, would collapse entirely. My time at

Padres would be poisoned for the duration of our stay in Mexico. Take the other and, well, who knew.

An incipient moment. A moment balanced on a fulcrum that could tilt one way or the other, depending entirely on what I did next.

Of course, I didn't then think through my options. I didn't analyze the situation. I stood up. I must have looked a sight, my face covered in frosting. I'd known something was up, that a prank was in the making. I'd seen the winks and heard the chuckles. But still I'd walked into the trap. I could have lashed out then … or burst into tears … or sought the safety of my mother's arms. Instead, I opened my mouth and laughed out loud, along with all the others.

Torta put a hand on my shoulder. "Sorry, amigo," he said. "It *is* a tradition, like I said – but most Mexican kids never fall for it." And he laughed again, which set off a fresh round of mirth in all the others.

I ran a finger down my cheek, scooping up a great glob of frosting, and popped it in my mouth. "It's delicious," I said. "Want some, everyone?"

Forty years later, the incipient moment of this latest turn in my life, the start of this most recent hero's journey, was not, I think, the moment I nearly wiped myself out against the back end of a 20-ton garbage truck. It wasn't the moment I found myself covered in a cold sweat wondering what the hell I was going to do with my life. It wasn't the moment Andrew Grauer pulled the lever that saw me plunge through the trapdoor.

It was the moment I picked up the phone and dialed Jim Donovan's number. It was the moment I decided to become the active agent of my own future – just as I had, for less conscious reasons, decided to laugh at myself back on my birthday in the January of 1982.

Of course, moments like these are simply signposts for a more profound change that is on the very verge of happening. They are the tipping points, the first tumbling stones of an avalanche of change.

But, helping to shape and transform them into spurs to action are the men and women who serve as your mentors, who point the way, who urge you to ask that fundamental question, the answer that will define the direction your life will take.

What do *you* want?

Every day, in every way, things go faster and faster. Change upends our expectations. We're surfing an ever more unpredictable wave – and no one, *no one*, knows where it'll end.

In this chapter, I picked out just a few relatively undramatic but, nevertheless, devastating episodes from my life in which change confronted me with difficult challenges.

Now, I want to suggest three simple exercises that'll help you develop the capacity to cope with and manage change. The first of these might seem trivial, but it's designed to help you accustom yourself to the *idea* of change as a constant feature of life.

I call it Baby Steps.

EXERCISE # 1

Take Baby Steps often
And you'll see why in a minute.

Baby Steps is an exercise designed to introduce very small changes into a life that is in danger – as all our lives are – of becoming moribund, so predictable that it no longer offers the sort of stimulation and provocation that keeps us alert to our potential, and to the infinite opportunities that surround us.

Today, think of something you can do that you haven't done before. Don't think big; think small. Visit your local Starbucks. Instead of ordering *the usual* – your espresso or Americano or cappuccino, let your eye run down the list of all the other options on offer. How about a caffè mocha? A vanilla latte? Or lash out on a cinnamon roll frappuccino? Today, try something you haven't drunk before. And then, savor it. Identify, if you can, the various ingredients. Drink it, as they say, *mindfully*.

Tomorrow, instead of driving to work, ride to work on your bike. Or take a route you haven't tried before. It might be longer, so give yourself a little time. Instead of going down the boulevard, meander through the park. Focus on your senses: what can you hear, what can you smell? Pause at a bush and rub its leaves between thumb and forefinger. *Savor* the difference.

You see where I'm going with this?

Examine your routine, introduce a small change to it and savor the difference. This isn't going to change your life, and nor is it designed to. But, if you're diligent about it, pretty soon you'll establish a habit of trying new things.

Do you remember the Jim Carey movie, *Yes Man*? He plays a depressive trapped in a dead-end job as a loan officer, who has fallen into the habit of saying "No". But then he meets an old buddy, who encourages him to attend a seminar led by a charismatic guru, and this guru persuades him to say "Yes" to every opportunity.

It transforms his life.

Now, I'm not advocating anything as radical as that. But I do believe – and my life is testament to this – that saying "Yes" to change opens up possibilities and opportunities, and encourages you to embrace life, rather than shelter from it.

And it might all begin with ordering a cinnamon roll frappuccino.

EXERCISE # 2
Share the change you want to make

You can react to change in your environment – new competitors, a new boss, a failed relationship – or you can make changes in order to improve your life in one or other way. Baby steps help produce the mind-set that welcomes change, that identifies opportunities, and that makes you the master rather than the victim of your fate.

Eighteen months or so ago, I was invited to talk to the operations team at Unilever here in Santiago about making positive changes happen in their lives.

I began by asking them to close their eyes and breathe deeply for a minute or two: taking four seconds to draw in a breath; spending six seconds to release it. When they'd thoroughly slowed down, I invited them to think of something they'd like to change in their lives. It could be anything. It could be relatively minor, or relatively major. It could be quitting smoking. It could be getting healthy and fit. It could be reading more. It could be related to the business, or be purely personal.

Once they'd settled on a change they'd like to see happen in their lives, I asked them to write it down.

So far, so easy. Now came the tough part.

I asked everyone there to take out their phones, unlock them, and send a WhatsApp message, to five people in their contacts, in which they spelled out what they hoped to change and promised to keep them updated on progress toward that goal.

This is the essential part of the exercise. You have to make yourself accountable to others. When you enlist them as *accountability partners,* you increase, exponentially, the chances of achieving your goals. I consider it so important that I've devoted a complete chapter, Chapter 5, to accountability.

I made myself accountable to a number of friends and family members when I committed myself to writing this book. I was reminded of that covenant when a friend phoned to wish me a happy birthday. He asked what I was up to. I told him one of my most exciting projects this year was writing and publishing this book. Instantly, I made myself accountable to him because I know that, in six months' time, when we speak, he'll ask, "How's the book coming along?" And if I haven't finished it, I'll feel bad. That's a powerful inducement to keep to my commitment, believe me.

Another way of making changes in your life is to recognize it's not very different from establishing a useful or productive habit. James Clear is the go-to man when it comes to habits. His powerful book, *Atomic Habits,* is the most useful guide I, and millions of other readers, have found on the subject.

Here's a third exercise that, like the last, asks you to take a considerable risk.

EXERCISE # 3
Start, Stop, Continue?

This is an exercise I picked up a few years ago from a fellow coach. It begins with a series of WhatsApp messages to people you know well, but who are not intimate friends and are definitely not members of your family.

Each message consists of a request to them to do three things. Ask:

1. What two or three things do I do that I should *Continue* doing?
2. What two or three things do I do that I should *Stop* doing?
3. And what two or three things should I *Start* doing?

The sequence of questions is important. The first question is biased to the positive. You're asking for affirmation of something that your friend approves of. "Continue to be as energetic as you are. Continue to be cheerful. Continue to communicate well." This makes it easy for people to give feedback and get started since they inherently prefer to be liked.

The second question relates to an activity or an attitude that, in your friend's eyes, at least, is a big fat zero. "You can stop talking about how you wished you'd invested in Apple twenty years ago. It's boring."

And the third relates to something you can do that'll improve your effectiveness in some way. "Start praising your subordinates' contributions more regularly."

Now, it takes a strong person to invite this sort of feedback. But if you believe you can take the criticism, it's a very powerful exercise, especially if the feedback you receive reveals a trend. For example, if half the responses suggest you don't give credit where it's due, then you can be pretty sure that's a habit you need to develop.

And this informal survey also enlists these contacts as accountability partners. You've asked for their advice; you can be sure they'll take an interest in whether you *have* made the changes they suggested. And this knowledge will help turn the changes you make into habits.

Key #1

FIND YOUR PURPOSE

"I hope you live a life you're proud of. If you find out that you're not, I hope you have the courage to start all over again."

—*The Great Gatsby* – F Scott Fitzgerald

"What do you really want, Patrick?" said Jim during one of our first coaching sessions, a series that would span nine months.

I listened to the faint hum on the telephone line while I thought about my answer. It was summer, I'd finally turned off the heating, and it wasn't hot enough to warrant a/c. Just as well, given the fact that I was scraping the bottom of the barrel. The last thing I needed was a higher electricity bill.

I felt stumped. Coaching was hard. It was such a simple question, but with such a complex answer.

"You've asked that already. I've *answered* it already."

I had. I really had. We'd been at this coaching thing for a month and I can't tell you how many times Jim had asked, and I had answered, that question. I didn't want to be the victim, *again*, of yet another startup CEO's misguided preconceptions of what marketing was and what it wasn't. I didn't want to go back to doing the same thing I'd been doing over and over again for the past fifteen years. But, apparently, that wasn't good enough for Jim.

He wanted me to develop a series of positive answers that summarized the central drivers of my life. What did I want, and why?

To me, the answer was simple: I didn't want to go on working for other people, pushing products I didn't believe in, or reporting to some 20-something CEO, who knew fuck-all about marketing but insisted the five blog posts they'd read on Medium made them an expert on the subject.

After a few minutes, I blurted out: "I just want to have control over my life. That's it."

"Well," Jim said, "that's a beginning. But what are you going to do about it?"

My answer was simple. Over the following weeks, I established my own company – Mad Mork Enterprises. I briefed a designer on Upwork, who came up with a great logo. I cobbled together my first website on Wix. I reached out to my contacts in the Valley. I hadn't spent ten years in San Francisco for nothing, I told myself. I was filled with energy. I had a firm grasp on the handlebars of my life. Now, all I had to do was develop some momentum. I had no doubt that I had what it took to steer an independent course through the tech jungle of Silicon Valley.

Within weeks, I was talking to venture capitalists and startups about how I could help them devise winning marketing strategies.

Just the realization that I wasn't prepared to work for anyone else again – ever! – was liberating. It was also terrifying. So, of course, I was still stressed. Redwood City, California, is one of the most expensive locations in the world. I had two kids to support. I had alimony to pay. I had savings, of course – but, month by month, I watched them dwindle as I lashed out on the inevitable expenses of getting my consultancy off the ground. Managing my little savings became a maniacal obsession. I reached a point where I was even buying milk, not based on the brand, but on which brand was cheaper. Frankly, it was hard to believe it had gotten that bad.

One of my biggest investments was Jim. Top-notch coaches don't come cheap and, although we only communicated once every two weeks for an intense session over the phone, the bill still made me feel sick to my stomach. But this was money I was happy to invest, I have to say, because he was helping me – a 45-year-old marketing pro, whom some would say was over the hill – make some profound changes in my life. Not easy. Not simple, although at that stage, just a month or so after the Course Hero fiasco, I needed a lifeline and these coaching sessions were it. They felt absolutely indispensable.

Something else struck me during those strange months. As I said, I paid strict attention to my network, meeting old buddies, colleagues and acquaintances regularly at one of several of the Valley's coffee shops – Café Borrone in Menlo Park, or at the famous Coupa Café in Palo Alto. At times, it began to feel like my new status as a one-time insider, now floating on the margins of the tech universe, prompted some of them to come clean about their own doubts on the direction their lives were taking. I remember having coffee with a friend, a hardened professional in her mid-30s, the epitome of success, with an impeccable CV, and a stellar career at Apple.

Over a macchiato, she confided that, one day, she'd woken up and realized the cost of her success. "I have no kids, and no prospect of having them. I hardly ever see my friends. You remember how much I loved surfing?" I did. She'd been a fixture at some of the most challenging beaches on the coast. "Well," she said, eyes downcast, "I can't remember the last time I went surfing." She sighed. "Tell me, Patrick, what's the point of it all? Is being a success at work the be-all and end-all? Why do I feel like I've worked so hard, but still can't see the end of the rainbow?"

I didn't have an answer for her. Except: change. Do *some*thing. *Stop.* Curiously, I went back to some of Jim's toughest questions, and specifically the single question that trumped all others. I looked right into her eyes and asked: "What do you really want?" Little did I realize it, but I had just taken my first step towards becoming a coach.

I'd been there. My experiences at GetJar and Course Hero had taught me that, sometimes, you have to change – or you just wither and die. And if that sounds melodramatic, think of my own narrow escape. I'd reached the end of my rope. I had decided to go it alone, without the baggage of bosses and quarterly reviews, without the burden of meeting other people's expectations. It was nothing short of a revolution. Although I was scared, I felt liberated of all the bullshit I'd lived through for the past 20-plus years working for others. I felt free.

What I didn't realize, during those early sessions with Jim, and during those endless conversations with burned-out marketing execs, was that it wasn't enough.

I don't know if you're familiar with the South Bay coast, south of San Francisco. It's an endless series of bays and coves. Sometimes, the cliffs rise high above the ocean and, in other places, they swoop down to meet the beach. The variety of vistas and vegetation is amazing.

Both before and after my divorce, I'd taken our two children, Natasha and her big brother Raphael – names we chose to help them fit in wherever in the world they found themselves – to various beaches. Our favorite was, I think, Miramar Beach on Halfmoon Bay.

It was the very first beach I'd discovered when we settled in the Bay area in 2008. I remember visiting the Miramar Beach Restaurant – it's right on the beach, with tables that look out over the ocean – and ordering a volcano chocolate cake. The cake is filled – yeah, you guessed it – with molten chocolate and, when you slice into it, the chocolate simply oozes out. It's like an orgasm in your mouth and it's delicious, believe me.

As the kids grew, our visits to the Miramar Beach Restaurant became a tradition.

"So, what do you guys feel like eating?" I'd ask. Both Raphael and Natasha knew where this was going and they'd fall in with my routine.

"Maybe a burger with fries?" Natasha said, innocent as the day she was born.

"Uh huh. And you, Rafi?"

He'd think hard for about a millisecond, and then pop out with something like, "Hot dog?"

"You both happy with your choices? Burger and a hot dog?"

And both kids would nod, solemn as judges.

"Nothing else?"

"No. We're good." More solemn nods of assurance.

"You quite sure?"

And then either Natasha or Raphael would get this sly grin and they'd say, "Well, maybe just one other thing—"

"You name it, I'll tell you whether I can afford it."

And they'd both burst out together: "Volcano chocolate cake!"

Usually, we'd go to the restaurant after we'd walked the Half Moon Bay Coastal Trail, or after a bike ride along the seafront. Both kids loved a house we passed on these journeys. It was covered in the most intricate shamanistic carvings and they'd imagine the wizard who lived there, casting his dark spells on anyone who disturbed his peace.

Miramar triggered a great many positive memories. But a particularly bitter one as well. It was at Miramar that Laura and I took the kids that fateful day, after we'd told them we were splitting up. We bought ice-creams at the restaurant and walked up and down the beach, allowing them to run around and climb a nearby tree, hoping, praying, that they wouldn't be crushed by the news. We told them our bad news as gently as we could. "Daddy and Mommy are going to live in separate houses," Laura must have said, as a million mothers or fathers have said before her, "but we both love you as much as ever and you'll see Daddy every week."

Natasha, five at the time, took the news pretty calmly. She probably didn't realize its significance. But Raphael burst into tears. He let us know in no uncertain terms that he "didn't like the arrangement" and crawled into my lap as we sat on the floor of their playroom back at the house and sobbed uncontrollably.

That was one of the hardest days in my life and one I'll never forget.

That was also our last visit, as a family, to Miramar.

Ironically, our divorce was probably the best thing that could have happened for my relationship with Natasha and Raphael. Of course, it was sad, but the reality was that, while I was living with Laura and the kids, I spent surprisingly little time with them. Or, perhaps that wasn't so surprising.

It wasn't that I didn't care for them. But my mind was constantly fixated on my job, deadlines, money issues and finding the next great unicorn to be a part of. And, yes, the children were everything to me, but like so many type As in the Valley, I left most of the child-rearing to my wife as I obsessed over my career. As much as I was "there" on weekends, I really wasn't. I was never really mentally and emotionally there.

And then we separated and, in the blink of an eye, when the children were with me, as they were every second weekend and for an annual holiday, *I* was the primary caregiver. It was up to me to feed and entertain them and keep them busy. I had to figure out what interested them, what bored them, what they enjoyed. I had to be present physically, mentally and emotionally.

So, the divorce was, in a way, a boon rather than a problem, certainly when it came to me and the kids.

But there was also a dark side to this newfound relationship with the kids. Whenever I dropped them off with Laura at the end of our weekends together, I'd feel torn apart, robbed of an essential part of my life. The hours we spent together were awesome – but, in the days between, there now was a large, gaping hole in my chest that sometimes felt like it almost physically hurt. My small, two-bedroom apartment would go from a bustling hive of laughter, yelling and activity to being as quiet as a tomb. Just me, my plants and the television. I had never felt more alone in my life than in those days after the kids had gone.

It wasn't a long drive from Laura's house in Menlo Park to my apartment in Redwood City. It would take no more than fifteen minutes or so in traffic, and less off-peak. But every time I drove back from dropping off the kids, I'd consider the role they played in my life. Because, the fact was that, no matter what was happening, no matter how tough things got – and they got really tough in these first few months after Course Hero – I felt I could endure anything if I was able to spend days with them in the park or on the beach, on horseback or in an amusement park, racing down a roller coaster. Often, my best times were spent simply wandering through woods with the two of them or playing basketball in the park with Rafi. The time I spent with the kids was my lifeline to some sort of normalcy. They became the oxygen and me the air-starved patient.

Of course, when it came to money, I'd set myself up for failure. I'd been booted out of an extremely well-paid job at a flourishing startup and, instead of looking for a job, I had decided to set up my stall as an independent marketing consultant. Fortunately, I had an impeccable reputation in the industry as a marketer – regardless of the fact that I'd been fired twice in eighteen months – but I knew it was going to be tough landing the clients I needed to pay the bills.

So, when Andrew Lee, a former Googler who had sought me out for mentoring back during my Google days, called while I was having a coffee at a Starbucks in Redwood City, and suggested we meet to talk about a problem he was trying to solve at his company, I instantly agreed. Problems meant consulting, consulting meant fees.

Andrew was the chief marketing officer at a tech startup called Weedmaps. It was a tech company serving the cannabis industry, established years before weed was legalized for recreational use in California. Then, when the floodgates opened in 2016, Weedmaps found itself surfing the crest of a wave. They were like the Google Maps of weed and helped consumers find legal dispensaries where they could shop in cannabis heaven.

Andrew and I had worked together and struck up a friendship during my days at Google in 2012 and '13. We met to discuss his problem. "We have a founder who's a super-smart guy," he told me. "He's really good at business and an excellent strategist—"

"But—?"Andrew grinned. "But he really doesn't get marketing."

It's a problem throughout the tech industry. Startups build astonishing products. They imagine, then, that the world will beat a path to their app or website. They see marketing as the ugly step-child, a poor cousin:

tolerated, fed the odd scrap but, in the bigger scheme of things, not really important. This view grew out of Google's experience because, as we all know, the world *did* beat a path to its door.

But that isn't true for most tech companies. Most have to blow their own trumpets as loudly as possible to attract customers and get noticed. They need passing trade. Creating that, effectively, takes good marketing.

When Andrew said he'd like to hire me as a consultant for three months at a monthly fee of $25 000, I blinked and said yes. The money would get me out of the hole I was slowly sinking into. It would give me breathing space while I built my practice. It would give me a fighting chance to succeed in the crazy endeavor I'd committed myself to.

Jim was noncommittal when I reported Andrew's windfall offer to him. "What exactly does he expect you to do?"

"Well, to start with, I'll be helping them build a brand book to figure out the positioning of their brands. It's the sort of thing I can do with my eyes closed."

"And?"

"And, secondly, and maybe this is even more important to Andrew, he wants me to help him convince the CEO of the importance of marketing."

"Think you can do that?"

"I'll give it my best shot."

To begin with, the thought of the paycheck, awaiting me at the end of my first month, was a great motivator. I worked on the marketing plan with Andrew, and I helped present our ideas to Justin Hartfield, founder of the company. I was earning a lot of money, sure, but I reckon I gave back as much in value, if not more.

But, by the time the third month rolled around, I was feeling a little frustrated. To my surprise, working out the nuts and bolts of the marketing plan had felt … boring. Been there. Done that, I thought. Hadn't I been here, done all this before? Not once, but repeatedly. Wash, rinse and repeat. That was basically what I'd been doing for the past fifteen years.

Despite the money, to my chagrin I just could not summon the passion or the enthusiasm that had once been my stock in trade. The spark had died. Yes, I was working as a free agent, and that did make a difference.

But not enough to have me wake up each morning buzzing with ideas to transmit to Andrew.

Slowly, but surely, I started to ask myself a single, nagging question: had I come to the end of the line as a marketer? That realization started to slowly creep up on me, like a snake slithering up on its dinner. Worse, it scared the shit out of me because, if the answer to this question was "yes", then the next question was worse: "What the hell do I do now?"

But, during those three months with Weedmaps, I learned a second lesson that was even more important. It determined what I was going to do with the rest of my professional life.

I found that, what I really enjoyed wasn't the marketing consulting. What I really enjoyed was mentoring and coaching Andrew. I spent a lot of time with him, both in his office, and over lunches and coffees. I saw him as a kind of younger version of myself, and I was determined to help him avoid the pitfalls and mistakes I'd made in my own career. I set out to transmit as much of the wisdom I'd gleaned in the fast tech lane as I could.

These discoveries both exhilarated and scared the hell out of me.

"Why does it scare you?" Jim asked, on one of our calls.

"Because I'm known as a marketing guy, Jim. Marketing's been the basis of my career for 20 years. Mention my name in Silicon Valley and, if they've heard of me, people will associate me with marketing. It's the *essence* of who I am." Even the title on my business card at Google, to the horror or humor of many, read "the Marketing Guy".

"There's money in marketing," Jim said.

I was pacing furiously up and down my tiny apartment now, earbuds threatening to pop out, waving my arms about.

"Fuck, it's not about the goddamn money."

"You liked what Weedmaps was paying you. I remember you saying—"

"I know what I said. But something's changed. Think about the blogs I've been writing."

Once I'd established my website, I'd started developing more and more content for it. This took the form of long-form blog posts, for which I drew on my experience of working in the Valley. I was writing one or two of these pieces every week. Not only did I post them on my own website, but I syndicated them on other websites like Business Insider, Medium and LinkedIn. I even managed to have half a dozen or so published in the knowledge blog of my alma mater, INSEAD – the French-based business school whose MBA program is acknowledged as one of the best in the world.

"You invest a lot of time in writing those posts," Jim remarked. "Do you know why?"

Well, obviously, they formed part of my personal marketing plan, getting my name out there, associating it with stimulating and provocative articles.

Jim had a knack of cutting through the BS and zoning in on the essentials. "I sense there's more to it than that," he said. "Why do you *really* write them?"

"I like … helping people," I said slowly, coming to a halt at my window. "I do. That's why I've enjoyed mentoring Andrew."

"So, let's sum up where you've got to, Patrick."

"The lessons I've learned?"

"Exactly."

I thought about it for a minute, but then the words rushed out.

"Well, to begin with, I do think I've made some progress with you, Jim. I know that I want to work for myself and not for some startup or other.

"I know that I want to … help others. People like Andrew. I mean, if I can't help others, like me, avoid the career mistakes I've made, then what's the point of anything, right? I want to make a difference in the lives of others."

"That sounds suspiciously like you've made your mind up to switch lanes," Jim interrupted me. "Can you be more specific? Put it into words."

Suddenly it was obvious to me. "I want to be a coach," I said slowly, feeling as if I stood on the cliff-edge of possibility.

"Good. So, describe to me, then, what that would feel like."

I wasn't sure what he meant and said so.

"Imagine a moment at some point in the future. You've got the training you need, you've enlisted a few clients, you're on your way as a professional coach. How would doing that work, make you feel?"

I thought about it. I really tried to inhabit that future me, who had successfully switched tracks and was now speeding towards a destination of his choice.

I began slowly. "I think I'd be happy." I felt my heart pick up speed. It had been a long time since I'd been truly happy. "I'd be filled with purpose. I'd feel good about the work I was doing." I was going like Usain Bolt now. "I'd be helping others and that would make me happiest of all."

There was a pause on the line. I knew what Jim was about to say, before he said it, because he and I both knew that, while insights were great, and daydreams could be motivating, it took action to make them mean something.

"What are you going to do about it, Patrick?" I stopped. As one of my idols, Tony Robbins, had once said: "There can be no result without massive action."

The coaching with Jim had given me an understanding of some of the tools required to operate in the field but, to acquire the skills I really needed, I'd have to enroll in a course.

I spent a few days researching what was available – California is a coaching hotspot – and eventually settled on an outfit called the Coach Training Institute (CTI), based in San Rafael, north of San Francisco. I knew little or nothing about them apart from what Jim had told me and what I read on their website. They were the largest coaching training institution in the world, run by a couple of people who pioneered the concept and practice of co-active coaching, Karen and Henry Kimsey-House.

Now, let's think for a second about what I was considering doing. I was about to ditch a career at which I had excelled. (Despite the trauma it can cause, getting fired in Silicon Valley is common and is actually seen as a badge of honor by many.) I was known, as I've said, as a serious, experienced, chief marketing officer who'd helped launch Google Play, who'd (briefly) put GetJar on the map, and who was sought-after by startups to help them cut through the noise and get noticed.

In place of that, I was proposing to reinvent myself as a coach, in a territory where coaches were a dime a dozen.

I had just turned 46, had limited savings and inescapable obligations to an ex-wife and two children whom I loved and wanted the very best for.

At Google, my handle had been madmork@google.com. The question I had to ask myself now was: "Am I really crazy or just plain fucking stupid?" There was only one way to find out...

The CTI course took place over seven consecutive weekends from late April to early June. Every Saturday during this period, I made the hour-and-a-half drive from Redwood City up through the San Francisco area, over the Golden Gate Bridge through Mill Valley, to San Rafael.

On my first trip up, I was fired-up by a mixture of fear and a sense of freedom. That's often the case when you've made a decision to upend your life. I was tearing down the highway in my Mini Cooper S, electronic music blaring, thinking of the possibilities.

On my left, the city, on my right, the gleaming waters of the bay. I considered what the cost of signing up with CTI represented. The cost was not insignificant for someone who was counting every out-going cent. Any rational assessment of my situation would conclude that I couldn't really afford either the cost or the risks involved.

Think about it. I was starting from scratch. My 20+ years in tech and INSEAD MBA were interesting features of my CV, but they told potential clients nothing about my worth as a coach. I had no idea whether I was going to succeed. This decision could mark the start of a downward spiral from which I might never recover.

And yet, as I made my way up US101, I had this sense, deep inside, that I was doing the right thing, that this was going to work, that coaching and helping others was my future.

It was a fine spring day, the first time I weaved my way up the peninsula. The drive wasn't long, it wasn't arduous. And yet, like a hero on a legendary journey, I was leaving one world, the world of technology, the world of startups, lines of code represented by Silicon Valley, and entering another, the world in which the values were people-centered and not monetary, in which the human spirit was more important than algorithms and coding. A world in which empathy, asking questions and soft skills mattered and made a huge difference.

The hills I passed through were green and verdant, the skies bright blue, the water of the bay silver and gold.

I felt as if I were casting off the shadow of the past and entering a brave new world of promise and possibility.

The first thing that struck me about the other members of my class – 40 or so of them – was their commitment to *people*, to making a difference, to improving the lives of others. I don't mean they were do-gooders, wannabe missionaries or Sixties-style hippies hoping to build a utopian society.

No, many were hard-headed business people. Some performed HR functions in their companies and wanted to add another string to their bows to help them do their jobs more effectively. Others were former tech executives from companies with household names: Facebook, Microsoft, Uber. A former female Uber executive, with a flaming red head of hair, was one of the most striking of them all.

There was no doubting their commitment. One woman, whom I got on well with, had flown from the UK for the seven weeks of the course. Think about that. She had to pay, not only for her course, but for seven weeks of board and lodging, car hire and all the other incidental expenses of a long trip.

And another was an inspiration all on her own. April Holmes, originally from New Jersey, had specialized in track and field events at Norfolk State University. She'd been building her career, establishing herself in the telecommunications industry, when she was involved in a train accident, which resulted in her left leg being amputated just below the knee.

Fitted with a prosthetic leg, she allowed the tragedy to rekindle her enthusiasm for athletics and, within a year, she was competing on the field. In the 2004 Paralympics, April won a bronze medal in the long jump; in the 2008 Paralympics in Beijing, she finally snagged the gold in the 100-meters sprint. And in London in 2012, bronze, again in the 100-meters. I'll never forget the day she brought her gold medal to class. I still recall the feel of it and the glint of pride in her eyes as she shared it with us.

And now, April was in San Rafael, working to equip herself with the skills she reckoned she needed to make her foundation an agent of change, diversity and hope.

I felt honored to work alongside her. She's an amazing person.

"I feel like I'm wrapped in a cloud of warmth," Brian said.

"A moment ago, you said you were feeling a little nervous about being coached in front of all these people."

"Oh," he said, "that's gone. I feel a lot more stable now. I don't feel rushed. I'm also aware that I'm actually taking time for myself in this moment and I probably haven't been doing that like, in truth, for really … months or years."

Brian, I'd learned, was working for the HR department of a startup in Silicon Valley. I could understand that he'd lost touch with himself in the rush everyone in the field experienced. I feel for you, buddy, I thought, but didn't say. Instead, I referred to my notes.

"What is happening inside your body right now?" I asked.

"Right now, I'm feeling pretty clear, although there is a bit of tightness in my shoulders and my chest… But that's easing even as I talk. I could do with a lot more clarity in my life, I can tell you."

Co-active coaching involves, among other things, really listening. I'd sensed the intensity with which Jim listened to me. Now I was learning the skill of that kind of focused listening myself.

Every Saturday, we'd have sessions in which co-active theory was explained to us. And then we'd practice coaching ourselves, one-on-one, with our fellow wannabe coaches. Brian and I were exploring what it really meant to become aware of *the moment*. At no point does the coach impose his interpretation on his client. He learns to ask simple, powerful questions and then simply to listen to – and, just as importantly – respect the innate wisdom of his client.

What we learned was that we needed, as coaches, to encourage and support our clients' belief in themselves, in their ability to find solutions, in their own resourcefulness, creativity and resilience. *They* have the wisdom and the answers within themselves. It's our job as coaches to help turn the key to these resources, to be, if you like, the locksmiths of their better selves. "You can lead a horse to water", was one common phrase. "But you can't make it drink."

It's not a matter of looking for solutions, for quick fixes; it's much more important to develop a relationship based on trust, which encourages the client to seek clarity and find the solution for themselves.

Now, one of the remarkable consequences of this approach is that every coaching session helps the coach develop a deeper understanding of their own processes and motivations. In helping others, you help yourself. We grow along with our clients. That's got to be a big plus, right? In fact, it seemed a much bigger pay-check than any I'd received in 20 years in marketing, that unexpected cash injection from Weedmaps included.

Part of our homework, over the seven weeks of the course, was to recruit clients between Saturday sessions – guinea pigs, on which we could practice our developing coaching skills.

I turned to people I knew and was friends with in the tech industry.

"Hey," I'd say, "I'm doing a coaching program and I'm learning these new tools. Would you like to have a free coaching session? I'd like to try these tools and see how they might help you."

A surprising number of people agreed instantly. Well, however much you're earning, I guess the offer of free coaching is irresistible.

One of my test subjects was a close personal friend, Gopi Rangan, a venture capitalist in the Valley. We'd both been to INSEAD (different classes) and Gopi had also been the president of the Bay Area Alumni

Association. He'd been a close friend for years and was someone I really respected and admired.

He was blown away by the experience. I won't take the credit for his enthusiasm; well, not altogether. I think he was responding to the tools I'd learned, as much as he was to my fumbling use of them. "Wow," I remember him exclaiming. "This is powerful stuff. I really uncovered some insights that feel incredibly useful."

In fact, before I'd even concluded the course in San Rafael, I was already actively seeking paying clients. My first was also a fellow INSEAD graduate, a young head of marketing for a tech startup that sold wine online.

One client doesn't make a summer, of course, but recruiting Mark Alexander opened a door on the possibilities that lay ahead. The more I coached, the more my confidence grew and, more importantly, the more I got to see the impact of my work on people's lives first-hand. The satisfaction and reward for helping people, not just to find solutions to mundane, work-related issues, but also to support them in making life-changing, career- or relationship-related decisions, was like nothing I had even remotely come close to feeling in the 20+ years I'd been working. It was an awakening.

For the first time, I felt like I was doing something many tech people and INSEAD grads had often complained they didn't have in their lives: I was making an impact and, even if it was limited, it was deep and it was real.

The thing that stops most people from getting what they want, or making significant changes in their lives, basically boils down to one thing: taking consistent and constant action towards their goals. (As Tony Robbins says: "Massive Action".)

This isn't rocket science. Even in the Valley, this is not a secret. It's been the subject of a hundred self-help books, which have pointed out the importance of developing daily habits that promote your ambitions: they range from Steven R Covey's blockbuster, *The 7 Habits of Highly Effective People*, to James Clear's explosive *Atomic Habits*.

Habits are behaviors we incorporate into our daily lives. It's a fact that good habits are as easily adopted as bad habits, so it's a no-brainer deciding which sort we should embrace.

But good habits can only help us achieve our goals if we know what those goals are.

So, at the heart of CTI's co-active coaching program, was a focus on establishing what our purpose was.

Notice that I said "purpose" and not "goals" in that last sentence.

"Purpose" is subtly different from "goals". My goal is the object of my ambition, something I've set my mind on, something I might devote my life to achieving. Something I can measure and that I strive for.

But "purpose" is bigger. It feels like something you seek rather than select. It's a calling rather than the object of a desire or an ambition. It's something that drives you and gets you up in the morning. Even on those days, particularly for startup founders, when you really feel flat-out tired. At least, that's the way I see it.

Of course, goals are important. One of my goals might be to have the means to give my children the best start in life possible. That's crucial, both for them and for me. But it's not my purpose. My purpose is what I'm here to do. It is what gives my life meaning. It's what makes me, *me*.

Now, with all due respect to Weedmaps and all the other startups I've worked for, my goals might have been to promote their sales and their profits, but I can't honestly argue that that was my purpose. I guess that's partially why, one day, my tank just ran out of gas. I looked around and was, like, "Really? This is it? I'm just here peddling mobile games, app stores or somebody's next gen mobile ad network?" The answer was obvious.

I could see, during the initial sessions at CTI, that my purpose was to help others through coaching, helping them avoid the career mistakes I'd made; to find *their* purpose and, therefore, fulfilment and, yes, happiness.

But my purpose needed to be refined, it needed to be stripped down to a single sentence, and it needed to feel powerful, inspiring and, more importantly, mine.

The coaching class wasn't just a series of lectures and group exercises that taught us the theory and practice of co-active coaching. It was also a series of introspective exercises that challenged us to explore and share who we were and what we wanted to become.

Throughout this process, we had to develop and share, as a group, our visions for the future. At the end of the journey, we had to declare, to all our fellow students, the purpose we'd sought and found, and that would drive us for the rest of our lives.

I remember the day well. It was 10 June 2018, a good sunny day in northern California, and the final day of our CTI experience. On the road up that morning, I'd honed my purpose in my mind until I had it pitch perfect.

Now I stood in the center of the circle of 40 of my fellow aspirant coaches, and shouted, as loudly as I was able, my challenge to myself and the universe.

"I am the magnetic energy that inspires people to live careers of meaning and impact."

I was finally free and I knew, at last, what I had to do.

And everything changed.

I was a certified coach with the skills and, I hoped, the sensitivities, to help others navigate the trickiest path through their professional lives, deepen their engagement with their most authentic selves and become more productive in the process.

I felt on top of the world. Yes, my savings were still under siege. I'd recently been told by my landlord he was increasing my rent by ten per cent. But I had the means, now, to establish myself in my new career and, hopefully, earn the sort of money I needed to live a reasonably comfortable life, and to create the sort of environment in which Raphael and Natasha could flourish.

Before I could call Laura to tell her the good news, she called me.

Let me give you a little insight into my relationship with Laura at this stage. We had been one of the happiest married couples we knew. People remarked on the fact that we got on so well. So, why had Laura asked me, back in 2015, for a break?

Well, it was obvious to me, in hindsight, at least.

In the early days of our marriage, Laura and I celebrated *Miercoles Feliz,* Happy Wednesdays, every week. We'd cook something delicious together and share an intimate dinner by candlelight. At the time, we were young and often poor. But, whether we were living in Madrid or, later, in Leamington Spa in the UK, Wednesdays were sacred – and, over the stove or the dinner table, we'd talk about what we were up to, what our plans were, what our dreams were.

It was a wise way of nurturing our relationship.

Later, when we moved to the US, the tempo of life increased, the demands on my time rocketed, the children were born … and our Happy Wednesdays fell by the wayside. By the time I woke up to the reality, our marriage had withered and died.

There was no massive crisis. No infidelity. No throwing of plates. Like many couples, we just drifted apart, stopped investing in the relationship and, one day, woke up to the realization that the only thing holding us together was the kids. Rather than wait for the inevitable squabbles or boredom to tear us apart, we just made the call to take a break. That break ended up becoming permanent.

But, we were still friends and we were, after all, the parents of children we both loved.

Although we were human and squabbled about trivial things from time to time and had little shake-ups over the children, on the whole, our relationship in separation was better than it had been during the last few years of our marriage.

When we met at the beginning and end of my weekends with the children, or over coffee or the odd meal, we did so as friends. We were interested in each other's lives. I had high hopes that the business she'd established some years earlier would thrive. And she hoped that my dream of becoming a coach would be achieved.

This might explain why, when Laura phoned and asked for a meeting, it struck me as no big deal. Something to do with the children, I thought. Or perhaps she wanted my thoughts on her business.

But, after we'd made the arrangements and ended the call, something niggled. Something in her tone. An edge of anxiety, perhaps, a touch of defiance? I wasn't sure what it was, but I knew that, whatever she had to say to me, would not come as a pleasant surprise.

"This letter arrived for me on Tuesday." Laura laid a sheet of paper on the table between us.

Bearing in mind my slight disquiet, I'd suggested coffee in Starbucks. It was full of people. Animated conversations were happening all around us, bursts of laughter punctuating the morning.

"Read it."

I picked it up. I recognized the letterhead. It was Laura's landlord. Oh, great, I thought. She'd been hit by an increase, too.

"Me, too," I said. "My owner increased my rent ten per cent, can you believe it? It's bad, but we'll just have to find a way of managing it."

"You haven't read it all," she said, levelly.

I dropped my eyes to the lines of type. And realized it wasn't an announcement of a rent increase. Her owner, who'd bought the house – not a big one, just 1 200 sq ft with a small yard – two years before for $1.5 million, was putting it on the market for $2.4 million.

And was giving Laura 60 days to vacate the premises – unless she was willing to make an offer to buy the house.

The Silicon Valley housing market, that had been booming ever since the recovery after 2008, continued to waterboard renters.

"Well, I suppose we can't blame him," I said, laying the letter down. "He's cashing in while the going's good. But it'll be difficult to find something else for what you're paying."

"I don't want to look for something else, Patrick," Laura said.

"I can understand that. But I can help. We'll find a way, I promise you."

"I don't want to look for something else," she repeated, "because I want to go back to Chile." She paused, her eyes fixed on mine. "With the children."

EXERCISE #1
Focus on Five

There's a famous story told about Warren Buffett's advice to his personal pilot. "Write down 25 goals," he is said to have counseled. "Decide which five of the 25 are the most important. Then focus on those, and cross out the rest."

The article in which this story was told went viral and has cropped up in blogs all over the web, and is used by coaches on every continent.

The only trouble with the story is that … it's not true. When quizzed about it at one of Berkshire Hathaway's annual shareholder meetings, Buffett said he'd never heard of it and that he'd "never made a list in his life".

And yet, decoupled from the Sage of Omaha, the advice is still excellent. It works.

It might seem difficult to identify 25 goals but, believe me, it's possible. List all of the projects you're currently working on, both at home and at work. List all of the things you want to do but feel like there's no time. List at least 25. More is better.

Next, review that list. Which goals are most appealing? Which cause you to feel that flutter of enthusiasm, that could even be said to be "a calling"? Do some soul-searching, it doesn't matter how, and narrow the list to the five highest-priority objectives. Just five. Circle them (or copy them to another piece of paper). If you find it difficult to identify the key goals, then rate each on a scale of 1 to 10 based, first on how interesting it is, and, then, on how important it is. Then multiply these two numbers together. For instance, if one of your goals has an interest rating of 9 (very interesting) and an importance rating of 3 (not that important), its score would be 27. Compare the scores. Higher is better.

Finally, commit yourself to pursuing the five surviving goals, and set aside all the others. They consume energy, they consume time – and they don't get you anywhere near achieving the really important things in your life.

Angela Duckworth, who's written a book on tenacity, called *Grit*, adds one further step to this process. She advises you to ask to what extent your five goals serve a common purpose. The more closely aligned your top five goals are, the better you'll be able to focus on what she calls your passion, and I call your purpose.

EXERCISE #2
Thanksgiving Dinner

Here's another exercise that's common in self-help manuals and I use this with every client who coaches with me personally. You're going to contemplate and describe the personal legacy you'd like to leave in this world.

Imagine it's your seventieth birthday. After an illustrious career, you've invited a whole bunch of your friends, family and colleagues around to help you celebrate reaching this milestone. The dinner's been great – a true thanksgiving occasion, in every respect. The mood is mellow and forgiving. At the head of the table, you're filled with the joy of having the people who've always meant the most to you gathered in one place.

Guests are invited to raise a glass in your honor, and say a few words.

Imagine that the first person to stand and toast you is someone who represents your family – a grown-up child, a spouse, a life partner or a sibling. Now, imagine what that person might celebrate about your personal life. Write it down: just a paragraph or two that notes your accomplishments in this area of your life.

Once the applause has died down, and the glasses recharged with fine champagne, a second speaker rises. This one's a close friend, someone you've known for years, and has a deep idea of your personal strengths – and vulnerabilities. He or she now toasts that aspect of who you are and what you mean to him or her. Write their little speech down.

Thirdly, someone you've worked with stands up and tells the gathering about your contribution in your professional life. They'll remark on your most significant accomplishments in this area, on the accolades you've been granted, on the skills you've acquired, on your judgment and your effectiveness. Write down the highlights of this speech.

And, finally, someone who knows you from the work you've done in service to the community – in your church, perhaps, or any community organization dedicated to the upliftment of people, generally, and the less fortunate, in particular. They will talk about the values that drove you to make your contribution in this area of your life, and the life of your community.

The speeches you imagine these people would make will give you insight into what you believe your purpose in life is. They will also reflect the values that underpin and inform that purpose. But, don't worry, your values are the subject of the next chapter of this book.

EXERCISE #3
Ikigai

You might have heard of the third exercise I'm going to recommend to you as a way to identify your purpose. It was originally developed in Japan and, like so many great ideas, has spread across the world and been developed and adapted to suit a whole range of applications.

Ikigai is a Japanese word meaning a reason to live or, to bring it down to Earth with a bump, it's a reason to get up in the morning.

The first exercise in this chapter identified the four characteristic arenas in which we live our lives: family, friends, work, and, if you like, duty.

Ikigai also assumes there are four areas in which we operate, but it defines them slightly differently.

- You have those things that you love doing.
- You have the ability to offer the world what *it* needs.
- You have the skills that others are willing to pay for
- You have your passion

Let's illustrate these ideas graphically:

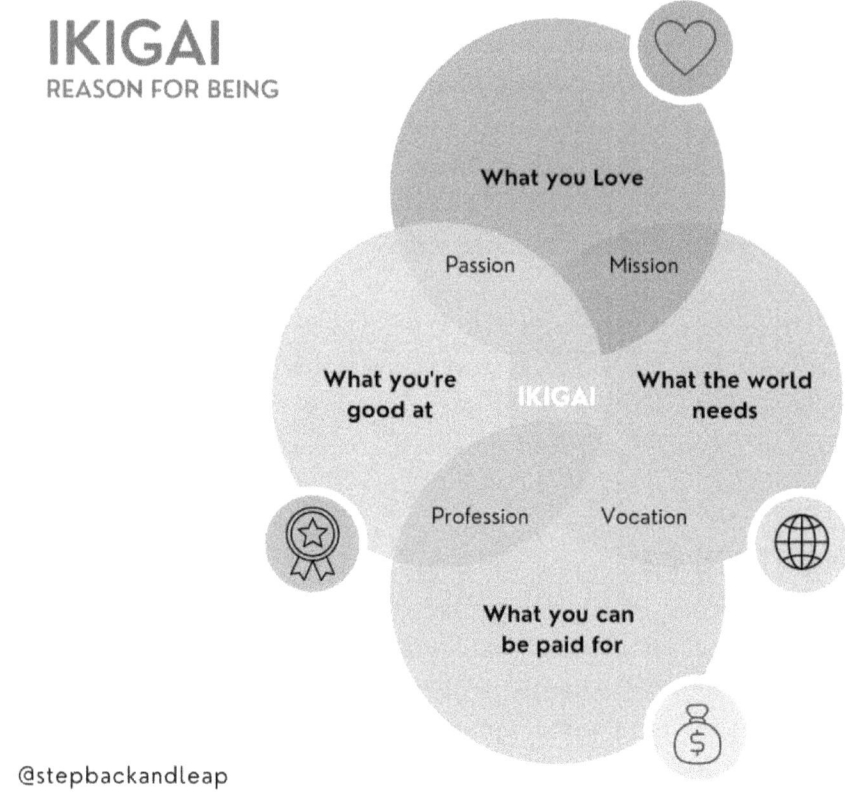

IKIGAI
REASON FOR BEING

What you Love

Passion   Mission

What you're   What the world
good at   IKIGAI   needs

Profession   Vocation

What you can
be paid for

@stepbackandleap

Your ikigai, your reason for getting up in the morning, the meaning of your *life*, is contained in the area in which all four circles overlap with each other. This is the magic spot, where your talents, your training, your vocation and the real world in which you have to make a living, converge.

So you begin, again, with a list. This time it's a list of all the things you do that give you pleasure. Think only of the satisfaction these activities give you, the joy you take in doing them.

Then, make a list of all the things you believe the world – call it the market, if you like – needs most.

Third, make a list of your marketable skills: the things you can do that you might be paid to do.

And, finally, identify the things you are really good at.

Naturally, there will already be overlaps in these four lists. After all, we naturally derive pleasure from doing the things we're good at. Our skill-set is the product of what was probably a long educational journey, and it is therefore likely to be in demand somewhere.

Your analysis will reveal which items on these four lists converge.

Take my own case, as an example:

I might decide that, at the top of the list of activities that give me most satisfaction, is helping others realize their potential. I love to help people grow. This is not entirely altruistic: helping others feeds my ego and, in some cases, it's also great for my business. I enjoy being the center of attention. I enjoy earning the gratitude of others.

Then, I might identify the fact that the world needs more soft skills. There's a lack of empathy in society and the world of business and tech. People seem not to be able to give positive feedback to their subordinates. They're impatient, lack understanding of the needs of others, don't realize the importance of communication – and the key role that active listening plays.

Which of my skills are people and businesses willing to pay for? Well, I could be paid as a writer or as an entrepreneur.

And I'm good at writing, at public speaking, and at motivating others. I'm good at leading teams. I'm good at inspiring others.

You can see at once where this analysis is going. Maybe I should go into coaching. Oh, wait…

This exercise is especially useful at a time in which change threatens to upend your world, or when you're faced with important decisions about your future: when you've graduated from college, say, and are about to choose a career. Or when you've been fired (as you've seen, I can talk from experience about that). Or when you're deciding to expand your skill-set at Graduate School.

Key #2

UNCOVER YOUR VALUES

*"People can't live with change if there's not a changeless core inside them. The key to the ability to change is a changeless sense of who you are, what you are about and **what you value**."*

—Steven R Covey

"Forget it," I said. "You can do whatever the hell you want, but you're not taking the children with you."

I slammed my cup down. Coffee surged out onto the table.

"Patrick, please, let's not fight over this."

"I'm not fighting." But I could feel the rage bubbling inside me. Laura had just announced that she was taking my children 6 000 miles away, and now she was telling me she didn't want a fight. I took a deep breath. So be it. No fighting.

"I'm just informing you," I said, aware of a tremor in my voice, "as firmly as I can, that I won't let you take my children away from me." I found myself lining up the items in front of me: the paper serviette, the notebook I'd brought with me in case Laura was late, the wallet I'd used to pay for our coffees, my latte. It was as if I imagined my little palisade could keep Laura's threat at bay.

To be clear, this wasn't, in fact, the first time Laura and I'd had this conversation. She'd mentioned the possibility of returning to Chile before. It was understandable. She came from Chile. She was born and educated there. Her family was there. Her oldest friends lived there.

But this was the first time she'd stated her intentions so boldly: "I want to go back to Chile with the children."

I suddenly flashed back twelve years to a conversation I'd had with my father when I'd told him I had proposed, and that Laura had accepted.

"You know, Patrick," he'd said. "At some point she's going to want to go back to Chile."

"No problem," I'd said. "We can go to Chile as often as we like. Christmas, holidays. Introduce our kids, if we have any, to that side of the family—"

"I don't mean that. Not on holiday. Permanently. They all want to go home at some point."

I'm not sure who he meant by "they" – but I didn't take him seriously enough to challenge him on his use of the indefinite third person pronoun: Chileans? Latinos? Any foreigners? Women?

"Maybe so," I'd said equably. And over the years, I'd always assumed that, even if my father was right, Laura would wait until our children were grown and educated. I saw Chile as, maybe, a retirement destination, somewhere we could go when our careers were done and we were happy to grow old together.

Of course, I had no clue, then, that our marriage would end in divorce before our children had even reached their teens and I certainly hadn't imagined myself living in California by myself with my children 6 000 miles away.

Now, at our table at Starbucks, I recognized that the surest way to settle this issue once and for all was to use the most reasonable arguments available.

"Listen, I can understand where you're coming from—" I began. But she'd started a sentence at the same moment:

"You know what I think of this so-called Silicon Valley culture—" Laura said, a flash of contempt in her eyes.

She thought it superficial and artificial. She found Americans brash and chafed at the pressure to demonstrate political correctness.

We each paused.

"You go first," I said.

"There are a whole lot of factors. The traffic on 101, the insane cost of living, the homeless people everywhere – I mean, have you seen the armies of poor people living under highway underpasses lately? Seriously, Patrick, even you don't actually like living here, do you?"

Whether I liked living in the Bay Area or not was beside the point. This is where I'd made a career and, more importantly, had my friends, had created a network and where I was attempting the difficult task of switching careers in mid-stream. So, I wasn't actually prepared to ask myself whether I *liked* living here. I had finally found something I enjoyed and all the people I could coach and help were based here. In the Bay Area. It was a simple matter of priorities.

I took a little time to point all this out and, although she listened and nodded, I could see that I'd lost her.

"There's another other thing. Victor has cancer—"

"Yes," I said, soberly, "you told me." Laura and her stepfather had always enjoyed a good relationship, the sort of relationship that, honestly, I'd like to establish with both my children. She respected him, she enjoyed his company, she loved him. And, just months before, he'd been told he was suffering from throat cancer. The condition was not life-threatening, but Laura had missed being at her mother's side to help care for him and support them both.

"So, go back to Chile for a few weeks. I can handle the kids. If need be, I could even move into your place—"

"I've thought of all the alternatives, Patrick. I've thought of going back, briefly, asking you for help. I even thought of suggesting you move to Menlo Park—"

"So, no problem then."

But she was shaking her head.

"It wouldn't work. Victor's cancer's not going to go away, he's not going to be back on his feet in three weeks. Plus, my business in Chile needs me and, the more it grows, the more it's going to need me. I have clients there, a business partner and employees. I can't continue to run things from here."

Laura had always been an entrepreneur at heart. She had tried her hand at multiple companies and had finally started a business in Chile, which she had, somehow, miraculously managed from Silicon Valley. It was a services business focused on events designed to bring innovation to the Chilean economy, and now it was starting to thrive.

I sighed and glanced at my phone. I'd run out of time.

"I'm sorry," I said. "I've got a meeting in 20 minutes—" I started dismantling my palisade.

"Will you think about what I've said?"

"Yeah, of course," I said quickly. But I knew, even as we exchanged a brief hug, that I'd already made up my mind. There was no way I was moving to the ass-end of the Earth and there was no way I was going to allow anyone to rob me of my children.

She was still at our table when I got onto my bike outside. I could read the words she mouthed at me through the glass as clearly as a headline on a billboard: "Think about it. Please."

When I got home, I made a quick call to a friend who worked in IP law. I put my question to him. As I'd expected, he said that, although he'd studied it, he'd never practiced family law and, for all he knew, there'd been a revolution in family law since he'd graduated. He was nevertheless pretty sure a wife had to have the signed agreement of her husband to take their children out of the country.

Well, it was no more than I had vaguely understood – but, hearing it from the lips of a lawyer was deeply reassuring.

My meeting was with my new coach. I was by this point no longer working with Jim. I had decided I needed a different perspective. Jim, by his own admission, excellent though he was, was not formally certified as a coach. Having immersed myself in the disciplines taught by CTI, I wanted to work with a coach trained in the same methodology.

Rachel Peterson sensed my ambivalence about switching coaches. She's more mothering than Jim could ever be, or would ever want to be, but she's also loud, funny and tough. And her methodology simply felt clearer and sharper than Jim's. Plus, she had the tools to match.

My nine months with Jim had changed my life and put me on a new career path. Now, I felt that I needed someone with more structure, more tools and exercises to tackle things that were deeper down and which, I knew, I had neglected for way too long. I felt a bit rudderless and without direction. I just didn't get what my purpose was and, although I had some idea around my values, they were not crystal clear either.

Purpose that isn't informed by a clear sense of what's important to you is, well, interesting without being particularly significant.

Rachel was also a graduate of CTI, with a long history of working with Valley types like me, executive survivors of the tech rat race.

Of course, I felt bad abandoning Jim, although he assured me that he understood my decision.

My goal was to identify the key values which I hoped to live my life by and practice my new profession.

I get that, for some of you, this will probably sound like touchy-feely BS. I can understand that. But bear with me while I sketch out the process, and describe what came of it.

Values aren't invented, they're unlocked. This means the process of listing the key values you hope to live your life by is kind of like a detective story. What is most important to you? What accounts for those "peak moments" that we experience as epiphanies, or OMG moments, moments of acute happiness, or serenity; those "aha" moments when we feel as if we have a finger on the pulse of the universe?

The thing that underlies those moments of supreme clarity are generally your core values.

And then, by contrast, what accounts for that burst of what you felt at the time was irrational anger? When you felt your blood boil and you lashed out, verbally or physically? Was it in response to what you perceived as something unjust? Did you experience it as an assault on your ego? Were you responding to a comment that targeted a vulnerable area?

Usually, what underlies these flashes of rage are core values. When someone says or does something, or when you read or see something on social media that just makes you want to scream or freak out, that's generally because one of your values has been trampled on.

Why did I feel like I really needed to come to grips with my values? Simple. I deeply suspected I hadn't been living my life according to my core values. Both professionally and personally, things just felt out of whack. There were things that really bothered and frustrated me, which I couldn't quite put my finger on. I needed someone on the outside to probe and ask tough questions. Someone to shake things up. Someone to help me see the obvious things I wasn't seeing.

Rachel fired question after question at me during our video conferences: powerful questions aimed at unearthing clues that would help me formulate my own unique set of values.

Now the fact is, we're all humans, so it follows that we share a great many values. If we didn't, life on Earth would be riven by conflict. Oh, wait...

But seriously, motherhood and apple-pie are virtually universally acknowledged as the touchstones of a certain kind of value-set.

And that's true of values in a much broader sense. In fact, you can find online lists of values, some of them over 200 items long. They include such things as accomplishment, altruism, truthfulness, empathy, fortitude, integrity, and so on.

You could, I guess, run your shopping cart up and down the aisles of a values Walmart and pick out the values that strike your fancy.

But there aren't really any shortcuts. The tough part – where you have to cut through the undergrowth of memory and feeling to find your compass, your true north – is the only sure route.

"Tell me about the feelings you experienced when you crossed the finish line?" Rachel asked me. The race she was referring to was the Sequoia Century cycle race, which I'd just taken part in, and which forms the basis of the next chapter in this book.

The Sequoia played a big role in what you might loosely call my psychic rehabilitation, after the blows I'd suffered to both my ego and my career.

Remember that, having recently separated from Laura, I was fired twice in relatively quick succession. Critically, the ride restored my confidence in myself and proved to my own satisfaction that I possessed a streak of bold fearlessness.

"It felt amazing," I told Rachel. "I mean, I was so exhausted I could barely stand up – but I felt on top of the world."

"Was it a peak moment for you?"

"Absolutely. No question."

"Try and unpack those feelings, Patrick. What does being on top of the world mean to you?"

As we pierced deeper into the feelings triggered by my completion of the race, we started putting together a value-set that I called, "The Century Ride". This value was actually a cluster of the following values: striving, driving, questing, curiosity, resilience; the quality of being present, tolerating no bullshit, being willing to commit to people, having no limits, and, yes, being both bold and fearless...

In identifying this value, I also committed myself to *upholding* it. "The Century Ride" is both a description and a prescription. If, having named "fearlessness" as one of the values I hold dear, I then chickened out of a challenge, I would feel bad, no doubt about it. I would feel disappointed in myself. I would feel that my actions were not aligned with my core beliefs in myself.

Defining "The Century Ride" was the first step in my quest to find what my most important values were.

The next time I saw Laura was at the weekend, when I was picking the kids up. She stood at her front door with her arms crossed, watching me as I settled the children into the back of my black and red Mini Cooper S, a car Laura had never liked, particularly when compared to the sleek and somber Audi S5 I had owned during my time at Google. It probably sounds trivial and childish but, somehow, buying that car felt like my last, single act of defiance towards the end of a marriage that was heading off a cliff.

"I hope you've been thinking about … Chile," she said.

"I checked my legal position," I shot back. "You can't do a thing without my permission. That's the law."

I slammed the door and left in such a hurry that I think I left scorch marks on the asphalt.

"What did Mom mean?" Raphael asked. "That thing about the law? And Chile?"

"Why're you fighting, Daddy?" Natasha said.

Laura and I took care not to express any discord in front of the kids. We tried never to argue about things within their hearing. We attribute their relatively easy acceptance of our divorce to this habit. But the flip side of the coin is that, when there *is* a disagreement, the kids pick up on it very quickly.

"It's nothing, guys," I said. "Just something Mom and I were talking about."

"Chile?" Rafi repeated.

"Yeah. Victor's sick and we were talking about that. He's in Chile. You know that."

Raphael knew that wasn't the whole truth, or even an approximation of the truth, but he also knew I wasn't about to come clean.

"You're going too fast," he said a few seconds later.

"Daddy, can you change the lights to pink?" Natasha said with a great, big smile. She loved how I could change all the LEDs inside the car, the doors, dashboard and floor lighting, to her favorite color. She also loved it when I drove fast. They are so different.

"Tell me about Mad Mork," Rachel said.

Another video conference, another episode in the search for my true values. Of course, everyone believes in a whole stack of values. Most of us would endorse every one of the values listed on that site on the internet. We all believe in honesty, fair play, love, loyalty, endurance, courage, and so on. In reality, it's all bullshit because, sadly, most of us never really clue into our real values and, even if we did, many of us don't live our lives by them. The only time we start to seriously think about our values is when our lives have felt really off, for a seriously long time.

The question that we each have to work out is, which four or five values – or *clusters* of related values – constitute our moral compass. Which four or five values should work as our guide when we make important and consequential decisions?

I'd earned the Mad Mork moniker back in my business school days at INSEAD, after I and some friends pulled an outrageous stunt which involved me pouring a can of beer over a visiting McKinsey partner's head while he was giving a talk in one of the auditoriums in front of 300-or-so MBAs. It was all staged, of course. The McKinsey guy, himself a member of our class, was in on the deal.

But the staged incident so shocked the audience of incoming MBA candidates that a number of them petitioned to have me expelled and instantly vilified me as Mad Mork. The name stuck, even after the whole thing was explained and they came to realize that this incident, as well as many other inexplicably strange things that week, had been part of a performance.

I explained all this to Rachel. "You rather like the idea that you're a … a provocateur, a disrupter, a rebel?"

"Absolutely."

In fact, I'd liked it so much that, over the years, I'd used the name as my handle at Google (madmork@google.com), something which Lorraine Twohill, Google's chief marketing officer, had often chided me for. It was even the license plate on my Mini.

"Tell me what it means to be Mad Mork?"

And out of that discussion emerged another value. "Mad Mork" is independent and free-thinking. He lives the life he chooses. He possesses an innate drive to challenge. He stands for fairness and justice, he's anti-establishment and he hates being politically correct.

And, when I looked at that value written on my google doc, a number of things suddenly became really obvious. People have often asked me, for example, why I left Google. A perfectly good job, at a great company, on a cutting-edge team with a pretty decent pay package. I had often struggled to put the answer into words. But, looking at the Google doc and the words, Mad Mork, it started to make much more sense. I'd left Google because I felt stuck. I'd left Google because Google Play, the startup I had helped build, had grown into a serious business and, with a serious business, came serious rules, processes and oversight. I left Google because I could no longer be "Madmork". The way they wanted to run the business, and manage me, was no longer in line with my values. I had to leave.

"Good," Rachel said, as I shared that sudden insight with her. "It looks like we're really getting somewhere."

The kids and I spent Sunday at Half Moon Bay, walking the coastal trail. It takes you three or four miles from Miramar up past Manhattan Beach and, if you're in the mood for golf or just an expensive meal overlooking the bluff, through the course at the Ritz Carlton.

It's a perfect walk for me and the kids, not too strenuous, with truly wonderful views of the ocean, and the chance to talk – or not. In fact, for me, half the value was in reconnecting with nature. It soothes me. It calms me. It's better than a hot stone massage.

And then Rafi asked me whether I was still mad at Laura.

"I'm not mad at her," I said. He gave me one of his looks that said, who was I trying to kid? "Seriously, buddy. She wants to go to Chile. I want to stay here. Parents sometimes have to sort out disagreements like that. It doesn't mean we're mad at each other."

"You sure *sounded* mad," he said.

I realized the muscles in my shoulders had tensed up again. "Give me a moment, guys." We had just crossed a little creek that runs down a gulch into the bay. I paused, looking down to the beach, took a deep breath and tried to erase from my mind the possibility of losing the kids.

I explained all this to Rachel during our next session.

"So, nature's important to you?"

"Isn't it important to everyone?"

"Maybe so," she said thoughtfully, "but you seem to use it consciously as … therapy?"

"It's more than that."

I've always loved nature. Going to the beach, or to the woods, as I often did with the kids, was a way for me to recharge my batteries and get reconnected with the natural world. It must be a connection we're programmed for, something established by thousands or maybe millions of years of evolution. It's hard-wired into our DNA.

For some reason, a visit we'd recently made to the Japanese Friendship Gardens near San Jose sprang to mind. It's a beautiful, tranquil place, with large ponds filled with enormous koi. Both I and the kids had been mesmerized by the fluid dance of the fish among the water lilies.

Watching them was like meditation.

I mentioned this to Rachel. She chuckled. "You know what koi symbolize in Japan? Let me see: good fortune, yes, success, certainly, prosperity and ambition."

"My kind of fish." I laughed.

"More seriously," she went on, "nature seems to be another touchstone for you, the basis of another value."

And that's how Tranquility joined the Century Ride and Mad Mork in my hall of values. To me, it represented peace, simplicity, gratitude, an impulse to get back to basics, a refuge. It was embodied in the natural world. It went hand in hand with good health and a sense of natural belonging. But it suggested a deep connection with self, with family and, most fundamentally of. all, what it means to be human.

A few days passed and Laura called me. "I want to talk a little more," she said. I felt my hackles rise at once, all my old suspicions returning in a rush. I had visions of Laura abducting the kids, smuggling them out of the country, and flying to Chile, like some Bad Mom in a Netflix series.

Of course, Laura was anything but a Bad Mom. She put the children first, every time. She'd never deliberately rob them of their father. In all fairness, she'd been a good wife too.

But, despite all that, would she be tempted to smuggle the kids out of the country?

When it came to my kids, I knew I was getting a little paranoid. That's why my response was suspicious: "If it's about you going to Chile with the kids, haven't we said all we need to say?"

"I want to go about it a little differently this time. I want to bring in a mediator."

For a moment, I thought she'd said, meditator. Well, I was all for meditation. My reaction to the koi in San Jose was testament to that. In fact, as part of my new, post-tech detox, I meditated every morning for 20 minutes. It was part of the process of reinventing myself. Better yet, it worked.

But then I did a double take and realized she'd said, not "meditator" but "mediator".

"Tell me more," I said cautiously.

"I've been recommended to this guy in Menlo Park. He's not expensive, and I hope he'll help us work through this, whichever way it turns out. We're just going to talk and he's going to help us understand each other's perspectives a bit better."

The best thing to do in any negotiation, when you're confronted with an invitation to commit, is to delay. "Let me think about it," I said.

Long story short: I thought about it, concluded that it was an entirely reasonable suggestion and tucked into my pants pocket the thought that, if the mediation looked as if it were turning against me, I could always walk. It wasn't a court of law, after all.

The mediator was a nondescript guy in his 40s, the sort of man who might as easily have been an assistant sales manager for a small-town car dealership, or an English teacher at a high school. He was mild-mannered, soft spoken, with a comb-over that didn't really conceal the fact that he was completely bald on top. Laura had booked three sessions up-front.

I wondered whether she wasn't being over-optimistic. We were going into the negotiation with totally opposite agendas. How on earth would we be able to arrive at a mutually satisfying agreement after just three hours of talking?

"I'd like to begin," the mediator said, after we'd concluded our introductions and settled into more or less comfortable chairs in his office, "by asking each of you in turn to state as clearly as possible your side of the story. I want you to explain to each other what you each want."

That sounded like a coaching mantra to me. Tell us what you *want*. It was the basis of every coaching session I'd ever witnessed – or run. Until you know what you want, how can you put together a plan designed to *get* you what you want? Mediation was, if you like, a coaching session for two.

Problem was, of course, that what I wanted was X and what Laura wanted was Y.

The mediator – I'll call him Larry Chalmers – explained the first of the ground-rules of mediation. While one person was spelling out what they wanted, how they felt and the consequences of their situation, the other party should not interrupt at all, except to ask for clarification. When one of us had finished, he'd ask the other to summarize what they'd understood: in other words, play it back to the first. Later, as I became a coach, I would come to know this as active listening and it would even become a core skill that I would teach my clients.

"Got that?"

Well, it seemed simple enough. I suggested Laura go first. As she outlined her desire to return to Chile, Larry noted each of her talking points on a large whiteboard on his wall: her concern for her step-father; her desire to take charge of her growing business there; her dislike of Silicon Valley's values; her appetite for contact between the children and their extended family; the fact that life in Chile was less expensive and intense than the Valley... It was a long list. She was clear and direct in her declaration and I hardly needed any clarification.

I was tempted to object to some of the points she raised, but a look from Larry reminded me of the rules of engagement.

Then it was my turn.

I started by paraphrasing her arguments. I realized, as I did so, that, coming out of *my* mouth, they seemed pretty reasonable. Life in the Valley

was intolerable, and insanely expensive. People *were*, by and large, monoma-
niacal – single-mindedly pursuing their tech and financial goals without
paying enough, or any, attention to the other priorities of life. Bridges over
the highways had become refuges for RVs and the homeless, unable to afford the budget-busting rentals landlords were charging.

Finally, I came to her concluding argument. It had not been about
what she wanted, but what she believed the toll of living and working in
the Valley represented, for me. She didn't once point to my failures over
the past few years, I'll give her that. It would have been understandable if
she had. She pointed out that I wasn't working in tech anymore and that,
in her view, my experience and track record would be much more valuable
in Santiago than they were in Silicon Valley, where CMOs were a dime a
dozen.

I acknowledged, at once, that much of what Laura had said was true.

"The thing is, though, that, yes, I'm not in tech anymore, but nor am I
in marketing. I'm trying to build a new career as a coach. It's fucking hard,
excuse my French, Larry, but it is. I'm 46, and I need all the help I can get.
That help is here. My network is here. My friends are here. My former colleagues are here. Who do I know in Santiago? Nobody!"

I realized there was a note of panic in my voice. I took a deep breath.

"Take your time, Patrick," Larry murmured.

"Look, Laura, you need to give me a few years, that's all I'm asking. To
establish myself as a coach, to work up a decent client base. To get some
money in the bank."

When I'd finished, Laura reflected – very fairly, I thought – what I'd
said back to me. Larry thanked us, and said he looked forward to the second session, at which we'd explore options for compromise.

He seemed to be happy with our progress. Laura seemed satisfied. I,
though, was left with the sense that all we'd done was spell out the reasons
we could never agree.

I was still adamant that I was not prepared to let her take our kids to
a distant foreign country. At night, sometimes, particularly in the evening
after I'd had the kids for a few days and driven them back to Laura's house,
I'd stare at the ceiling in my little, ridiculously overpriced apartment, and

try to imagine weekends without them. My chest would tighten and tears would well up in my eyes. It was simply too much to bear.

The thought that Laura wanted to take my kids away, I guess, was what prompted me, that evening, to call up all the photographic albums I'd collected on my tablet. Many of the more recent ones were devoted to trips I'd taken with the kids.

For Thanksgiving a couple of years before, I'd planned a road trip to a horse ranch in Castaic, southern California. I was no cowboy, that's for sure, but I figured the kids would love to learn to ride.

I didn't have a lot of money – I seem to keep playing that tune – so the cottage we booked on Airbnb for the weekend was about as small-ass as they come. But we'd have access to ponies every day, so I reckoned a little hardship wouldn't be a bad thing. It would help strengthen the bonds between us, I thought.

I talked up the delights of horse-riding all the way down.

I didn't count on two things. One, I hadn't done the math correctly and, instead of taking a couple of hours to get there, it took seven and a half hours. We arrived well after sundown. The kids, especially Natasha, who was just four, were exhausted. I had to coax them to eat something before they fell into bed.

The second thing was that Raphael turned out to be allergic – extremely allergic – to horses, and almost instantly came out in a rash. So, no horse-riding for him.

But I do have pictures of Natasha on horseback looking quite the cowgirl. And a couple of pics of Raphael reaching out tentatively to – but not actually touching – a horse.

I was right about one thing. Cooking together, sharing the space of the tiny cottage, was fun. I enjoyed it, and the kids enjoyed it. Those pictures recalled just some of the fond memories I've built over the years of my trips with them. Priceless moments of pure happiness.

As I flipped through my albums and felt myself tearing up – because, despite my reputation for brashness and assertiveness, I'm a softie at heart – I realized how many of my peak experiences had happened in the company of Peanut, as I always call Natasha, and my "little man", Raf. Moments of happiness so extreme that, reviewing the pictures I'd taken over the years, I felt a resurgence of joy and a deep sense of peace and gratitude.

There wasn't much joy to be found in Larry's office during that second mediation session. By the time our hour was running out, Laura was tight-lipped and I realized I was as tense as a guitar string.

"I can't see what's wrong with my proposal," I said belligerently.

It was something that had occurred to me after I'd spent an hour checking out those records of my trips with the kids. I could understand why Laura hated life in the Valley. To a large extent, I shared those feelings. We were both stressed financially. We both found the values of the tech crowd alienating. So why not move … to Florida, to Miami?

Florida, because my father lived in Florida for part of the year, so we'd have a support network to help with the kids. Florida, because I had friends there, contacts who would help me establish myself in my new career. Florida, because it was still the goddamn United States, with its high-speed internet and Amazon Prime.

Laura killed that idea real quick with an adamant "no".

"Because it's not a compromise," Laura said. "It's not Chile. *My* business isn't in Florida, my parents aren't in Florida, my *home* isn't in Florida!" Her voice rose to a crescendo. "Either we move to Chile, or we're not moving."

I sat back, exasperated.

"Well," I said, "I don't see, then, that a compromise is possible. You want to go to Chile, I don't. It's as simple as that. All I can tell you, for the twentieth time, is that I won't have my children ripped away from me."

Larry stepped in then. "I don't think Laura's suggesting that she wants to rip your children away from you, Patrick—"

Whose side was this guy on, anyway? Perhaps the time had come to abandon this farce of a mediation. I was about to get up and get the hell out of there when Laura spoke again.

"Actually, Patrick, it's not simply that I don't want to take your children away from you—"

"You're proposing to take them to the ass-end of the Earth." I could feel my face flush with rage.

"Not without your agreement."

"Damn right. You legally can't do it," I fumed.

In fact, my father had stepped into the fray and sent Laura an email threatening her with "legal Armageddon" if she tried to deprive me of the kids.

"Whatever the law said, I would never take them away from you."

I felt the steam go out of me. "What are we talking about then?"

Laura composed herself for a moment, then spoke calmly: "What I'm saying is that, if you refuse to come to Chile yourself, then I'll stay in California. I'll run my business from California. I'll go back to Chile to see Victor for a few weeks. If I need to go back repeatedly, I'll do that. I'll just have to scrape the money together. Not impossible."

"So, you'll just give up?"

"Let's say, I'll put my dream on hold, that's all. The children are more important. It would hurt them to be deprived of their father. I won't do that to you or to them."

And that more or less brought the hour with Larry to a close. I walked out of there and back to my bike in a daze. Laura was willing to concede on *everything?*

"One thing's clear," Rachel said in our next session, which took place just a couple of days later, "and that is, your ex is clearly prioritizing your relationship with the kids ahead of her own dreams and desire to move back to Chile."

"Come on. She's not giving up her business. Far as I know, it's doing very well."

"That's the business she runs in Chile?"

"Remarkable, right?" It was. Because Laura ran her business in Chile from her dining room table in Menlo Park – and ran it very successfully. Not sure that I could have done as much.

"Your decision not to move," Rachel said, "is about your career, isn't it?"

"Sure." What else could it be about? "Working here in Silicon Valley is a smart career decision. It puts me in reach of my market, it gives me access to the world's best communications tech… Well, you know the arguments."

"I just wonder how consistent these *career* decisions are with your values?"

I thought back over the three value clusters we'd already identified: the Century Ride values, which identified my driving curiosity, my commitment to boldness and fearlessness. I considered my Mad Mork values: independence of thought, my anti-establishment bent, my belief in justice and fairness. And finally, I ran through the values attached to my love of nature: my love of peace, my sense of gratitude for being in the world, my deep connection to my family and my common humanity…

Thinking about that last commitment sent a shiver up my back, I wasn't sure why. Perhaps, in putting my career first, I was doing Laura an injustice. Had I always put my career first? I had an uneasy feeling that I had, from the start. We'd always gone where my career took me, across oceans and time zones, from Spain to England and on to California.

All the decisions I'd made in the past had been about me. My career. My job. My money. My promotion. My dreams.

Me. Me. Me. Me. Me.

My silence was eloquent. Rachel – who sometimes astounded (and astounds) me with her ability to read my mind – said: "And then there's the value that I think we should talk about now."

I'm not sure why I hadn't started with this, final, value. It was so obvious. Who did I value most in the world, above my career, above my drive to prove myself, above my appetite for challenge? My children, Peanut and Rafi.

"Being a good father," I said.

And we dug into it, in the usual fashion, with Rachel asking me count-less probing questions and, by the end of the session, I'd fleshed out my final core value: "The Good Father".

The Good Father value is all about mentoring, coaching, helping and being there for others. More importantly, the Good Father is exactly that: a good father. And there were only two people in the world that mattered from that perspective: Natasha and Raphael Mork, Peanut and Little man.

It required of me a total commitment to being really present and en-gaged in the way I *hadn't* been in the final years of my marriage; to being prepared to play, have fun. It implied spending quality time, not just with my family, but with my clients as well. And it mirrored a generally optimis-tic take on the world and the future.

As I wrote down that final feature, a memory flashed before my eyes, of Peanut asking me earnestly one evening, when I was putting her to bed: "Daddy, why are you always so mad?"

I didn't want to be remembered by my children as the Mad Dad. I wanted to be the Good Father in my dealings with them, and with the world.

"You look as if you've just hit the tape on the finishing line," Rachel said.

She was right.

This time, the decision had to be about something else. It had to be about someone else. I still remember getting off the video conference with Rachel, sitting down on the edge of my bed and looking at the piece of paper with my Good Father value scrawled on it. It was then that I real-ized I had to rethink my position. I had to step outside myself and look at this entire situation from a different perspective. I had to make a change.

I had come to a turning point in my life. To be certain that I was making the right decision, I did what I always did under circumstances like that: I drove out to the beach to clear my head and think.

I booked a room at the Pacifica Beach Hotel, just ten miles north of Miramar Beach. I'd never stayed there before but, every time I'd passed by, I'd felt an urge to stop and explore it. It sat perched, like an eagle, overlooking the sea. At the center of the hotel was a 1920s-style glass structure that sheltered an indoor pool. Whenever I'd driven by that place, for some reason I'd thought about F Scott Fitzgerald's *Great Gatsby*.

The Pacifica has great views out over the Pacific but, for the most part, sitting in my room on that first evening, I was immersed in my thoughts – thinking of possibilities, crunching numbers – and ignored the sun sinking into the ocean. I grabbed a meal at a nearby Peruvian restaurant. I'm sure it was great, but I was so preoccupied that, honestly, I don't remember what I ate.

When you're confronted with the need to make a potentially life-changing decision, you start by being practical or, at least, I do. Although I was familiar with Chile, and speak Spanish fluently, it was 20 years since I'd spent any time there. I was unfamiliar with the business scene, and I knew next to nothing about its economy. Crucially, I knew nothing about the difficulties of raising money there to fund a business.

The calculations I made about potential income were so vague that, after a couple of hours playing with numbers on Google Sheets, I gave up in frustration and went to bed, with the sound of the restless ocean echoing my mood.

First thing in the morning, I reached for a towel and went for a swim, then, chilled but very awake, walked along the beach, skirting the surf line.

Thinking.

Laura had argued that she believed moving to Chile was best, not just for her, but for the kids.

In Chile, they'd have family. Their grandparents, cousins and extended family. In Chile, they would have a nanny and a better quality of life. More importantly, they wouldn't be subject to the stress of two separated parents living a frenetic and stressful Silicon Valley life and struggling to keep their heads above water.

She had also argued that the move would be good for me. I could start over with a fresh slate, a *tabula rasa*. I could build my coaching business. I could work to develop the entrepreneurial ecosystem. There were probably not too many Belgians living in Santiago who spoke several languages, including Spanish, and who had lived in eleven countries and worked at Google and several startups.

But, on the other end of the scale, I had to weigh the following facts: I had spent ten years of my life in the Valley. All my friends were there. I had a professional reputation, even if it was a bit blemished. I loved my cycling and I loved living in the States. I just couldn't imagine moving to a small, Latin American country on the other side of the world, where I'd have to start all over again at the tender age of 46.

How was I going to break the logjam of these competing options? I thought back over my session with Rachel and, without warning, out of the blue Pacific, came a single, simple question:

What would the Good Father do?

And, all of a sudden, it was painfully obvious.

I'd come to the end of the beach. A path led up a bluff. I followed it until I stood well above the ocean, heaving and surging below me.

I don't think I'll ever forget that moment. I looked out over the Pacific with the cold wind blowing in my face. I'd made up my mind. Now I needed to communicate it to Laura.

I decided to drive to Menlo Park for our final session with Larry, although it was only 20 minutes there on my bike, and I usually relished the exercise. But I wanted to waylay Laura when she got there, and I reckoned I'd be better off waiting for her in a car.

I recognized her BMW X5 when she arrived just a couple of minutes before the mediation was due to begin. Enough time, though, to tell her what I'd decided.

I greeted her as she got out of her car.

"Hola." We often spoke Spanish between us.

She paused at the entrance to the building, frowning. "I don't think Larry wants us negotiating out of the room."

"And I don't want to negotiate—"

"Oh, god, Patrick. If I have to listen to another of your ultimatums—"

"It's not that. It's just that I've come to a decision and—"

"Can't it wait?" She glanced at her wristwatch. "We're going to be late. And haven't you got it, yet? It's not about you making a decision – it's about the two of us talking things through. It's mediation, not you decide or I decide. I've had enough of—"

I put a finger to her lips. She recoiled from my touch.

"Hey!"

"Listen to me for a moment, will you. Thirty seconds, that's all it'll take."

She sighed. "Okay, then. What's this latest decision of yours?"

I spent the first few minutes of our final mediation session explaining a few things to Larry. I'm not sure why I wanted him to understand. Perhaps I recognized that this was my final opportunity to justify my decision. I'd already put Laura out of her misery. I wasn't doing it for her benefit and there was no reason to seek Larry's approval, so my little speech must have been for my own benefit.

"I know I'll be repeating myself," I began, "but I'd like to run over the reasons it would be madness for me to go to Chile."

I went through the by-now familiar terrain. The difficulties of raising finance or seeking investors in Chile. The lack of a sophisticated communications network. The lack of a personal or professional network. The lack of friends and being even further from my aging parents.

And so on and so forth.

"So, you've decided to stay in Silicon Valley?" Larry said. "Well, Laura told you last week that if you did make that decision, that she would—"

"Wait, I haven't finished." I glanced at Laura. She was perfectly composed, happy to wait for me to finish. She'd managed, somehow, to bottle her usual volatility.

I told Larry about my work with Rachel on identifying and defining my values – and I spent some time talking about The Good Father and what that meant to me.

"When I stood out there on the beach at the Pacifica, I asked myself what the Good Father would do under these circumstances. And the answer was immediately clear to me."

"What Patrick's doing," Laura cut in, "is taking a thousand words to tell you what he could have told you in ten."

"And what was the answer?" Larry asked.

"It's the story-teller in him," Laura said. "He looks for drama, always. It drives me crazy."

"My answer is: It's time to be true to who I say I want to be. I'm moving to Chile."

Discovering your values can be frustrating, because isn't it obvious what they are? You value … honesty and integrity and compassion. Add to that spontaneity, rebelliousness (like me), your middle finger held up proudly at conventional wisdom, plus justice, fairness, generosity, and … and…

You need to take your values into account when you're making important decisions. But, can you take them *all* into account? The 200 values in your Values Walmart are simply too overwhelming to serve as a practical set of criteria to use at any given point of crisis, or decision.

You have to know what lies at the *core* of your values. What four or five values form the absolutely essential set, which you hope will serve you through life and guide your most important decisions?

Here are two exercises that helped me and, I believe, will help anyone identify their core values.

EXERCISE #1
Billboard
Imagine that you've had a very successful career. You've done well, you've received the accolades of your peers, and you've made good money along

the way. You're at the top of your game, you've mastered the skills that enabled you to climb the ladder to the top. You're now heading towards retirement.

An organization in your city has decided to honor you by giving you a billboard in a prominent place, overlooking a highway leading into the city. It'll feature a picture of you – and a message from you that captures, in just a few words, some idea or advice that you'd like to transmit to as many people as possible.

That message is what we'd like you to compose now. It is what you've learned over a lifetime of experience. Perhaps it's the distillation of the wisdom that enabled you to succeed, or to overcome the hurdles life placed in your way, or the inspiration that gave you wings.

When I did this exercise for the first time, the message I wanted inscribed on the billboard was this: There's no such thing as failure – only learning. (Have a look at the final chapter of this book.) But equally, it could be something like: Face your fears. Or, Do unto others as you would have them do unto you.

Give it some thought. After all, your message to the nation … to the universe … is one of your fundamental values, your north star: it lies at the heart of what you believe most passionately.

By the way, the exercise in the last chapter, which I called Thanksgiving Dinner, can also serve to identify your values. Have another look at it now.

EXERCISE #2
I'm mad as hell and I'm not going to take it anymore

You'll recognize the quote from the 1976 movie, *Network*, in which Howard Beale (played by Peter Finch, who won an Oscar for his performance) makes an impassioned rant, which ends with that wonderful line. It's worth quoting something else he says in the same speech: "I'm a human being, goddammit. My life has value."

That's what this exercise zooms in on: the values that are revealed by rage.

Cast your mind back to an incident that really pissed you off. It might have been a conversation in which someone dismissed your argument contemptuously. It might have been that you witnessed some injustice – a homeless person being mocked, or a black person being beaten up by a white cop. You might even recall that indelible memory of being teased at school for wearing the wrong shoes, or an unfashionable blouse.

Remember how you clenched your fists so tightly that your fingernails threatened to slice into your palms. You had to control yourself from lashing out physically. You might now, in retrospect, regret *not* retaliating.

Now, try to recall the feeling that lay under the rage. Take your time. Feel the emotions flow through you. Try and put a name to each emotion.

Very often, when we get mad at someone, when we feel our blood boil inside, or a film of red spread across our vision, it's because one of our fundamental values has been flouted. Bullying is outrageous because it's so *unjust*, right? Having your views dismissed is cause for anger because it's so *unfair*. Reading a news report about a child being abused makes you angry because *children are sacrosanct*. Witnessing someone being discriminated against on the basis of their race makes you indignant because *people should be judged by the content of their character and not the color of their skin*.

Justice, fairness, equity, compassion: these are all values that determine how we live our lives. When we see them transgressed, we get upset.

By analyzing what upsets you, you can find your way back to the values you hold dear.

The flip side of this exercise is a more positive one. Think now about what last moved you to tears of joy. You might see a clip of a man throwing himself into a raging river to save a child who'd slipped and fallen in.

You might see two senior citizens, well into their 80s, holding hands and clearly still in love… Or a mother glowing with pride as she watches her child recite a poem on the school stage… Or a disabled person struggling to accomplish a task, but insisting they do so without help.

You might recall being praised by your boss for something you did that you thought, perhaps, would never be noticed.

Anything that inspires strong emotions in you can be a clue to your values.

I know that, when I witness someone behaving arrogantly – say, somebody obviously wealthy who pushes to the head of a queue, insisting they be served first – I get really mad. I want to step out of line and smack some sense into this person.

I know that, when I encounter closed minds – people who say they've always done something their way, and damned if they're going to change – I have to restrain myself. I value very highly the capacity of people, whatever their situation, whatever their past, whatever their age, to grow, to push beyond their comfort zone and change their behavior.

So, when my father, now in his late 70s, insists that he's too old to change, that an old dog can't learn new tricks, I lecture him sternly on the need to remain open to the possibility of changing. The refusal to expand our horizons is simply not acceptable to me. After all, if we're not willing to grow, then we're standing still and, since the world is constantly evolving and changing – remember Heraclitus's river? – refusing to change means we're going backwards. It means we drown. It means we die.

And who, in their right mind, wants to shrivel up and die?

Key #3

UNLOCK YOUR GOALS

People who don't have goals end up working for people who do.

—JACK CRANFIELD

In the months after my marriage fell apart and I moved into my shitty little apartment in Redwood City, I became seriously depressed. I'd been through the worst two years of my life. Almost everything that could go wrong *had* gone wrong.

My marriage had imploded.

Although I still saw them pretty often, the fact was that I'd lost my kids – or, at least, that's the way it felt at the time.

I'd left our beautiful three-bedroom home and moved into my pitiful apartment, which was so dark I had to leave the lights on through most of the day just to see where I was going.

And I'd been fired, not once but twice, in the space of just eighteen months. My career was a train wreck.

And my self-confidence was in ruins.

A year or so before, when my father was visiting the Bay Area, we both agreed I really needed to step up my exercising. I landed on the brilliant idea that I'd like to buy a bike and start riding. I'll never forget our trip to the bike store right near my apartment in Redwood City. My dad ended up coughing up something like $500 for a hybrid bike (one that could be used as a mountain or street bike). He joked that I would probably never end up using it. It wasn't a great machine. In fact, to tell the truth, it was far too heavy and unwieldy for the type of riding I would end up doing. But it had two wheels, a saddle and handlebars, and it did its job: it got me out on the road, exercising.

Less than six months later, while I was up in San Francisco for meetings, the bike was stolen. I'll never forget the day. I came out after a session in Starbucks and the bike was nowhere to be found. Initially, I cursed and raved but, later, I found myself bursting into laughter when I told the story to my dad over the phone. My life was such shit those days that losing the bike was just the icing on the cake.

Regardless, I'd started to get more and more serious about cycling and, the more serious I got, the more my friends urged me to get a "real" bike. I finally settled on a Cannondale Synapse which, at $2 500, was a lot of money for me at the time.

It still didn't rank with bikes that some of my buddies in the tech industry rode, high-end machines like the Cervelo or the Pinarello carbon-fiber models that retailed for $20 000+. My Cannondale was nothing to write home about, but it did the job and took my cycling pastime to a whole new level.

What does bike riding have to do with my catastrophic collapse of self-confidence? Well, stick around and you'll see there's a very obvious connection.

I've previously mentioned the group of INSEAD graduates to which I belonged, who got together from time to time to share war stories, compare career challenges and swap advice. We called ourselves the INSEAD Personal Board of Directors or IPBD.

Now, one of my fellow directors was a guy called Paul Bromley. He was a senior executive at a large semiconductor company – but, more important than that, he'd been a keen cyclist for many years.

When he heard about my first cycling expeditions – to work and back, sedate rides round the neighborhood – he took me aside and said, "Next Sunday we'll start with a quick ride up into the hills and back."

That sounded ambitious to me. "No," he insisted. "It's no more than ten miles. You could do it with one foot in a cast."

The following Sunday, we met by arrangement at 8 am, at the Woodside Road United Methodist Church on the corner of Alameda de las Pulgas and Woodside. Usually, at eight on a Sunday, I'd be rationalizing staying in bed for an extra half hour or making the kids their breakfast. I was only prepared to meet Paul at this ungodly hour because of the promise he'd exacted from me.

"Which way're we going?" I was a little nervous. Paul, as I said, was a veteran rider with one of those lean, pared-to-the-bone bodies of someone who routinely racks up a couple of hundred miles or more a week.

"That-a-way," he said, pointing at the mountains to the west. "Follow me."

That day we did, as he'd promised, a ten- or twelve-mile ride, some of it up fairly taxing hills, but Paul's strategy, looking at it now with the benefit of hindsight, was to reel me in slowly. At the end of the ride, I was a little tired, but exhilarated.

"Now for our reward," he said, as we freewheeled past the parking lot where we'd left our cars. (Thank you, United Methodist Church of Woodside Road.) A few minutes later, we drew up outside Bucks, a coffee shop we both knew well, and tucked into cappuccinos, eggs and bacon.

We rode once a week for the next few months, establishing a habit that I came to rely on. But, every couple of weeks, he'd suggest we try a new route that stretched me a little more. "How far is it?" I'd ask suspiciously.

"Oh, probably just about twenty miles," and then, in response to my expression – I'd probably winced – he'd say, "C'mon, Patrick, we cycled over fifteen miles last Sunday and you were fine with that. No real sweat to do twenty."

So, we'd ride the 20-mile route through the hills west of Redwood City, passing stands of majestic redwoods, swinging down through long, looping curves of the road – and racing each other for the last couple of miles to Bucks.

Then, one Sunday, Paul said casually, "Let's go to the beach."

"The beach! Christ, Paul, it's got to be 50 miles there and back."

"You got anything better to do?"

So, we went to the beach. Getting there was not too bad. For one thing, there was more downhill than uphill. The forest was, as always, great, a reward all on its own. And racing down Tunitas Creek Road and catching that first glimpse of the immense Pacific made all the sweat – and there was a lot of sweat involved, despite Paul's assurances – worthwhile.

But even as I enjoyed the ride there, it didn't take a tech genius to realize I'd pay for it on the way back.

Tunitas Creek Road is deceptive. There aren't that many truly steep bits, but the road goes on forever. It took me a full hour to make it to the summit and, by the time I got there, the muscles in my calves were cramping. Bear in mind that we'd already ridden something like 35 miles, more or less as much as I'd ever ridden on a single ride before. And then this long grind. By the time I got to the top, I was cursing Paul.

And yet, our bacon and eggs after the beach ride was the best breakfast I'd had in years.

That's when Paul said, in that throw-away style he'd perfected: "You know something, Patrick, I think we're ready to sign up for the Sequoia Century."

Let me tell you about the Sequoia. It's an annual bike riding festival that offers cyclists a choice of several routes. Each is more challenging than the last. You could, for instance, choose to do the 45-mile route. If you're slightly more ambitious, you could sign up for one of the two intermediate routes of between 60 and 75 miles.

Or there's the big one, the Century, which, surprise, surprise, runs through 100 miles of the most beautiful terrain in California, and that takes riders up 10 000 vertical feet. That's 100 feet per mile on average that you have to climb. Now, that might not sound much to someone who hasn't done any biking – a mile, after all, is 5 280 feet, so that means you're pedaling uphill, on average, at a very modest gradient.

But on the road, 10 000 feet is monstrous. That's a third of the height of Mount Everest, more than double the height of the United Kingdom's highest mountain. Think about that. And you ride up it in just a few hours.

I'd followed the Sequoia Century in the media for a couple of years. It was one of the highlights of the Northern Californian cycling calendar. Every year, news reports would feed us titbits about the race: who the winners were, naturally, but also included each year were a couple of human-interest stories. About the grandmother who completed the race ahead of her grandson. Or the competitor who spun off the road and hit a redwood. You know the sort of thing.

So, naturally, when Paul suggested signing up for the Century ride, I said: "No, Paul, are you insane?"

Of course, Paul finally talked me around. There were still a couple of months to get really fit. We could increase our weekly target so that, by the time we did the Century, it wouldn't be much more than we were used to doing habitually.

The clincher was when he said, "Besides, it'll be good for your confidence, a big ride like that."

"Which is totally beyond my capabilities," I pointed out.

"That's precisely the point. There's no big deal in setting a goal if it's easy to reach. You need something that really stretches you."

He was right, as he so often is.

You can see how my depression, if that's what it was, fits into the story of the Sequoia Century. If I could somehow get race-fit in time, it would, without doubt, be a great boost for my flagging self-esteem.

The secret to any crazy goal of this kind, where you're faced with a massive challenge that, in your more sober moments, you doubt you can meet, is to develop habits that make the goal achievable.

By this time, thanks to my weekly outings with Paul, I had developed the habit of riding every morning for an hour, no matter what the weather, or what other pressures were bearing down on me. I would get up at five, even as winter closed in on us and the sun began to rise only after seven.

In winter, I wore gloves and a ski mask because, although California isn't anything like as cold as the East Coast, it can still get pretty cold in the mornings.

I didn't let the dark or the cold deter me. Riding my bike down the mostly empty streets of Redwood City had become part of my identity. I was proud of my status as a cyclist. In my bathroom, I stuck a Post-it note to my mirror with the words: I am an athlete.

In the pitch dark of early morning, I'd cycle ten miles or so before heading home, having a long hot shower and making myself a breakfast of champions.

The breakfast was my immediate reward. But, of course, the larger reward was my increasing fitness. After cycling every day for several months, with a longer ride on Sundays with Paul, I was in the best shape of my life, and the prospect, the following June, of the Sequoia Century, didn't scare the hell out of me the way it had when Paul originally suggested it.

But the thought of all that cycling. and the 10 000 feet of climbing it entailed, was still pretty intimidating.

And then, just weeks before the race, while I was playing basketball with Rafi, I slipped and fell. I landed heavily and knew at once I'd damaged something in my ankle. I limped off the court, dropped Rafi with Laura, and made my way home. A hot shower and a dose of aspirin would, I was sure, do the trick.

But, of course, it was a little more serious than that. I managed to get my foot into my cycling shoe, and I went out for my ride the next morning but, I have to tell you, it was hell on wheels. Every time I applied pressure to the pedal, I felt as if all 27 bones of my ankle were grinding against each other. I have no idea whether there are 27 bones in your ankle, but that's what it felt like.

I persisted, though. I mean, what else can you do when you've built an inviolable habit? I rode my bike for an hour every morning. That was part of what I did, it was part of who I was, so how could I stop just because I had a bad ankle?

After three weeks, though, the swelling hadn't gone down, and I went to see my doctor. A sprain, he said. You've sprained your ankle pretty badly. Well, thanks, genius, I could have told him that by looking at it. What was he going to do about it? He told me he'd have to put my foot in a brace. "That's just great," I muttered.

"Am I going to be able to continue training? I've got this big race in two weeks' time and—"

He stopped me right there. His eyes widened incredulously, "You've been *cycling* on that?" He pointed at the ankle.

"Sure, I'm a cyclist and—"

"Mr Mork, you've got a grapefruit for an ankle. There is no way you're going to ride again this summer."

That news pretty much wrecked my plans to ride alongside Paul in 2017, so we put down our names for the 2018 Sequoia Century and, for the next ten months, trained methodically.

By the time June 2018 approached, I was as ready as I'd ever been. But then, the week before the race, Paul called and told me something had come up at work that required him to make an urgent business trip to the UK.

I was on my own.

At dawn on an early-June day in 2018, I turned up at the start of the race with my bike in the trunk of my Mini-Cooper. I was one of several hundred other cyclists. The mood was festive. This wasn't a highly competitive event. That morning, we were brothers united by a common enthusiasm for cycling and for nature.

Of course, I regretted not having Paul as my riding buddy. But I reckoned it wouldn't be too big a problem. I planned to Instagram friends and family along the way to let them know my progress. I wouldn't feel lonely. Besides, there were all the other riders who'd be keeping me company on the road.

At 6 am on that cool morning, a whistle sounded and we were off.

I faced a mountain of a different kind two years later when I finally agreed to leave my burrow in California for Chile.

The more I thought about the challenge of abandoning what I'd come to see as my base and moving to a foreign city, the more I appreciated just what a risk I was taking.

It was all a matter of confidence – or lack thereof. As I've said before, my confidence had taken a beating, and now the prospect of beginning again in strange surroundings, in a foreign language, in the context of an unfamiliar marketplace and business culture, was a daunting one. You're standing on one side of a turbulent river. What's on the other side of the bridge is an unknown. You can't even be sure the bridge can be trusted, or whether it'll collapse when you're halfway across, tossing you into the torrent.

My career as a coach was still in its infancy, my client base extremely limited. But I had promised Laura and the kids I would throw that away and begin anew.

Was I nuts?

Over the weeks that followed my decision to leave, I can't pretend that things were easy. The harsh reality of my situation, my age, my lack of connections in Chile, and the complications involved in moving to a foreign country, were not lost on me. I would wake in a cold sweat, surrounded by half-packed boxes, questioning myself and my decision.

I wondered how I'd make a living. What it would be like to start all over again. How I'd manage to make friends in a foreign country and in a foreign language.

I grew increasingly anxious as the date of my departure got closer.

But in the end, the challenge all boiled down to just one thing: The Good Father. I relied on the fact that my decision had been based on my core values and what mattered to me most: my kids, and being an important part of their lives. Viewed from that perspective, my decision was pretty straightforward. It was also a lesson I'd preached to the clients I'd coached over the past year. Once you really know your values and commit yourself to living by them, many of life's most important decisions just become a lot simpler.

On 29 of September 2018 at 8:50am, I touched down at the Arturo Merino Benitez International Airport in Santiago, Chile. My luggage consisted of three suitcases and a bicycle. These were the sum total of my possessions until I moved into a permanent apartment.

The first few miles of the Sequoia went reasonably smoothly. I was surrounded by fellow cyclists, some of whom were no more experienced than I was. We exchanged jokes, got to know each other and talked about how we planned to reward ourselves when we'd finished the race.

Not everyone I talked to had signed up for the Century. In fact, a number of them were doing one of the less ambitious races. I felt pumped up that I'd had the balls to go for the big prize.

I wondered why I'd been so anxious in the run-up to the race. All that preparation, I realized, had not been for nothing. Yes, I might be older than most of the participants but, hell, I was fit. And I'd done all the prescribed immediate planning: I'd slept well – no pre-race insomnia for me! – I'd had a great pre-dawn breakfast, had hydrated well while I was waiting for the bell to ring, and had a pack of peanut butter and jelly sandwiches, and a more than adequate supply of protein gel. This is a source of instant energy that riders rely on during long and grueling rides. It's not particularly tasty but, man, does it pack a punch. The only problem ends up being what it does to your stomach after ten or so of these. Yuck!

Ten miles into the race, I was totally and utterly committed to completing it, and I had no doubt I'd be able to do that. I still felt fresh and, although we had yet to tackle one of the long uphill slogs – Tunitas Creek Road was the big challenge in the closing stages of the ride – I had no doubt I'd crush it.

The views were spectacular: we caught glimpses of the Pacific and of the distant hills covered in towering redwoods.

The first rest stop came up. There were seven in all, at roughly ten- or twelve-mile intervals. Each was manned by volunteers, cheerful types who offered us water and pointed the way to the restrooms. I paused, but decided not to dismount. After all, I was still feeling like a 25-year-old, fully primed and straining at the leash. I told the volunteer who rushed up to me that I had enough water. I took a selfie and shared it on Instagram.

Within seconds, I scored a dozen likes and a handful of messages: "Keep it up, Patrick", "Go for it, bro!", "Nice!" I felt like a million bucks.

I had a particular reason for Instagramming the stages of the race. Not only was I celebrating my progress with friends and family (and inviting their encouragement and support), I was also recommitting myself to finishing it. I'd made a promise to my kids and others in my circle that I'd complete the Century. The selfies were my reminders of that promise.

It would be shameful for me not to keep it.

I took an Uber from the airport to the Airbnb apartment I'd rented online in the US. The drive through Santiago was surreal. I'd lived there for three years between 1996 and 1999, in the early days of my career as a marketing brand manager for Pepsi. But the city had changed enormously. Back then it had felt like a provincial capital, apparently reluctant to drag itself out of the twentieth century.

But Santiago had succeeded. Tall, modern skyscrapers rose about me, and the city's streets were much, much busier than I remembered.

My Airbnb wasn't at all shabby. Located on the top floor of a pristine new apartment building, it had a panoramic view of the entire city. It wasn't much bigger than my old place in Redwood City, but it was stylish, with modern furniture and a beautiful flat-screen TV.

First things first. I checked into Facebook to let friends know I was now resident in Chile. I WhatsApped my parents to assure them I'd landed safely. It was too late to phone the kids. I'd only let myself into the apartment after ten that evening. It wasn't too late, though, to order a meal through Uber Eats. I was starving.

Half an hour later, I sat on the balcony looking out over the Andes, a glass of Chilean cabernet sauvignon in my hand. The night sky was crystal clear, perfect for a little reflection.

Of course, I was totally out of my mind. But then I considered the huge advantage I enjoyed over others in my situation. After all, as the son of an expat, I'd lived in eleven countries in my life. I was used to making changes. In fact, the river from this side of the bridge didn't look as dangerous as it had from the other.

It was, after all, the perfect opportunity: a new country, new clients, a new career. I'd left my baggage behind, literally and figuratively, and was ready to reinvent myself as a coach.

Confidence, I told myself, is a muscle, and muscles that aren't exercised, atrophy. I would exercise my confidence muscle by throwing myself into my new life.

I hadn't built confidence riding my bike around Redwood City. I'd built it by following Paul's lead and riding to the coast. I'd proved to myself what I could do. And when he'd slipped out the color pamphlet on the Sequoia Century, although my instinct was to turn down the challenge, I knew in my heart that it was, in fact, a key step in what I might call my rehabilitation.

Unless you cross the bridge, you'll never know what's on the other side. But, more than that, you'll never know whether you've got what it takes to tackle the challenges you'll meet over there, in alien territory, where you'll encounter unfamiliar tests and trials.

Most of us are creatures of comfort. We settle into a groove and do what we're comfortable doing, day in, day out. Stepping outside of our comfort zone scares the hell out of us, so most of us simply never try to see what's on the other side. But it's on the other side of fear that growth lies. Life really begins at the edge of your comfort zone.

For me, the Sequoia was a means to an end. My goal was to build confidence – or, to be more accurate, to rebuild the confidence that life had knocked out of me.

And the move to Chile was *precisely* the same sort of challenge.

It scared me shitless. And my point is, if it hadn't, it wouldn't have been worth doing.

◆　◆　◆

The second, third and fourth stages of the Century ride weren't that much more challenging than the first. I hooked up with a guy who seemed quite happy to cycle at the speed I found comfortable. We talked about life in the Bay Area. We agreed the traffic was terrible, the pace of life relentless, the cost of living absurd, but that cycling gave us access to some of the most beautiful areas in the country, and that we were loving the Sequoia.

After an hour or so, though, my buddy excused himself, increased speed, and slowly drew away from me.

That was okay. I wished I'd asked for his contact details. It would have been good to keep in touch, especially on those occasions when Paul's business commitments kept him away.

The next rest stop appeared round a long curving incline. It was good to take a break. I slipped off the bike, took another selfie, posted it on Instagram, got the flood of responses I'd come to rely on, and then took a quick bio break.

I'd gotten unusually thirsty. Maybe it was the damn protein gel capsules. I suspected I'd been swallowing more of them than I needed. That last one had seemed to stick in my throat. And, while underhydration can be dangerous – especially on hot summer days, which this one was rapidly becoming – overhydration creates problems of its own.

I was aware that there were fewer cyclists at this rest stop than there'd been at the last. Reviewing the last half hour in my mind, I realized I'd been overtaken more and more frequently by other riders. Oh, well, the point was not to win. I'd never even remotely been on the hunt for glory.

No, I was in it to get to the finish line, to prove to myself, and no one else, that I, Patrick Mork, was capable of taking on a formidable task and completing it.

Naturally, I wanted to meet my goal: to ride the Sequoia Century at the age of 47, to make my dad proud of me, to hear my kids boast to their friends about their father, who'd crossed the finishing line like a champion after 100 miles under a smoldering sun.

I dashed cold water over my head and shoulders, got back on the bike, and set off again. Sixty miles down. Forty to go.

Three months later, sitting in my local Starbucks, I thought back ruefully to my early optimism. What I hadn't taken into account back then was the awesome power of habit, or momentum, or inertia, call it whatever you want. There's always a tendency to stay with what's comfortable, what's familiar. A tendency to keep the boat steady.

When I arrived in Santiago, even though I was in a different city, a different country, a different *hemisphere*, immersed in a different culture, the tendency was to go back to what I'd been doing in Silicon Valley, which was to return to Starbucks, drum up a little business, and start doing consulting work again.

So here I was, slurping a decaf mocha, waiting for a potential client who wanted me to help him formulate his product branding. The problem was, of course, that I could do this stuff in my sleep. Sure, it was still interesting. Sometimes even fun. But I couldn't escape the feeling that I wasn't pushing myself anymore. There was just not much of a challenge. Especially since I was just doing this for someone else, not for my own company.

Back in the Valley, I'd learned my coaching skills in order to escape all that crap. Now, it felt like I was trapped in Groundhog Day, caught in a time-loop, doing the same shit, which I'd sworn to give up, over and over again.

On this day in early November, 2018, my client arrived and, with a sigh and a hearty handshake, I got down to business...

In my defense, I have to say that my first priority was to earn a living, and the first few clients I managed to bag, while they said they'd value coaching, really wanted me to tell them what to do. They wanted marketing advice, they wanted me to help them strategize, they wanted me to be the me I'd been in Silicon Valley. So, reluctantly, I accepted these jobs. But I knew that, if I wanted to achieve my goals and build this "new me", I'd have to make a decisive break with the past, even if it cost me financially.

I drew the line outright, however, at accepting any of the job offers that came my way, lucrative as at least one of these was. With innovation and entrepreneurship becoming all the rage in Santiago, plenty of companies were actively looking for chief marketing officers, heads of strategy, and innovation gurus with Silicon Valley experience. Making a lot of money would have been easy. But I'd learned the hard way in Silicon Valley that it was *not* what gave me joy. It didn't fill me with purpose. It no longer energized me, even if people were willing to throw boatloads of money and fancy titles at me.

Chile was my chance to dig deep. To go somewhere new, scary and challenging.

Transforming yourself isn't something you can do overnight. It's all about taking small steps, one day at a time, one week at a time. Baby steps. My first big decision was to rent office space at WeWork. Doesn't sound like much, I know, but psychologically it was critical. Of course, it gave me some overhead, although nothing like what it would have cost me in California. But now I was surrounded by other people, all serious about building their businesses – and not simply by a bunch of people consuming their cortados and flat whites. Sure, every startup story seems to start with a meeting in Starbucks, but the reality is, most people go to Starbucks to buy lattes or mochaccinos or frappuccinos. They're not there to change the world or to find their purpose.

Sitting in my modest, shared office in WeWork, I could hear, not just the hum of traffic from the street far below, but also the buzz of business taking place around me. The outfit I shared offices with, for instance, was headed by a Brit called Matt, who worked as a consultant doing market research for the seafood industry. He had an assistant called Orianna. Flanking him was a Chilean entrepreneur called Jose Manuel, who was building a startup in the mining sector, manufacturing small robots armed with cameras and various other instruments useful to mining companies wishing to investigate dangerous areas underground.

One of the things I learned from my earliest days at Padres in Mexico City and, later, working at Pepsi and Google, is that your working environment affects your commitment to achieving your goals. It's the difference between people who work-out alone at home, versus those who go to a gym. In a gym you're surrounded by others who're also working out. Some have bulging biceps and six pack abs; others are comfortably flabby, but they're all there with serious intent, and you feel the pressure to work-out with them. It's really simple and obvious. We're a product of our environments. If you surround yourself with folks who are super-fit, eat healthy and work-out, there's a high chance you'll eat well, get super-fit and work-out yourself. Sadly, the flip side is also true.

Matt's assistant, Orianna, impressed me. She struck me, from the start, as someone who was smart, hardworking, diligent, and she seemed hungry to learn. Occasionally, I'd eavesdrop on her phone calls or observe her working with Matt and, slowly, it dawned on me: how much more might I accomplish if I had someone like that to work with?

"Hey, Orianna," I said one day, after listening to her expertly fielding questions from a client on the phone. "You wouldn't happen to have a twin sister who's looking for a job, would you?"

"No," she said with a smile, "but my boyfriend's moving to Santiago next month. He's a pretty switched-on guy who's done a lot of freelance work creating websites, ad campaigns and working with small businesses. He's actually starting to look for work here in Santiago. Would you like to meet him?"

Seventy miles, heading for eighty. Not many cyclists left around me. Slowly, but surely, I'd drifted to the back of the pack. Sure, I'd slowed down, but I was still feeling strong, if a little stiff. And those damned protein capsules were starting to make themselves felt – and not in a good way. I felt a certain churn in my intestines.

But the ride was still doable, despite the burn in my calves. A couple of times, on an ascent, I found myself weaving across the road. But all it took to correct that was focus and concentration.

I stood on the pedals and forced myself to keep to a line. I have to admit I wasn't paying much attention to the environment. My gaze was fixed on the tarmac beneath the bike.

Someone grunted as they passed me.

"Hey," I said. "Any idea where the summit is?"

It was a stupid question, and they didn't bother to reply. There was no summit. Or, at least, there were too many summits for the question to make any sense. I was riding through hill country at this point, but I was pretty sure we hadn't yet started the ascent up Tunitas Creek Road.

The rider disappeared round a bend in the road ahead.

I soldiered on, feeling the burn of acid reflux deep in my throat. I reached for the bottle of water in its cage on the down tube and took a swallow. I stretched down to replace it, but the bottle somehow slipped from my grasp. Fuck. Instinctively I reached down in a futile effort to catch it, my front wheel spun to one side and I only just managed to stop myself crashing to the ground.

I had to pay more attention to ... to *everything*.

I picked up the bottle, remounted the bike and managed, with a wobble, to get going again.

Getting an office was a nice first step. But every transformation requires *lots* of baby steps.

The second baby step I took in that first year in Santiago doesn't seem earth-shattering, but it signaled my realization that, if I wanted to do anything substantial, not to mention earn a decent living, I'd have to significantly scale up the way I was working.

My father, who had always been like a mentor and big brother to me, especially when it came to my career, helped steer me in the right direction. I talked to him frequently on WhatsApp on weekends, to share some of my challenges, fears and frustrations. After hearing me complain about the consulting trap I found myself falling into yet again, he remarked that I was thinking too small.

"But I'm a one-man band, Dad," I said. "I'm already busier than I want to be. I can't do any more without help."

"Well," he said, "find someone then."

Taking offices had been a first, vital step. Taking on my first employee was the second.

Orianna's boyfriend, Jose, was, like her, a Venezuelan. Unlike her, though, he was still stuck in Venezuela, although eager to find a way to join her. I interviewed him on Zoom.

"What experience do you have in marketing?"

"None," he said with disarming frankness.

"None at all?"

"I'm an electrical engineer, but there's no electrical engineering happening in Venezuela. I've been working as a sound mixer in a sound studio. And as a bartender – oh, and I train other bartenders, too. But marketing? I've helped design some webpages and done the occasional banner for online ads. Does that count?"

"What about Hubspot?" I asked. "Have you ever used a CRM?"

"I'm a fast learner and taught myself how to use Adobe Illustrator and a bunch of other design apps, but I can't say I've heard of Hubspot or CRM."

"What about Canva?" I said, feeling a bit exasperated. "If you've done design work, have you ever used Canva?"

"Sorry, Patrick. I've never heard of it," he said in a very open, apologetic manner.

Oh boy, I thought. This guy doesn't know shit. I'm going to have to teach him literally everything.

Over the course of the interview, though, I learned that, while Jose had no marketing experience and didn't know any of the most common tools I was using, he measured up well against the three criteria that management guru Patrick Lencioni tells us to look for in potential employees: he was humble, hungry and smart (emotionally as opposed to intellectually), not to mention friendly, curious and open to change.

It was also clear to me, even on Zoom, that Jose was scrappy.

Scrappiness is one of those rare skills highly prized in the startup world. Scrappy people can make the difference between success and failure in early-stage companies. Scrappy people figure out how to get things done without being told and are adept at finding new ways to get more done with less.

Given the situation in Venezuela, Jose had to deal with things, on a day-to-day basis, which seem unimaginable in more modern countries where things actually work. He partially built his own laptop from spare parts because he didn't have the money to buy a new one. He had to stay up half the night uploading files for clients because Venezuela's rickety broadband infrastructure was so bad. At times, Jose would have to use his university's facilities because someone had stolen the cable box for his home broadband modem. When he couldn't do a project or lacked the skills, he built a network of freelancers with different skills to deliver on client projects. He taught himself Adobe Illustrator on YouTube because he couldn't afford a class to learn the skills.

Most importantly, this was a guy who was always positive. Always upbeat and always had a smile on his face. When I told him I couldn't pay him much and that the best I could do was give him a three-month, part-time gig to help me with some projects, he was delighted. The only thing he wanted, he said, was to learn. I loved that about him, and do, to this day, over three years later.

So, despite my doubts – I mean, the guy really had no tangible marketing qualifications – my gut screamed at me to offer him the job. That was how Jose came to be LEAP's employee #1.

I was now starting to feel seriously sick. I put it down to the damn protein capsules. How the hell had they ever been recommended for cyclists? I wondered how far it was to the final rest stop. Twenty miles more after that and I'd be home and dry.

I was coasting down what felt like a rare decline when I felt the gorge rise in my throat and, before I knew it, I was vomiting all over my handlebars and the front wheel.

Emptying my stomach seemed to clear my head. I held on to the handlebars with grim determination. Ahead of me I caught sight of a fork in the road. A line of red traffic cones blocked the road forking off to the right. I consulted Google maps on my phone. This should be the last rest stop.

A couple of volunteers were loading empty plastic water bottles into garbage bags. I coasted to a stop on the side of the road.

"Hey, what's going on?" My voice was a croak. I was acutely aware of the stink of vomit that seemed to hang like a cloud about me. Startled, the older of the two volunteers, a slim woman in her late 50s, in a stylish track suit, turned to me.

"Oh," she said. "I didn't realize there were still riders coming through."

"I'm the last?"

"Well, of course I can't be sure. Which distance did you sign up for?"

"The Century."

I think she caught a whiff of me then. Her eyes widened with what I think was compassion – or, at least, pity. "You poor thing."

And the truth was, I was feeling plenty of pity for myself too. If she'd embraced me and told me I should get off the bike and rest under a tree, I think I'd have followed her orders without question. But then the second volunteer came up. He was young, and there wasn't any compassion in this guy's eyes.

"You're a little old for the Century, aren't you? It takes a lot of stamina."

The first volunteer chipped in then, I think to soften the edge of what her colleague had just said: "Take the left fork and it's only a couple of miles, mostly downhill, to the finish line."

"The right fork's the Century," the young guy said. "But I wouldn't even think of it in your state. Besides, all the volunteers have pulled out. That's why we've put the cones out. You won't have any support at all—"

"So, if you get into trouble," the older woman said, "there won't be anyone to help you."

But I'd already made up my mind. Too old? Not enough stamina? I could feel a few embers of pride burst into flame in my gut.

"I signed up for the Century," I said with grim resolve, "and I'm going to finish the Century."

A second later, I was wobbling off through the traffic cones onto the right fork. Behind me I heard the young volunteer say, "I guess we'll have to alert the marshal. They'll have to send out a vehicle to pick him up."

But then the forest closed in around me and I was on my own with 20 miles to go.

Over the course of the next few weeks and months, I networked like a madman. I went from meeting to meeting, learning about the challenges facing Chilean startups and medium-sized businesses. After each successful meeting, I would make a polite request for two or three introductions to other businesspeople.

Everyone seemed to know everyone else. I learned very quickly how close and tightly knit the Santiago business community was. Within months, I felt I knew half the people in the ecosystem. I was soon astounded, and even amused, that everyone I met was connected to someone else I'd already, and sometimes only recently, met.

And, to my huge relief, my instincts about Jose turned out to be on the money.

Within days and weeks of arriving in Chile and starting to work for me, he assumed many of the tasks that were costing me valuable hours, hours which I needed to coach, sell projects or prospect for new clients. Although most of the tools I used were new to him, Jose was a quick and avid learner and pretty soon he was translating my old blog posts into Spanish, sending out email newsletters using Hubspot, creating graphics in Canva and editing our videos and podcasts. The change was gradual at first and, I have to admit, I didn't find it easy to delegate responsibilities, but the more I did and the more I also accepted that he was going to make some mistakes, the more things got done. Little by little, I found I had the time to get more clients and build the business.

Perhaps the most important part of having Jose join me was the psychological impact of his presence. I would walk into the office on a Monday morning and there was someone to talk to, exchange stories and share coffee with. We would go for lunch and walks together. I spent hours teaching him about marketing, coaching, tech and managing a business, all of which he absorbed like a sponge.

Not only was Jose a quick learner, he also asked great questions, was constantly coming up with new ideas and eventually started to serve as a thought partner for me.

In time, he would go on to help me design the new LEAP.cl website, recommend a different vendor for our email platform and even start to build and automate all our outbound email campaigns, set up our website tracking and analytics and manage our remote digital marketing team.

While Jose was an essential stepping stone to scaling what we were doing in marketing, I quite quickly came to another realization: if I wanted to help my founders and coach more organizations, I was never going to be able to do this alone. I was going to need help.

I took my third baby step when I joined a WhatsApp group of coaches called La Red de Recursos Humanos (the HR network) – and met two coaches, Maria Paz Rioseco and Felix Arias. Talking to Maria and Felix led to a crucial insight: if I worked not as a lone-wolf coach, but hand in hand with other coaches, together we would be able to serve more clients, deliver more complex projects, and perform deeper leadership work. Most important of all, I would be able to scale my efforts and build LEAP into a real business.

Because, as I think I've said before, if you don't aim high, what the fuck's the point?

The last two hours of the Sequoia were among the worst in my life. My legs were shaking with exhaustion. I wasn't over the gastric upset that had caused me to throw up. After seven grueling hours under the mid-summer California sun, my ass ached and felt like it had somehow merged with the saddle.

And what lay ahead of me was not just 20 miles on a road along which, as the volunteer had so kindly informed me, there was no assistance to be had. Part of this final stage was the ride up the Tunitas Creek Road and Bunker Hill, a short but brutal little climb that the organizers had added from the previous year just to make the event "a bit more challenging".

On those occasions when Paul had coaxed me into tackling the monster, I'd thought the hour-long stretch of uphill taxing. Now it was completely and utterly overwhelming.

Every time I heard a car approaching from behind, I was sorely tempted to stick out a thumb and beg a lift. But then I'd remember the words of the volunteer: "You're a little old for the Century, aren't you?" And I'd feel a sudden surge of energy rise up from god knows where and I'd put my head down and pedal as hard as I was able.

The memory of my rage worked – but only for short bursts.

For a while, I let myself sink into a sea of self-pity. If I hadn't screwed up my ankle the year before, I'd have been a year younger and therefore perhaps just a little more able to tackle the race… If Paul hadn't pulled out, I'd have had his constant encouragement and support all the way… If I hadn't relied so heavily on the bloody protein capsules, perhaps I'd be in a fitter state than I was now… If it hadn't been so freaking hot…

The slow rise of the road seemed inexorable. I'd look up ahead and see it snaking into the middle distance.

I slowed more and more, it felt as if this were the road to hell, and that I'd be condemned for all eternity to be cycling up … and up … and up…

But then I applied a little technique I'd learned that made a real difference. Instead of thinking, OMG, there's still fourteen miles to go, I identified a landmark a couple of hundred yards ahead: a boulder perched beside the road. I'll aim at that, I thought. That's a doable target.

And when, a minute or two later, I passed my goal, I'd look ahead and pick out another boulder, or a tree, or a signpost. And after that, another and another.

And so, despite my doubts – because there's always that doubter inside you, ready to tell you that what you're trying to achieve is impossible – beat by beat, goal by goal, I chipped away at the miles remaining.

Ten … nine … eight.

My legs were lead, my muscles burned with fatigue, my throat was parched, my stomach felt like stir-fried shit and all this under the hot summer sun that beat down mercilessly.

But I remained on my bike, resisting the temptation to call it a day and collapse on the verge.

Six ... five ... four.

And then, what seemed like hours later, I saw ahead of me the race organizers packing up. But the markers indicating the end of the Century were still in place. I put everything I had into a final pathetic sprint. It didn't matter to me that I was last. To finish at all was what mattered. I crossed the line, threw my arms wildly in the air.

And crashed.

I was aware of a burning pain in one knee where I'd grazed it on the tarmac. I sat up, blinked, and burst into tears.

The only way – the *only* way – you can really grow is by stretching yourself on the rack of experience. And the best way to do that is by taking on challenges that, like the Sequoia 100, you really think are going to push you beyond your comfort zone. Because it's only when you step out beyond your comfort zones that life truly begins.

The first couple of bigger clients we took on I would not have been able to cope with without the help of Maria Paz, Felix and the other coaches I managed to call on. Keep in mind, I had very little experience in the field myself. When I sold myself to a client, I promised outcomes that were frankly beyond me, working alone. In some cases, I admit I wasn't quite sure what the hell I was doing. In Silicon Valley, we used to say, "Fake it till you make it." In Santiago in those early days, I did a lot of faking.

At times, I would write proposals outlining our philosophy and recommendations that I'd swear would solve their problems – but, truthfully, I didn't have any fucking clue how I was going to do it. "Yeah, yeah," I would say, "we can fix that, no problem." And then, the moment I left the meeting, I'd start scrambling. I'd get on the phone and call every coach I know and say, "I have this job. Fantastic opportunity. Any idea how we can really do this?"

And, fortunately for me, people like Maria Paz and Felix actually knew what they were doing.

These projects were really the beginning of building a serious business. We were working on scale, coaching the founders of each company together, doing six different workshops over six months, working on a systems-wide basis.

All well and good. But then I was approached by the CEO of Athena, a large chain of cosmetic retail stores. I started to think I might have bitten off more than I could chew. Helen Garnier was a Frenchwoman, a formidable executive with a Harvard MBA and an intimidating level of self-confidence. She was tough, didn't tolerate bullshit, in herself or others, and, in some cases, downright scared the shit out of her people.

"Let's walk and talk," she suggested. We headed for the nearest park and, while we made our way along verdant paths between the museums that are a feature of Quinta Normal, she told me about the problems the company was struggling with.

"The culture at Athena's screwed up," she said. "Plus, I've got issues with the board and, to lead the company effectively, I need the best possible team surrounding me. And I need to know who I can really depend on. I need an outside perspective."

Now, let me make something clear. The companies I'd worked with up to that point were almost exclusively startups and small outfits. For the most part, I'd coached the founders on a one-on-one basis. They were usually young and inexperienced and lapped up the advice and coaching I gave them.

But with Helen, it was different. She was a seasoned and sophisticated professional with a star-studded cv. She headed a company with upwards of 80 outlets in Chile and several hundred million dollars in revenue. Athena was owned by a consortium of one of the most renowned Chilean families, which controlled a nice little slice of the Chilean economy. In other words, this was the real deal.

Now, I'm not saying I'd ever bullshitted my clients but, for the most part, I relied on my relative experience and their relative inexperience.

Helen was much more experienced than I was. She'd spot any bullshit in my behavior at once.

"What do you mean?" I asked cautiously.

"I want you to assess whether my team has what it needs to take Athena to the next level," she said, and then, after a pause, added, "And I'd like you, personally, to coach me."

Her request filled me with a mixture of feelings. What if I screwed up? What if I found myself completely out of my depth? What if I simply couldn't give her what she and Athena needed? It would not just dent my reputation, it could well destroy it. I'd become known as the man whose ambitions outran his talents. Santiago was a small place. Everyone knew everyone.

On the other hand, I felt a surge of excitement: if I cracked it, I'd have a considerable scalp hanging from my belt. Bragging rights. A fat fee. And I'd have broken through the glass ceiling of small startups into the much more lucrative world of big corporations.

But I took the coward's way out.

"Let me think about it," I said.

What I meant by, "Let me think about it", was really, "Let me talk to Maria Paz about it".

Now, Maria Paz was not part of my business. She wasn't a business partner or a shareholder. She ran her own coaching business. She taught at one of the top Chilean universities. She was also a much more experienced coach than I was – and I wasn't shy to ask her advice.

"You're serious about building a bigger business, aren't you, Patrick?"

Yes, I was. I didn't want to return to the frantic days of Silicon Valley, but I did want to see what I was capable of.

"So, what does that mean?"

It's a classic coaching question. Don't tell your client what you think he wants. Ask an open-ended question and get them to say what they really want.

"If I want LEAP to become a serious business," I began slowly, "I have to take on more challenging projects." I warmed to my subject. "If I want to be of value to our clients, we have to grow ourselves, take on more difficult work, get better at what we do."

And so, faced with the challenge posed by Athena and Helen, I overcame my natural caution and put the pedal to the metal.

One of the first things I'd actually done when I started LEAP was to write down our four core values. One of those was simply to be *bold*. "You have to live by the values you preach so, if we're not going to be bold now, we might as well pack up and go home, isn't that right, Maria Paz?" She smiled at me knowingly.

"I think you know what you have to do, Patrick. You've always known."

I went all in.

The corporate part of the Athena gig was relatively easy, but that's because I had Maria Paz's help. We devised the curriculum, set up workshops for Helen's team, and set the process in motion.

And I started meeting Helen for coaching sessions. I decided I would be as ballsy in my approach as I could be. I would either transform her life – in the way that coaching had transformed *my* life – or I'd get fired for overstepping my boundaries. There was no point in being any less than totally bold.

I devised a diagnostic questionnaire that I got both her and the members of her executive team to fill out, to give us a 360-degree view of her in the context of her working environment.

In our sessions, I posed a series of challenging questions: why was she doing what she did? Was she living her values? What would happen to her if she did nothing? Why did she think she was so exhausted?

I was aware that I was having an impact on her. And then, in just our third session, she said something that shook me to my foundations:

"I've told the board that I'm quitting, Patrick."

"Look, I know things with the board have been challenging, but are you absolutely sure?

"The reason I'm so exhausted, the reason I'm so frustrated, is that I'm living outside my values," she said steadily. "The board micromanages me and treats me like a ... child, and now, with this diagnosis, I've actually realized that, in turn, I treat my team in the same way. That's not who I am. That's not who I want to be."

Helen's decision was the bravest and most honest thing I've ever seen a senior executive do and I was blown away by it.

Today, Helen's an entrepreneur who started her own successful business and moved her family back to France. She made a huge life change and, to this day, she attributes a large part of that to coaching.

I regard those coaching sessions as amongst the most successful I've ever done. I helped Helen find her way back to the values she believed in most fiercely.

The work with Athena led me to conclude two things. First, none of this work, particularly the work we would later do with Helen's whole team, which continued with the new CEO after she left, would have been possible without Maria Paz. None of it would have been possible without help. Second, although I knew coaching was powerful, I realized I had just helped someone radically change their life. This work wasn't just powerful, it was life changing. This wasn't simply something I enjoyed doing. This was something I *had* to do.

Two of the organizers rushed over to me where I sat sobbing on the tarmac. One of them shouted over his shoulder, "Get the medics over here."

"No, no," I managed to say. "I'm fine, I'm terrific. It's just... It's just I've been training for two years to do this, and now I've done the whole 100 miles, and I'm just so happy, I'm so happy—"

I knew I was babbling, but I didn't mind because what I was saying was true. Ten minutes before, I'd been in a deep trough of anxiety and depression, at the end of my psychic and physical rope. Now, I was in paradise.

The organizers exchanged a look. One of them gave me a pat on the shoulder, and they returned to the task of wrapping the Sequoia up for another year.

A disheveled-looking guy with a camera dangling from his neck approached me.

"Hi," he said. "I'm Doug Johnson from the Redwood City Courier. I'm looking for a human-interest story for my paper."

I looked up at him and beamed. "I think you've come to the right place buddy."

As human beings, we're creatures of habit. We have our routines. Drink the same coffee each day, use the same toothpaste each morning and eat at the same restaurant every weekend. We don't like change. It's hard. It's scary and it's unpredictable.

But change is good. It's necessary and it's what helps us become better versions of ourselves. It forces us to stretch, get uncomfortable and break with our old ways and views. Every time we succeed, we grow bolder, become better and develop our self-confidence. When we fail, we learn from our mistakes and get better.

Here are some exercises to help you build change in your own life. I hope you'll share your experience on our Facebook page and I wish you luck.

EXERCISE #1

Define the identity you want to be

Part of the reason people never realize their goals is that they don't really envision what the goal will actually bring them. For example, someone who's overweight sets themselves a goal to lose 10 lbs. There's nothing wrong with that. Part of setting goals is making them measurable. But the question is, what does the goal actually look like and why have you adopted it?

The first step is to envision why you're doing this or that, and how that manifests itself in your life. Going back to the "losing weight" goal, it's really about what it brings you. Maybe you're losing weight because you want to "feel good". Maybe you just want to be fit. The point is to tie this to your identity. I don't cycle, do yoga or work-out with a specific goal in mind. I do these things because my identity is about "being fit" and "being athletic". That's just part of who I am. I go to the gym or do yoga each morning because being an athlete and being healthy is part of who I am, day in, day out.

This exercise has three parts to it:

1. Define your identity. Manifest your desire to "be" a certain kind of person. I am an athlete. I am healthy. I am a good person. I am an entrepreneur. Whatever it is that's important and meaningful to you. Something which you want to be a core part of your identity.

2. Remind yourself of this identity every day. Some people do this by doing affirmations in the morning or evening. Others, like myself, have Post-it notes on their bathroom mirror and look at them every morning and evening when they're brushing their teeth. Every morning, I look at these Post-its (I have, like, ten of them) and I read them to myself as I brush my teeth or dry my hair. In the evening, I do the same. These remind me of the person I am or am trying to become. When I stumble, which we all do, I'll think of my Post-it notes and use that reminder to double down on what I need to do (go to the gym, do a yoga routine, work on my book, plan activities for my kids). If you constantly have ways to remind yourself of the identity you aspire to, it pushes you to take the actions to turn that vision into reality. Other people create personal boards or pin up pictures that visually depict the identity they are creating for themselves. This works particularly well for people who are more visually inclined and who actually need to "see" what it is they're trying to accomplish / change about themselves.

3. Share this identity with others. We'll talk more about the importance of accountability in the next chapter, but sharing this new identity with others helps make you accountable. If I share with others that I'm an athlete, good father or entrepreneur,

it'll be strange if I don't take action to make it real. Sharing forces us to be accountable to others. These "accountability buddies" become our cheerleaders. They ask how we're doing, they give us feedback or suggestions and they cheer us on when we're taking decisive action towards our goals. My aim in sharing my Sequoia pictures with friends and family on Instagram wasn't to show off or brag about what I was doing, it was more that I was reinforcing my identity as an athlete. As someone who aspires to be fit and healthy. I was holding myself accountable to them.

EXERCISE #2
Make your goals SMART

SMART goals have been around for a long time but it's amazing how few people actually put them into practice. Identity is the first thing you have to focus on because that's how you want to be, regardless of how quickly you reach your goals. My goal might be to bike 2 500 miles in a year, but my identity is to be fit and healthy. So, I don't stop biking and working out once I hit my goal. I keep going.

But, developing an identity is nothing without SMART goals. You can't become that person if you don't have measurable goals to work towards.

SMART goals are (S)pecific, (M)easurable, (A)ttainable, (R)ealistic and (T)imebound. Let's go back to the Sequoia ride. My Specific objective was to bike 100 miles and climb 10 000 feet in a single day. It was Measurable because, either I would finish the race, or not. In other words, it was binary. It was incredibly challenging for me but it was Attainable. With the preparation and training I had done for the two years before the race, I was able to get through it. It was Realistic. I was fully aware of all the challenges. I had biked most of the segments of the race in one way or another over the previous two years and under similar conditions (weather, hydration). Finally, it was Timebound. It was on a specific day of the month at a certain time and I, and all my friends and family, knew it.

EXERCISE #3
Break it down!

Most people never achieve anything meaningful because they look at the "top of the mountain" and are immediately defeated by the apparently impossible task of getting there. They think of all the work involved and it just overwhelms them.

The key to achieving any important goal is to break it down into smaller chunks that are SMART in the way we outlined in Exercise #2.

When I trained for the Sequoia, I didn't initially think I was going to do a 100-mile ride. If you remember, I started out really small and worked my way up. First 5 miles around the neighborhood, then 10, 15, 20, 30, 50, 80 and, finally, 100. It was a gradual process. Each step was SMART.

The day of the race, I had seven different rest stops. My goal was, naturally, to finish the race, but those seven stops gave me something to shoot for. During the last 20 miles, I had micro-goals, remember? I would aim for a tree, a mailbox, a certain curve in the road. I would just focus on hitting that goal and then move to the next. Writing this book involved the same process. My aim was to get a chapter done every four to eight weeks. I would revise the chapter with Richard every two weeks and would devise small milestones in between to keep ourselves honest.

Practically speaking, the best way to do that is to combine simple and complementary tools: a task management app or tool like Asana, Google Tasks or Trello, with your favorite online calendar.

I love Asana because I already use it for work, so using it in my personal life is a no-brainer. I can create a project, subtasks and then add due dates for each subtask. I might not hit every date, but this allows me to break down any projects into bite-sized chunks. I get reminders in my email and in the app and I know exactly where I am, when I'm late and what I need to do. In addition, using Asana allows me to invite "followers", or people I'm accountable to, in order to complete the goal or subtask. In the case of my book, Richard and Trish are my followers on many tasks, so they know when I complete a task, and by when, and they also know when I'm late (as I was, doing these exercises).

Breaking down our goals into bite-sized chunks allows us to see and "feel" our progress. Every time we "check off" a subtask, we get a little dopamine hit that makes us feel good. We see the progress and we maintain the momentum. When we combine this with accountability to others, we can do anything.

Key #4

BE ACCOUNTABLE

Responsibility equals accountability equals ownership. And a sense of ownership is the most powerful weapon a team or organization can have.

—Pat Summitt

My father had high hopes for me as, I guess, all fathers do of their sons. It's why he insisted I go to Padres: it was the best school in Mexico City, and so he believed it was the right school for me, despite, or *because* of, the hurdles it would force me to jump.

As I've already said, Dad was a corporate nomad, restlessly moving from country to country as he climbed higher and higher up the corporate ladder. In 1988, I was in my junior year at Pace Academy in Atlanta. I wasn't exactly a star student, but my grades were solid Bs and B+s with the occasional A in the areas I enjoyed (history or English) and the occasional C or D in things I hated (science and math). Things were relatively calm.

Then Dad landed a job as President of Canada Dry USA. Not bad from his perspective, disastrous from mine – because his new job was in Connecticut. My mother was less than keen on our moving and I, frankly, hated the idea. It didn't take a genius to recognize that it wasn't the best time to yank me out of Pace and enroll me in a new school in a new city.

"He's established himself at Pace," my mother argued, the morning Dad announced the job offer. She believed the schools I attended should provide me with a protective environment in which my natural talents could flower.

My father, on the other hand, believed the schools he sent me to should simply be the best available and that their prime duty was to challenge me, to stretch me. "Tough is good," he'd say. "It brings out the best in you and helps build character."

"So what?" Dad said at the breakfast table. "Brunswick's got a great reputation. Very competitive. We leave in three weeks."

"You didn't tell me you'd accepted the offer," my mother said.

"Didn't I? Anyway, got to go. I'll see you this evening."

My father always got his way. The job came first. Always.

Dad had done his research and hired a consultant, a Dr Thomas Aquila, a college guidance counselor and himself a graduate of Yale. The Brunswick School for Boys in Connecticut (motto: Courage. Honor. Truth.) had a stellar reputation. It was also tough as nails and ultra-competitive.

Three weeks later, I was sitting in my first class at Brunswick – and eighteen months later, graduated with an A- average.

Next question: which college should I attend? Of course, my father set his sights very high: Harvard, Princeton, Yale. But there was little chance I would be accepted with my grades, reasonable though I thought they were. Dr Aquila said there was a good chance my fluency in four languages would make me eligible for Georgetown University's School of Languages (nicknamed Ling Lang at the time) – no slouch by any measure. He was right. And then, prompted by Dad, I applied for a transfer to, and was accepted by, the Edward Walsh School of Foreign Service, arguably the most competitive arena at Georgetown. It was, in fact, as prestigious as Harvard and Yale.

There was no doubt about Dad's ambitions for me. And, in turn, I felt accountable to him.

That's what this chapter's about. Accountability. And how accountability helps us all achieve heights of performance that we wouldn't be able to without that sense of obligation to what I have chosen to call our accountability buddies.

But there is, of course, a difference between expectations and accountability. We'll explore that difference here as well.

And then, what did I do? Well, I'll let you connect the dots. My father had been a senior executive at Pepsi, so guess where, fresh out of Georgetown, I applied for a job?

I kicked off as an intern in Boca Raton, Florida, where Pepsi's HQ for Latin America is situated. My six months' internship came to an end without a job offer, but I took a chance, went over my boss's head, and groveled to the man who'd just become president of Pepsi in Brazil. That, and my command of Portuguese, which I'd learned as a kid when my Dad was based in Brazil for a couple of years, finally landed me a job there. It was the perfect opportunity to have fun and sow a few wild oats – hey, give me a break, I was just 21 and frisky – and I almost got fired for my trouble. But Pepsi gave me another chance, and I was sent on a Mission Impossible to Minas Gerais, where I pulled a rabbit out of the hat, more than met the expectations of the local GM and, perhaps, surprised my father. The real fact is, I felt a real bond of loyalty to the president who'd given me the chance in the first place. I felt accountable to him, just as I felt accountable to my father for getting me back on track.

My success in Minas Gerais, where I organized Pepsi's sponsorship of the 1995 World Championship Motocross Tour, earned me the spot as head of marketing for Pepsi in Chile at the grand old age of 25, with a budget of $6 million. I was flying high and enjoying every second of the ride.

But then I decided to add more qualifications to the mix. An MBA at a business school seemed to be the next natural stop on my inexorable rise to superstardom. And not any business school, but arguably one of the top five in the world: INSEAD, or to give it its full name, the Institut Européen D'administration des Affaires. The MBA it offers has produced the second-most CEOs of the 500 largest companies, after Harvard Business School, and it's consistently ranked among the top three business schools in the world and #1 in Europe.

Was it any coincidence that I chose to apply to INSEAD, considering that my father was a graduate and, now, a member of the board and a prominent donor? Well, of course not. With hindsight, it's easy to see that

I was either consciously or unconsciously following in his footsteps in an attempt to earn his approval.

But there was more to it than simply my accountability to my father. I told my boss at Pepsi and the others I worked for that my goal was to get into INSEAD and emerge with an MBA. By doing so, I made myself accountable to *them* too.

I guess that, at that stage of my career, I reckoned I could do no wrong. How else to explain that I took the Graduate Management Admission Test (GMAT) as casually as I did. And scored just 570 miserable points out of 800. That was highly unlikely to open INSEAD's doors to me, whether or not my father was a board member. So, I took a deep breath, resigned and flew to Washington, moved in with a couple of friends and a hair-shedding dog and, for three months, put my head down and prepared to retake the GMAT.

Every day, I'd pick my way over stacks of pizza boxes and empty bottles of beer, ignore the piles of dirty pots and pans in the kitchen, and make my way down to the nearest Kaplan Center. And there, I'd either take practice GMATs, or polish my math skills in preparation for the real thing. I hated every second of it and there was nothing like the math section of the test to make me feel like an idiot or a simpleton.

My dad thought I was crazy. On one telephone call, he told me as much. "You're not thinking clearly," he said. (He never was one to pull his punches.) "You've left a well-paid job, and now you're spending your savings partying in Washington—"

"Dad, I'm *studying*, not partying," I protested.

"Oh, bullshit. I know you. You're staying with this friend of yours, you're probably drinking until the early hours, then spending a couple of hours at this test center persuading yourself that you're being responsible."

"I *am* being responsible."

"Come on, Patrick, if you don't do well in this second test, then tell me, what the hell have you got planned?"

Good point. And the problem was, my scores on the endless practice tests weren't climbing appreciably. So, for the final four weeks before I'd booked to write the real test, I hired a tutor.

And I stopped partying.

That conversation with Dad made me acutely aware that I'd burned my bridges, thrown away a great job and risked everything to get into INSEAD. Walking downtown to the Kaplan Center through the chilly Washington DC spring mornings, I was understandably worried about the future. If I didn't get a good enough score to get in, what *would* I do next? Go back to Pepsi with my tail between my legs? Move back to Chile?

But then, thanks to the kindness of my friends (I forgive them the chaos in their apartment, but not the dog for its hairs), my tutor, my own belated determination, and, crucially, my sense of obligation to my accountability partners (including my colleagues in Chile), I took the GMAT and, thank god, emerged with a score that helped me scrape into INSEAD.

The Dean of the MBA program at the time was Prof H Landis Gabel, with a string of degrees behind his name, including a PhD in Economics. He welcomed the new MBA class of 2000 with an inspiring address that pointed out, among other things, that we were among the most talented people in the world, the business leaders of tomorrow, and so on.

I was feeling proud to be there, until I realized his piercing blue eyes had fallen on me.

"It gives me great pleasure," he said, "to note an unusual circumstance in this year's class. Patrick Mork, sitting here in the second row, is the son of one of our very first alumni, who is now a member of our board, and who is present here today as well. Welcome to INSEAD, Mr Mork. I hope you profit as much from your year here at Fontainebleau as your father did."

In the front row, my father and other members of the board turned to look at me. "Gee, thanks, Dean Gable. No fucking pressure now, right?" I mumbled to myself.

You have the right to assume that I instantly threw myself into the academic life of INSEAD with all the enthusiasm my father had obviously brought to his time there 30 years before. But you'd be wrong, for a few reasons.

Firstly, *I'd* assumed that, despite my initial failure to achieve a decent score on the GMAT, I was pretty good at business. After all, my success at Pepsi had persuaded me that I had what it took to solve just about any intellectual challenge thrown at me. In Chile, in the company of other marketing guys, I'd always felt like a rockstar and we did some very innovative and far-flung marketing campaigns, which were not only successful, but emulated across the region – like launching TV campaigns with soccer stars, including Marcelo Salas and Ivan Zamorano, Chile's finest soccer players. So, despite my hiccups with the stupid GMAT, I arrived at INSEAD confident and cocky about my abilities.

But I soon found that I was surrounded by some of the most exceptionally capable people in the world. People who'd worked in big pharma, others who'd already made their mark in private equity firms, or been strategy consultants for years. There was one guy who'd literally worked as a missile scientist in Russia, another who was a rising star in the semiconductor industry in India. Yet another Indian put on a show playing chess blindfolded against three opponents simultaneously. And fucking winning all three games.

Long story short, I realized I was no longer even close to being the smartest guy in the room.

My career had been limited to marketing, whereas many of my classmates had already had general management experience or worked as strategy consultants for top firms like BCG, McKinsey or Bain.

Hellish competition and brilliant people aside, the other thing that makes the INSEAD MBA program so tough is that it's just a year long, divided into five two-month periods, and it drives you through the material at breakneck speed. The first two periods are devoted to the MBA's core curriculum, which includes subjects like accounting, finance and operations management. I realized within a week or two that I was totally out of my depth. I didn't understand half of the lectures and discussions. While I comfortably aced marketing and organizational behavior, I was a disaster at just about everything else.

So, what did I do?

I played golf.

And had a fantastic time in the little chateau I roomed in, along with a bunch of other students. It was as cold as hell, but a wonderful entertainment venue. I'll never forget the grand dinners we hosted for guests, which invariably involved the consumption of endless bottles of fine French wine, and often ended with one of us – a Chinese classmate – singing opera arias. Wining and dining and general merriment would take us through to the witching hour of midnight, when we'd split our guests into groups of two or three and each of us would take a group on a candle-lit ghost tour of the chateau.

The point, of course, was to frighten the hell out of them.

Picture the scene: by the flickering light of the candle in my hand, I pause outside the tiny door to the attic. My guests, two attractive female visitors, huddle close. I speak in little more than a whisper:

"It's 1790, the height of the Terror. A lover of Louis XVI comes seeking refuge here at the chateau, occupied by a distant cousin of hers. Remember, back in Paris, the cream of the aristocracy are having their heads chopped off. She's frightened. The duke says she can stay in this attic. To keep her quite safe, he locks the door on her—"

As I talk, the shadows of my two companions dance flickeringly on the wall behind them.

"What happened to her?"

"Ah, very sad. Her hosts were taken by the mob the day after she arrived."

"And she was locked in?"

"Behind this door … without food or water."

"She died?"

"Her body was only found years later… But her ghost continues to pace up and down the attic… And sometimes you can hear her faint cries—"

"No!"

"Water!" I croaked. "Bring me water."

And then, by "accident", the candle would go out, and my companions would scream and seek sanctuary in my arms.

It was all great fun.

I had such a good time at INSEAD that I ended up failing the first two periods of the MBA program.

Dean Gabel called me in. He fixed me with those piercing blue eyes and said, "We're all disappointed with your performance, Mr Mork."

Of course, I had a dozen excuses lined up, but another look at his expression convinced me that excuses weren't going to cut it.

"The fact that your father is on the board won't save you."

I swallowed hard.

"If you don't cut back on the golf, and devote more time to studying, we're going to have to throw you out. It's up to you."

And that was the end of the interview – and my golf.

Fortunately for me, the next three periods consisted of elective subjects that I both enjoyed and excelled at, so at least I was studying stuff that I'd chosen. But it was also true that I put my head down and worked like hell – and emerged, at the end of the year, not only having passed all my classes, but actually with better grades than my old man, and an MBA from one of the best business schools in the world.

In addition, I also identified new accountability partners who really helped give me the motivation, not only to pass my classes in P3-5, but to excel.

And the knowledge that I hadn't let my father down. Yes, he had high expectations of me. But I'd committed myself to meeting those expectations, and so I was bound to a contract with him. I was accountable to him.

And accountability is a very powerful motivator, especially when you're accountable to a 6 ft 6 in, pissed-off Norwegian father.

That sense of accountability didn't last long. After all, with my INSEAD MBA tucked in my pocket, I was one of the masters of the universe, a superior being whose position at the head of whatever queue I joined had already been earned, or so I assumed.

I knew I was destined for big things, and so sought every opportunity to rise up the ladder. My progress was rapid, if a little checkered. Here's a telescopic view of my career for the next ten years or so:

Two years in a telecoms consultancy company in Barcelona. The rigidity and process-oriented nature of being a neophyte in consulting turned out not to be my thing, nor was doing research or writing long slide presentations so, when the dot.com bubble burst and clients began leaving in droves, I was happy to take a severance package. And I moved on.

I plowed my meager savings into a startup in the computer game space, but couldn't enlist any investors so, after six months, I wrote it off to experience and moved on.

I married Laura and joined a troubled cyber-café company as CEO, but was unable to fix things and, after a year, parted company with them. England beckoned. Pack your bag, I told Laura, we're relocating. And moved on.

I joined a video games company called Codemasters as brand manager but, when the company missed its numbers and I recommended the product we'd been developing be shelved because it couldn't compete, the project was canned and, as last in, I was first out – and after a year, I moved on.

I was recruited by a startup called Digital Bridges, making games for cell phones but, after a year in which Electronic Arts, whose licenses made up 80 per cent of our revenues, bought our main competitor, I realized the company was toast and moved on.

As Digital Bridges teetered on the brink of oblivion, I was approached by a much larger competitor called Glu Mobile, to run their marketing operation in Europe. Since Glu was about to go public, I saw big potential in being part of that success. We built a pan-European marketing team across five countries and launched some amazing games. But then, after the company did go public, the founders abandoned ship and, feeling anxious and eager for a new challenge, I accepted an offer from a little-known startup, headquartered in Vilnius, Lithuania, which had built the world's first app store, providing apps for feature phones. GetJar raised $6 million from the legendary investors at Accel Partners (think Facebook, Spotify and Atlassian, to name a few of their investments).

It took me six months to finagle a work visa, but I eventually left

London and moved to Silicon Valley, forcing Laura to abandon the salmon-skin fashion startup she'd founded. I spent three years with the company which, sandwiched between Apple's iPhone app ecosystem and Google's Android, began to implode. It didn't help, of course, that GetJar lacked vision and leadership. The rollercoaster hurtled on.

Not sure if you detect a pattern here? All I could focus on was my career progression. I rose from a not-so-humble consultant, to CEO of a small company, to brand manager of a much larger company, to CMO of an up-and-coming unicorn. I was a sought-after public speaker, I was interviewed by the media whenever they wanted a great soundbite about the booming app ecosystem. I was invited to speak at conferences as a keynote speaker and panelist. I blogged. I was out there. All the time. 24/7.

The world was my oyster.

But with a growing family – by now Laura and I had two children – there was very little stability. And, well, Google is another way of spelling "stability".

In 2011, I turned down an offer from Nokia as head of marketing in the USA and joined Google. I was finally where I thought I belonged – and the prospect of future rewards and promotions seemed limitless. Within a couple of months of my arrival, I was given the task of building the marketing team that would rebrand and relaunch Android Market into what would become Google Play. I was on top of the world.

Six months later, my first performance appraisal came up. I had every expectation that I'd be congratulated for my efforts in establishing Google Play on center stage. My team had won back-to-back platinum awards for outstanding work in marketing and I was in a chest-thumping mood.

I sat down in a meeting room at Mountain View with our HRBP (Human Resources Business Partner), and waited for her to spell out the many ways in which I'd impressed the company.

"Patrick," she said, "we've canvassed the members of your team—"

"Great people," I murmured.

"—and asked them what their impressions were of your communication skills."

No problem there, I thought smugly. I'd always prided myself on my ability to communicate and inspire. I was a natural speaker and had no issues giving direction and communicating.

"The team," the HR woman said quietly, "says you're a terrible communicator."

I froze. "WTF???" I whispered to myself. It took me a moment or two to get my head around that. She had to be joking.

"You're joking, right?" I said, aware that my grin was slipping.

"No. I'm very serious."

I shook my head. "That's impossible. I'm a fantastic public speaker. I can't tell you how often I was invited to address conferences before I joined Google, I—"

"There are two sides to communication," she said.

"Of course. I know that, but—"

"Your team says you don't listen. You don't ask questions and, when you do, you don't pay that much attention to the answers they give you."

I was shocked, and completely floored. Communication, in my book, had always been about making yourself completely understood. My father had been my role model. He'd been the authority at home. When he told us his war stories, we listened. Mom spent evenings listening to his stories about what was happening at the office, how this guy was sabotaging his project, what an asshole that boss was.

Of course, I listened to our HRBP and, for a few months, I invited members of my team to give me feedback on my attempts to listen more… But the idea, back then, of somehow being accountable to my team really shook me up. The notion that maybe I wasn't as good as I'd thought, cast a pall across the rest of my time at Google and, at times in meetings, I started to second-guess myself and wonder what the hell I was doing there or why they'd hired me.

In coaching and psychology, there is a term for this: Imposter Syndrome. And, before long, I was thinking actively about trying my hand at my own startup, about being my own boss again, about being accountable to no one but myself. After all, isn't that what the American dream is all about? I just felt like I had to regain control. Why did it matter what these people thought? I was destined for greater things than just working in corporate America. I needed to find my own space again.

Before I moved on, something else happened that shook my confidence on the personal side. I'd joined what we called an INSEAD Personal Board of Directors – a group of alumni who met monthly to discuss common problems, to lend each other moral support, and to give presentations on issues of interest to members. It used the Young Presidents Association (YPO) as a model, and operated like a professional self-help group. We discussed each other's careers, financial struggles, marriage issues and everything else you could imagine. It was a neutral and open place where each of us could share and get help on our most challenging problems.

It was a great group, the meetings were interesting, the discussions lively and productive. But I had other priorities at the time, missed some of the meetings, and arrived late for others. On one occasion, running 40 minutes late, I called to say I was on my way. Pierre, the guy chairing the meeting, told me not to bother.

After another meeting, a couple of the members, including Pierre, called me aside and asked me to explain my patchy attendance record.

"You guys don't understand," I said. "I work for Google. The pressure's insane."

"We all work hard," Pierre said, irritated. He himself was CEO and founder of a small biotech startup that he had been self-financing for seven years.

"Yeah, but Google's in a league of its own."

"So, what you're saying, if I understand you, is that your time is more important than our time, am I right?"

Well, actually, he *was* right, although obviously I wouldn't have phrased it quite so undiplomatically.

"No, of course not," I protested.

"It's bullshit, is what it is, Patrick," one of the others said forcefully. "You're not the center of the universe. We all have issues and struggles here. You should know that."

Pierre put a calming hand on his angry colleague's shoulder. "The fact is, Patrick, everybody agrees that, unless you make significant changes to your attitude and your behavior, we're going to have to ask you to leave the group."

No one was asked to leave an INSEAD group. For fuck's sake, I was one of the handful of founding members of the entire concept. I helped get it started in Silicon Valley. I looked around desperately for some support, but the rest of the group stared at me implacably. Their ultimatum was unambiguous, so I took note, made sure I improved my time-keeping, and made an effort to listen more carefully to what the others were saying.

It was a warning shot that I really should have paid more attention to – not just in my professional life, but in my private life as well.

It was not all about me.

There was a question I'd started to ask myself. The point of building a career is to climb as high up the ladder of success as your talents permit, right? But what if the ladder is leaning against the wrong wall?

After I left Google, to clear my head, I hiked through the Atacama Desert in Chile and visited Machu Picchu in Peru.

I've just said that I was tired of marketing. What I learned on my return to Silicon Valley was that marketing wasn't tired of me. My resume clearly underscored my experience in the field so, naturally, that's what people wanted me to do. But I didn't want to simply swap one business card for another and go from one large company to another, or even from one startup to another. I wanted to grow, learn and move out of my comfort zone, do something that was going to give me a different perspective and, hopefully, a whole set of new tools, skills and experiences. The other thing that started to dawn on me was that I was looking for something else. Something bigger than myself. I'd sold soft drinks, consulting services, video games and now "app stores" but, in the end, it didn't seem to really mean anything anymore. I started to realize I was actually looking for something deeper. I was searching for meaning.

But finding "meaning" is hard. Real hard. Though I spent hours reading books, attending seminars and talking to friends about what I should do, I was lost. So, I did what a lot of people do when they really don't know what the hell to do: I became a consultant. With the stash of cash that I'd accumulated during my years at Google, I freelanced, offering my expertise as a consultant to a number of startups. It was still marketing, but at least I was my own man.

Over the next few years, as well as trying and failing to launch another startup of my own, I worked with a handful of companies on everything from social messaging and geolocation platforms; from digital content to mobile advertising attribution platforms.

And then, in short order, as I've explored in earlier chapters, three sharp blows to the back of the head sent me reeling.

First, my marriage fell apart.

The night before the movers arrived to take us both away to our new homes, I couldn't sleep. The moon was up, the sky filled with scudding clouds. I made my way down the stairs in the half dark, checking, on the way, whether the children were asleep. I didn't bother to turn the lights on. The shadows and the occasional gleam of the moon high above suited my mood.

I sat down on the last step and looked out across our kitchen and the foyer to the picture window and, beyond it, the lights of Silicon Valley, ablaze even at this early hour of the morning.

The house was full of cardboard boxes containing all our stuff, the accumulation of a marriage that had lasted just about a decade.

I wondered what the hell had gone wrong. Two people who'd loved each other were now virtual strangers in the same house, bound by children they both loved. That day, the movers would come and make the separation a physical, final thing.

I remembered the Sundays we'd spent in this house, waking late and lazy when the kids bounced into the room, and all over us, yelling for us to get up, to make breakfast, to have fun with them.

That would never happen again.

I realized tears were running down my cheeks.

How had it come to this? Even then, I suspected I knew the answer to that, and it was no comfort.

For a decade, our marriage had revolved around me and my career. I had proudly been accountable to myself and myself alone. I'd decided on our destination, charted our course, stood at the helm. Now I stood alone, and the prospect terrified me.

I moved out of the family home, found my tiny, but expensive, apartment in Redwood City and felt sorry for myself. I joined a startup focused on mobile advertising, as Chief Marketing Officer – and, just months later, got fired on the phone by the CEO after the company failed to raise the funding it needed for me to build a marketing team.

The Course Hero debacle followed – and my near-brush with death, as you'll remember from the first chapter of this book.

You also know about my attempt to pick myself up, about my initial coaching by Jim, and how I took up cycling in order to inject discipline into my life, to give myself a sense of purpose and a clear and audacious goal to work towards.

That adventure climaxed with the Sequoia Century Ride, in which I deliberately drew in a circle of friends and family to make myself accountable to them. At every stop along the 100 miles of that ordeal, I took a selfie of myself and attached a short message to let those accountability buddies know where I was and how I was doing.

The messages of support they sent me, in turn, pumped me up and gave me the courage to press on.

But most important for me then, and for this chapter now, was that I felt it my duty to complete the race simply because I'd promised them I would. I felt obliged to them. I felt *accountable* to them.

When, at the end of race, I wobbled over the finish line, practically fell off my bike and burst into tears, the overwhelming emotion I felt was due, in large measure, to the fact that I'd kept to my contract with all those people who'd been following me, via Instagram, through the redwood forests of northern California. That feeling of accomplishment lasted for months after the race – and even today, years later, I continue to feel a flush of pride.

My father had high expectations of me when it came to my career. But expectations on their own don't generate that sense of accountability.

In coaching, one of the issues we talk about with our clients is the difference between expectations and agreements. A lot of the problems between people arise when they mistake one for the other. You might *expect* me to do something but, until I've *agreed* to do it, there is no contract, no obligation.

The biggest falling out I ever had with my father began when, after I was fired by Course Hero, I called him. First, I explained what had happened.

"Probably for the best," he said. "You need to find a better fit. Course Hero simply wasn't the right company for you."

"Dad, it's not really about Course Hero. I think I find corporate culture toxic and, frankly, I'm sick of working for other people."

"That's ridiculous. You were set for a great career at Pepsi—"

"That was 20 years ago, Dad."

"And what about Google? You loved your time at Google. You did well there."

"Maybe I did, but after a couple of years I felt like I was suffocating... I'm simply not a company man." I'd never told him about my negative performance review.

And then I told him I'd enrolled in a coaching program. "I'm starting a new career – as an executive coach."

Yeah, right, at 47? Well, he didn't say as much, but I knew that was what he was thinking.

And then a couple of months later, after I'd refined my understanding of my values, and specifically of the key value of the Good Father, I decided to make myself accountable to my kids, which meant I was moving to Chile. On one of my weekly calls to my father, I told him about my decision.

And he blew up.

"You're throwing away your entire career," he growled. "Chile? For god's sake, Patrick, I understand coaching really helped you through a tough time, but to actually become a coach? And now you want to do it in Chile? It's the ass-end of the world. I knew you fancied yourself as some kind of anti-establishment maverick, but this is crazy. You have kids, responsibilities … at some point you'll have to pay for Rafi's college. You need to get real at some point. You're 47 years old, not some recent college grad."

Our call didn't last much longer than that. What I only discovered much later was that my father then called my mother to discuss my recklessness.

Bear in mind that, after their divorce in 1997, they hadn't talked in nearly 20 years. By some miracle, he still had her number, dialed it, and spent an hour bemoaning the fact that I was throwing my life away. And yet, by the end of that hour, my mother reported later to me, they had both somehow managed to talk their way through their worst fears for my future and out the other side.

His last remarks to her were tentatively optimistic. "Perhaps this will end up being the best thing for him. Maybe he'll surprise us yet. Perhaps he needs a fresh start and an entirely new environment."

But that didn't stop him sending the incendiary email to Laura, threatening legal Armageddon against her for manipulating me into doing something entirely nuts.

But then, that's my dad. In his defense, I've always known that, no matter how tough the love, it always comes from a good place.

◆ ◆ ◆

Rafi and Natasha were, and are, my chief accountability partners, there's no doubt about that. It's my responsibility to support them, care for them, guide them and love them.

But not far below them are my employees. The LEAP TEAM, as we call ourselves.

When I took on Jose as my first employee, I explicitly and implicitly committed myself to a whole range of new responsibilities. Of course, the agreement between a leader and his team is reciprocal. When Jose agreed to join LEAP, he also committed himself to a range of responsibilities. Those are spelled out in his contract of employment. There's no mystery about them although, of course, I always hope for a level of commitment to achieving our joint goals that goes beyond, *far* beyond, the job description that employees sign up to.

And people like Jose don't disappoint. Despite his relative inexperience – well, let's be candid, Jose had *no* experience in marketing; he was an electrical engineer, after all – he has remained thirsty for knowledge, passionate and committed to what we are doing at LEAP.

My first responsibility to him was to train him, give him the tools he needed to do his job and to make his transition to Chile as painless as I could, at least on the professional side.

He's accountable to me, I'm accountable to him. That's the mark of a great company, at least for me. That the employees throw themselves into achieving the company's goals, and the company throws itself into helping their employees achieve their goals, develop and grow.

You begin by developing and honing their skills.

Jose and I would go for walks and I spent hours teaching him the basics of marketing, content, PR, building a brand and a business. Before long, he knew as much – no, more – than many of the tech-oriented founders of startups in Silicon Valley. And, in no time at all, he was making suggestions for improvements on everything from our monthly newsletter to how we published our podcast, wrote emails and managed our lead generation process.

But my accountability to Jose went far beyond training. He was, essentially, a refugee from his home country, which had been driven into the ground by the demolition crew supposedly in charge. It was inconceivable that I might fire him if the business took a dive. The consequences could be catastrophic for him and his girlfriend, Orianna.

I was also accountable to him, I realized, for helping him shape his career at LEAP. Since we were in the business of coaching, it was only right that I give Jose the chance to experience it first-hand. I asked Maria Paz, who had been the first coach I'd ever done projects with, to be his coach and to make his transition to LEAP, and to Chile, for that matter, as painless as possible.

The bonds that connect accountability partners can be very strong. As I took on more employees, new reciprocal relationships of the same kind were formed. Each new hire committed me to doing everything I could to make LEAP a prosperous and successful company. Much of our modest success – we're still only a tiny company in a small country – is due to the accountability that I feel to the handful of people working with me, and the accountability they feel toward me and the purpose we share in developing a company culture of meaning and purpose.

My move to Chile marked a turning point in my relationship with my father, and it was really high time. I was 47, my dad in his 70s, and the time had finally come for me to forge my own path, based on this new sense of personal purpose and values I'd developed with my coach.

Of course, it wasn't simply a case of a father resenting the independent decisions of a rebellious son. My dad was genuinely concerned about the wisdom of my decisions. He was baffled by my commitment to the sort of life he would never have chosen. Although my father had slogged through 30 years of climbing the corporate ladder, ultimately becoming Executive Vice-President and member of the executive board of Royal Ahold NV, one of Europe's largest retailers, and taken plenty of risk along the way, he had never started a company, been in a startup or decided to do a 180-pivot in his career at 47. If he was nuts, I was certifiably fucking insane.

Although I'd disappointed his expectations, for the first time, perhaps, our conversations revealed to him the nature of my purpose and the depth of my commitment to my values. In sharing these with my father, I made him a more powerful accountability partner than he'd ever been before, during my bumpy journey from one company to another. *Then* there'd been expectations and not agreement; *now* there was agreement and that agreement was that I was going to move to Chile and build a coaching business, with all the risk and challenges that came along with it.

To this day, we talk regularly on the phone. He's an old-fashioned kind of guy. Our conversations don't touch on our feelings. As a coach, my objective is frequently to ask the kind of questions that dig deep. They're designed to help people find their purpose and define their goals.

With my father, I discuss operational issues, and he gives me prescriptive advice. We don't always agree. For instance, when I was considering employing Jose, I asked my father for his advice.

"What's his experience?" was his first question. "What qualifications does he have?"

"He's an electrical engineer. He doesn't have any experience in marketing."

"How long has he been working in Chile?"

"He hasn't," I admitted. "He's a Venezuelan."

"Christ, Patrick, what are you thinking? You need someone with marketing experience, preferably someone who's got some kind of business qualification, someone who knows your business and is familiar with the market."

I knew that Jose hadn't ticked any of the obvious boxes – and, despite my conviction that his curiosity and drive would more than make up for that, I was grateful to my father for reminding me of the risk I was taking.

And the fact is that, when I described the talent I'd spotted in Jose, and his hunger to succeed, my dad got it entirely and, before the end of our conversation, he was as eager to hire him as I was.

"Coming from Venezuela means he won't be expensive, right?" Dad mused.

"Damn right. I'm not exactly swimming in cash over here, so that does help things a bit."

"You could get him to vamp up your newsletter, give it a few tweaks. And, come to think of it, marketing's not too hard to get your head around, hey? I mean, you did pretty well for a guy who couldn't crack the Ivy League."

This, uttered deadpan, was Dad's idea of a joke.

"Remind me of the Ivy League school *you* attended?" I shot back. Dad had gone to the University of Birmingham, not a bad school, but by no means Oxford or Cambridge, or even Georgetown.

And then Dad surprised me by WhatsApping me a few days later, asking if I'd sent Jose the offer letter yet and what his response had been. During subsequent calls, he wanted to know how Jose was doing. Was he turning out to be the ball of fire I'd described? Had I delegated any real responsibility to him yet?

Not every call was as amicable as that. We had some real differences of opinion; I'd rather have robust arguments about business than the polite exchanges that characterize so many father-son conversations.

But I wasn't ever entirely sure whether my father had ever come to accept my decision to throw in my corporate career and pursue my own course in Chile. Until a call not very long ago, when, out of nowhere, he said something that meant a great deal to me.

The conversation went something like this:

"I've never really understood your decision to leave Silicon Valley." It was, I suppose, evening in Brussels, mid-afternoon in Santiago. I'm sure he had a glass of something in his hand and I could imagine him sitting in his elegant living room, watching the evening slowly descend upon the city, between commercial breaks on CBNC, which he watches religiously.

I was at my desk. When he'd called, I'd set aside a proposal I'd been working on and was itching to get back to. But I always made time for our conversations. I sighed.

"I've explained, Dad. I just didn't fit."

"Don't understand that. I always imagined you taking up where I left off."

Dad had worked for some of the planet's most respected companies (PepsiCo, Cadbury Schweppes, Ahold). He had, as you've already learned, become one of INSEAD's superstars and a member of their board for eight years. I had, in fact, tried to take up where he left off. For those first few years, I was trailing, more or less directly, in his wake.

But it wasn't for me. I'd been climbing the wrong ladder. It wasn't so much corporate or not corporate. I had finally recognized something obvious that, sooner or later, most entrepreneurs realize: I fucking hated working for other people. I just couldn't handle having a boss and being told what to do. It went directly against one of my core values, which I call the Madmork value. I just have to have my independence. I can't be tied down.

"But you're not me, Patrick, never have been, never will be," he went on. "You've charted your own course. I was a company man, I needed the perks, the nice cars, golf clubs and the lifestyle that went with it. You're an entrepreneur – you enjoy the risks and the excitement. I would never have had the balls to do what you did, never. I give you a lot of credit for what you've done."

I sat in silence for a moment, listening to the faint sound of traffic drifting in from the street outside and soaking in what he had said. But he hadn't finished.

"I should have said this a long time ago, but better late than never. *Chapeau*, my boy, *chapeau*."

Which, in the French vernacular, translates as: Hat's off. Congratulations.

"Thank you, Dad."

We sat, thousands of miles apart, in silence for a few seconds. I knuckled my eyes roughly. It had been a very tough couple of years. Probably the toughest of my life. But, somehow, hearing him say that, helped make the frustration and pain all the more worth it. More than ever, I was convinced I was on the right path.

Something else happened more recently that I'd like to share with you. Rafi, now fifteen, got into a little trouble at summer camp. I won't go into the details, but let me at least say that it wasn't unlike the trouble I 'd gotten into at Padres all those years ago.

The school called and warned me that, unless Rafi learned to settle disputes without resorting to his fists, he was in danger of being expelled.

My first impulse was to shake some sense into the kid, to give him a stern lecture on behavior and morality.

But years of coaching clients had persuaded me that the better path was to take a deep breath, ask questions, and *listen*.

I took him out for a pizza and, while he was devouring a slice (and throwing anxious looks in my direction, because he knew what this was about), I asked him to tell me what had happened – and why he'd done what he'd done.

He went into detail. It was pretty shocking, but I managed to keep my cool and ask him more questions. He clearly knew what he'd done was wrong. I pointed out what he could have done, and he agreed.

And then he said something that blew me away.

"You've come a long way, Dad."

"What do you mean?" I managed.

"A year or two ago, you'd have gotten upset and angry and yelled at me. Now, you asked questions and you really listened."

I sat there speechless for a few seconds.

Right then and there, I realized I'd just passed the most important performance appraisal of my life.

If you want to be good CEO, a leader, or achieve something meaningful in your life, it's very simple: a good leader is everybody else's slave. If you want to be a good leader, you are the servant of others, and not the other way round. That's something it took me 20 years to figure out. Remember that: to lead means to serve others and put their needs ahead of yours. To be accountable to them. And when you're accountable to others, that will drive you to do things you didn't think were possible. It will give you the extra miles when your tank is running on empty.

Here are a few exercises you can practice to make yourself more accountable to others and towards yourself.

EXERCISE #1

The Buddy Report

First, pick something that you'd like to achieve. Anything. It can be personal or professional. It could be something you've been putting off doing for a while.

Second, try to break that down into bite-sized chunks. Most importantly, the thing you want to do has to be measurable. And it should be timebound. You need to have a date by which you want this task accomplished, as well as any subtasks associated with it. When you're developing your goal, a useful tool is to use the acronym SMART. I introduced SMART to you in Chapter 4. Here's a reminder of what it's all about:

- S: Specific / What do you want to achieve?
- M: Measurable / How are you going to know you've achieved it?
- A: Assignable / Are you doing this on your own or do you need someone else to do it?
- R: Realistic / Can you reasonably achieve this goal?
- T: Timebound / By when do you expect it to be done?

Third, pick a person to whom you're going to be accountable. This will be your accountability buddy. The key here is that this person cannot be a family member or close friend. It must be someone you know well, but who isn't going to let you off the hook if you don't deliver.

Fourth, share your goal and subtasks with your new accountability buddy. Explain what you're trying to achieve, how you're going to measure progress, the end date by when you want to achieve your goal and the various subtasks involved.

Finally, agree on how you're going to update your accountability partner on your progress. This could be a weekly text message, email or phone call. The important thing is that you update your partner on the same day each week, at the same time.

Bonus: The Price of Failure. If you want to make this exercise even more effective, agree to a penalty if you fail to report progress each week. Your penalty could be to put $10 into a glass jar, for example. Once the jar accumulates $50, you have to give your accountability partner a $50 Amazon gift card or something else you've agreed on.

For example, let's say I've agreed with my accountability buddy that I'm going to hit the gym for an hour, at least four times a week. Last week, I only made it twice. So, in this case, I have a penalty. I texted my buddy that I only made it twice and added $10 to the jar. If it happens five times, my buddy gets a free gift card. Not only am I failing to make progress towards my goal, but I'm $50 poorer.

EXERCISE #2
Spread the Word!

Spread the Word is a more extreme exercise than the accountability buddy. With Spread the Word, we start off with the same first two steps: we identify our goal, make sure it's SMART, and break it down into bite-sized chunks. Since this might be a more complex goal, like running a marathon, we need to ensure that each bite-sized goal, in itself, is SMART.

The biggest difference here is that we're making ourselves accountable to an entire group of people and not just one person. Two ways in which we might do this are either to create a group of accountability buddies on our favorite messaging app, like WhatsApp, Messenger or Telegram. Or we might even do this using a Facebook group.

The process is the same in that we share our goal and subtasks with the group and agree to report on the same day / time each week on our progress.

A noticeable difference, however, is that the penalty isn't to the group but to individual members of the group. Here's how we do that:

1. Again, use our friendly glass jar.
2. Each member of our group will then write down a penalty that you have to pay them if you fail to complete a given task each week. For example, one member might require you to buy them a cup of coffee. Another might require you to walk their dog. The important thing is that each member should provide enough penalties to

last the duration of your project. If the project lasts a month, and you report weekly, each member would fill out four small pieces of paper and place them in a jar.

3. If you fail in any given week, reporting through Facebook or your Whatsapp group, for example, you have to draw a single slip of paper from the jar for one person in the group and perform the action described on the paper. You should only perform one action for one person, although you're accountable to everyone. Note: if you want to make this extra tough on yourself, you could perform one action for each person in the group every time you fail to meet your weekly goal.

EXERCISE #3
Spread the Joy!

Spread the Joy is nearly the same as exercise #2 but, in this case, we take a positive spin on things. Instead of paying penalties to accountability buddies when we fail in a given week, we actually celebrate our success with them when we succeed. Otherwise, the process is exactly the same. We share our goal, milestones or subtasks and, each week, when we communicate our success, we pull out a piece of paper and reward ourselves and our buddy. This could be sharing a lunch, going on a small shopping spree or grabbing a drink after work. The point is, first, to create an occasion to share our progress and, second, to celebrate a milestone or achievement.

Key #5

ASK FOR HELP

One of the biggest defects in life is the inability to ask for help."

—Robert Kiyosaki

In Joseph Campbell's classic study of the hero's journey, the hero is called to go on an adventure. His first inclination is to refuse. Why? Because the call to adventure will demand that he leave his comfort zone and venture into new territory, where he won't know the rules, the language will be strange, and he fears there'll be dangers beyond every twist in the road. So, naturally, he is reluctant.

When Laura first asked me to leave Silicon Valley and go to Chile, I refused. The risks seemed insane. Even though I wasn't particularly killing it in Silicon Valley, it was the turf I understood. It was where I hung out. It was where I met my buddies for coffee at Coupa Café or Café Borrone. My entire network, the basis of my professional reputation and personal brand, was there.

For better or worse, it was home.

But it was also a jail that blinded me to the possibilities that lay beyond its walls.

It's only once you take that step over the threshold into the world of adventure, that you will grow and change and, like Luke Skywalker, become the hero you were always destined to be.

At this point, you might want to call out my bullshit and say, you're not some hero in an epic space opera.

Really?

Every time you experience something truly new, you're pushing against the boundaries of the familiar. You're stretching yourself. You're taking risks, including the risk of failure. It takes *cojones*, as the Spanish say or, simply, the courage of a hero.

And what do you need most when you're about to step out of your comfort zone? Advice. Support. A road map. Courage. Confidence. Someone who can sometimes challenge our perspectives and help us see things we might not.

And how do you get these?

You ask for help.

That's what this chapter is all about: the absolute necessity of asking for help when you find yourself facing problems and challenges that you've never faced before. I'm going to draw on a few key episodes in my own personal and professional life, to show how essential it is to ask for help and how you can go about doing it.

It was 3 December 2021. I and my partner, Jeanine Kenigstein, had been running LEAP for two years. We'd employed five people, and we were at last, I believe, making a difference in the business environment in Santiago. But we had a problem.

I was sitting in my office with LEAP's admin and finance person, Sofia.

"It's not looking good, Patrick. There are just fifteen days to Christmas, and we're way short of meeting our quarterly targets."

I knew, of course, that we were unlikely to meet those targets, which were, to be frank, ridiculously ambitious. But "way short" sounded ominous. I cursed myself for not keeping a closer eye on the numbers.

"How short, Sofia?"

"Right now, we've signed up contracts that amount to a little over 23 per cent of our quarterly goal."

That rocked me back in my seat. "Shit," I murmured. My mind raced. "Spell out the implications for me?"

"If we don't get any closer to target?" Sofia asked.

"Yes. Worst case."

"We've got enough money in the bank to cover our obligations at the end of the month, and most of January's—"

"Most?"

"Well, we've got to keep enough on hand to make that second payment on the bank loan, and that comes due in February." Sofia was managing to keep her voice relatively calm, but I could imagine what was churning below the surface. If we didn't make that payment, we'd be out of business.

"So, we'd have to give some of our people notice at the end of December. Nice Christmas present, right?"

I woke at two in the morning with cold sweat beading my forehead and my heart racing. I just couldn't face another professional disaster. Under-funded startups have to maintain a very delicate balance during their early months and years. We'd got by on loans and my own initial investment. But, as our overheads rose, we needed more and more money to fund our operations – and, although we'd made great progress, and had amassed a bunch of excellent customers, we were still sailing very close to the wind.

Twenty-three per cent! And essentially just fifteen good working days before Christmas to make enough new sales to guarantee our continued survival.

What the fuck was I going to do?

But let's step back to another dark day in my personal history. One of the darkest, in fact. You'll remember, in Chapter 1, my account of being fired by Course Hero back in 2017.

Cycling home from my last day at the company, I nearly wiped out against a garbage truck. If I hadn't managed to swerve out of its path at the last possible moment, I would now be part of that great, unlamented garbage heap in the sky.

But that moment was not, in fact, my lowest. That came minutes later, when I wondered whether it wouldn't have *solved* my problems to have face-planted right into that truck. One quick moment of sharp pain and then "lights out".

When I realized I was even thinking about ending my life as a solution to so many of my problems, it jolted me to pull out my phone and call Jim Donovan, a coach I'd got to know, and ask him for help.

I was down, metaphorically speaking, to my last dollar, so I was able to break the usual barriers we face when confronted with the need to ask for help.

More often, although we might recognize our need for help in solving a practical or existential question, we will be reluctant to ask for it. We all know the old tale of how women are able to ask for directions, while men declare they don't need help – and remain lost. Ladies, raise your hands if your partner is one of those guys who simply will *never* ask for directions, even when it's clearly fucking obvious that they're *so* lost. My dad is one of those. Google Maps? What for? I know exactly where I'm going...

The issue could be more important than simply not knowing the way to a particular address. It could be that you're struggling with one of the many addictions that seem to afflict modern society. Or, it could be there's something seriously messed up in your job or your marriage.

Men tend not to ask for help for ego reasons: we're reluctant to admit we've been unable to solve our problems on our own. This is particularly true in the chauvinistic societies of South America, the Middle East and Africa.

But none of us is happy to admit defeat – and asking for help is always, at least to some degree, an admission of defeat in our society.

What can you do to overcome your own reluctance? I have four suggestions.

1. Start by asking yourself what you really want. This will help you refine your understanding of the problem you want to solve.
2. Ask yourself what the consequences would be of *not* solving the problem, or just letting it fester, as so many of us do.
3. Then, consider what life would be like if you *did* ask for help and, in so doing, solved the problem you're facing. How would you feel? How might that impact people around you?
4. And finally – and this is a toughie – ask yourself what the impact would be, on those you love or value, of *not* solving the problem.

Let's say you're a nicotine addict. You smoke 40 a day. You know you shouldn't. Your doctors have told you to give up. But you've been smoking ever since you were in your teens and life without smokes seems impossible. But you know, deep down, that now's the time: you *want* to change.

Ask yourself these four questions: what do you really want? A healthy life? Or a slow decline into ill-health and emphysema?

What if you don't give up? Well, we all know the prognosis, the health risks, the shortened life expectancy.

But if, with help, you could give up, what would life be like? You'd be fitter, you'd have more energy, food would be more delicious, you wouldn't suffer from those terrible winter bouts of chronic bronchitis.

Finally and, perhaps, most importantly, what would the consequences to your family be if you *didn't* give up? They'd suffer, themselves, from lung problems as a consequence of passively inhaling cigarette smoke. They'd be more likely to become smokers themselves, since we're all a product of our environment and people tend to imitate the behavior of those around them. They'd suffer the agony of losing a parent too young.

By the time you've worked your way through these questions and properly weighed the answers, my guess is, you'd be ready to ask for help.

◆　◆　◆

From a coach's point of view, asking for help is not a sign of defeat or weakness. A coach will tend to turn the issue on its head. Problems are not burdens, but opportunities for growth.

As coaches, we offer our help in a very particular way. When I turned to Jim for help, what I really wanted was for him to say:

"Patrick, I think what you should do is X. That's my advice. And I've got more advice on how you can qualify yourself to do X. I'd also suggest that you seek professional psychological help. I have the names of three therapists in your area that I could recommend—"

So, when I'd explained to Jim what my situation was – the divorce, the debacle at Course Hero – I then asked him my question: "What should I do?"

There was a short silence on the phone.

"Jim?"

"I'm here, Patrick. But I think the better question is simply, what do you want?"

I couldn't work out why he was being so difficult. It was a simple question, wasn't it? I'd outlined the nature of my various mounting problems. Now, all he had to do was give me some practical advice.

But instead, after an awkward pause, he said: "Change is difficult, Patrick. And that's what you're having to manage right now. You're in trouble. You're uncertain of the future—"

I interrupted him: "And that's why I want you to suggest a few options—"

"The most important thing I can do for you, is help you identify what you *want* to do, what you think the options might be, what you want your future to be. If I give you a recipe, or suggest what you *should* do, you won't be committed to that. In a couple of weeks, you'll be back where you started… But if *you* think of the solutions, you'll be halfway there."

And so, we began the process which ended with me deciding to become a coach myself, and with the formulation of my own key values as well as my purpose for being here.

That process changed my life. It's why I'm in Chile today, managing the growth of a small but flourishing company, enjoying my relationships with the most important people in my life, my children, and looking forward to a future of continued growth and fulfillment.

And those conversations with Jim, conducted over a period of nine months, and what I myself later learned at the Coach Training Institute, points out the fundamental difference between *directed* help and *open-ended* help.

Let me share a conversation I had with my father. He's a practical guy, with vast experience managing large and complex organizations with thousands of employees and billions in revenue. He's a guru in his field. Ask for help from him, and he'll give it in spades.

It was at the stage of my life when I was trying to decide whether to go to Chile or not. I called Dad and asked for his advice.

"Chile?" he said incredulously. "Why on earth would you want to go to the ass-end of the world. Chile? Oh, my god, Patrick. You don't know anyone there. What the hell would you even do there?"

"Laura's taking the children there."

"Well, then, you've got to stop her taking them. Set the law on her. You're their father, Patrick, you can't allow that woman to rob you of your children."

"I could get a job there ... or even start a business."

"Without contacts? Without your network? How many people do you know in Santiago?" He didn't wait for an answer. "Two and a half?"

"Dad," I protested, "I worked there myself once."

"Twenty years ago," he reminded me scornfully.

"So, your advice is?"

"Whatever you do, *don't* go to Chile. It'd be the death knell for your career."

I'm not sure whether I ended the call or he did, but he left me in no doubt whatsoever what his advice was.

And then, as you know, I moved to Chile anyway. That had one unintended consequence: it irritated my father that, having asked his "expert" advice, I then ignored it – or, at least, appeared to ignore it.

What I didn't realize at the time was that, if you ask someone for *practical* advice – what, under these circumstances, should I do? – you are, in fact, half committing yourself to taking their advice. You are, to some extent, beholden and accountable to them. If you then ignore what they've said, they have every right to feel a little pissed or, at the very least, sidelined.

I was, in fact, asking the wrong person the wrong question. Dad is superb at giving practical advice about business matters: how should I go about raising capital for this or that project? What should I do about straightening out my balance sheet? Is now the time to launch a marketing campaign? And so on.

But my question – should I move to Chile? – was not amenable to that kind of hard-headed practical advice. Because the answer was predicated on what I wanted, and what my values were, and whether I was living my life in accordance with my values. It was also predicated on what type of person I wanted to be.

Compare that conversation with one I'd had a few months earlier with Jim, my coach.

After the first couple of months working with him, I finally got down to base-rock issues. I was sitting in my shitty flat in Redwood City, confused about my career, uncertain what my next step should be. I'd made my reputation in marketing. But now, that seemed a problem rather than a solution.

Outside, gusts of wind blasted in from the Pacific, sending clouds scudding across the sky. I was on my bi-monthly call with Jim. As he started talking, an image occurred to me: I was standing on a cliff edge. Behind me the chaos of an avalanche; before me, the void.

"How happy do you feel," he said, "working in marketing?"

The answer that rose up in my throat was: I *hate* it. But what I said was, "Well, I don't know, man. I mean, I can do the job blindfolded, and it's kind of challenging, I guess – but the truth is…" I *hate* it. "…I'm bored."

"What are the consequences of being bored, Patrick?" I valued everything Jim said, but sometimes his relentless questioning drove me up the wall.

"It's kinda obvious, wouldn't you say?"

"State the obvious."

"Well, because it doesn't excite me, I don't put as much effort into it as I used to. I don't give 150 per cent."

"And the consequence of that?"

Enough already, Jim! But I gritted my teeth and ground out an answer: "I don't feel satisfied with my work."

"And how has that left you feeling over the last few years?"

"As I said, I don't feel satisfied."

"And?"

I'd had enough of this. "What do you want me to say, Jim?"

"What I'm hoping you'll do, Patrick, is get to the bottom of your dissatisfaction," he said evenly. It was difficult, if not impossible, to provoke impatience in Jim.

"Okay, okay, I feel like I'm not growing, I feel like my career has stalled. I mean, for fuck's sake, I've just been fired twice in a row. *Something's* out of whack, isn't it?"

"And how does that make you feel?"

The classic psychiatrist's couch question. How *did* it make me feel? I stared out of the window at those rushing clouds, feeling as if *I* were being blown about by forces beyond my control.

"Nothing I do seems to *mean* much. I mount a marketing campaign, it succeeds or it doesn't, people buy more of the product, or they don't. But what does it matter? I'm not making any fucking difference, Jim."

"Ah," he said. "I think we're getting down to the core of your problem. The problem is not, you don't like marketing anymore, it's not that you're bored with it. The real problem is—"

I finished the sentence for him, because it suddenly made all the sense in the world: "I'm not doing something that matters."

And that's when things started turning around for me, because that realization led to my quest to find *meaning* in what I did and that, in turn, led me to settle on coaching as an activity I believed would have an impact on others and make a difference to the world.

And *that* was something I could commit myself to, body and soul.

After Sofia tossed her hand-grenade in my office, I spent the weekend thinking about what I could do to pull LEAP out of the fire. I tossed and turned and, only when the sun was lighting the mountains to the east of Santiago's city bowl, did the answer occur to me – finally.

I could ask my team for help.

First, I outlined the problem to them as starkly as I could. Of course, they had a fair idea that we were, as a company, falling short of our goals – but they, like me, were shocked by just how short we were.

"It's December 6, people," I ended. "We've got just over three weeks to make up 77 per cent of our forecast. I've spent the weekend racking my brains to think of answers and, frankly, I've come up with a big fat zero. So, I'm asking you for help. What do *you* think we can do to dig ourselves out of this hole?"

I left them with that thought, and then paid a visit to a good friend and successful Chilean entrepreneur, a man called Pablo de la Barra. Pablo is a former startup entrepreneur who has built a successful company on the back of a formidable record of sales and just getting things done.

"Pablo, if you have the time, I'd really value your help here. We have fifteen or twenty deals on the table, a fabulous sales pipeline, but we're simply not turning them into signed contracts. What are we doing wrong?"

"Let's have a look at your sales process," Pablo said wisely. "Step by step. Tell me exactly what your sales guys do, from prospecting, through constructing the proposal, to closing."

We spent an hour doing just that. Pablo scented the problem fairly early on – but it took our entire session for me to see the light myself.

"The thing is," he said, "your salesmen – and that includes you, my friend – are doing everything right, except … you're not asking for your customer's signature. You're not closing."

He was right. We were too "nice". We'd have these terrific sessions with our clients, at which we pitched our proposals, everybody would emerge smiling, and we'd say something like, "We're really looking forward to working with you. Let us know when you've come to a decision."

We'd walk away feeling these positive vibes, but without a commitment.

A week or two later, we'd call or email them to say, "Hey, how's it going? We're on standby and really looking forward to working with you."

Pablo summed it up succinctly: "You don't have a strategy to get your clients to make a decision: either yes, or no. When you give people too much time to make a decision, they kick the can down the road and don't do anything. Remember, people hate leaving their comfort zones."

It was all blindingly obvious, but I'd needed an outsider to point it out to me. I thanked Pablo profusely and returned to our offices to hear what suggestions the team had come up with to solve our problem.

Here's another thing about asking for help: it's often best *not* to ask close friends or family for advice, either of the directed, or the open-ended kind. The problem with asking people who have a vested interest in your welfare and your happiness for advice, or feedback, or commentary on your performance, is that they'll be loath to tell you the unvarnished truth. Their advice will always be slanted.

My father would never advise me to do something that could go drastically wrong and leave me stranded on the far side of the globe without a cent to my name or prospects for the future. He cares too much for me to suggest I take risks with potentially catastrophic outcomes.

No, the best people to ask are, in fact, those who know you well but are neither friends nor relatives. They don't have a vested interest in the outcome. They can afford to give you the cold, honest truth. Even if you fucking hate it.

When I was weighing the pros and cons of moving to Chile I was, as I've already mentioned, a member of just such a group of professional associates who, while they were friendly, were not, by any stretch of the imagination, best buddies.

The INSEAD Personal Board of Directors met every month for four hours. During these meetings we updated each other on what we were each up to and a couple of us, at every session, had the opportunity to make a presentation and ask for advice from our colleagues.

This advice could be professional or personal. On one occasion, I recall one of us asking for advice about the diagnosis of cancer he'd just been given. Our response was to give him intense emotional and practical support. On another occasion, one of our members asked for advice about his son, who was about to leave home for college. How would he, his father, maintain a strong relationship with his son?

And I, inevitably, shared with them the dilemma I faced when Laura told me about her fateful decision to move to Chile.

"Guys, I have to make up my mind whether to leave Silicon Valley and go to Santiago, of all places. My father thinks I'm crazy to even consider the move."

Before I asked for their advice, I outlined the pros and cons of the move as I saw them; I gave them a fuller account of my dad's opposition; and I told them what my two coaches, Jim and Rachel, had said. It was a thorough briefing. I didn't just want their opinions, I was seeking their considered, impartial recommendations and cautions.

And they asked questions, good and searching questions, like: "How could you contribute to the entrepreneurial ecosystem in Chile?" and, "You have a Google background, you've worked in technology, you're a smart guy, you've moved around, you've reinvented yourself five million times, what's the difference here?"

At one point, someone said, "What's the very worst that could happen, Patrick?"

"I suppose," I said slowly, "I'd fail at setting up my own coaching business. Not enough contacts, not enough introductions to the right people—"

"And if you failed," my fellow INSEAD alumnus said, "what would be the worst that could happen?"

I shrugged. "I suppose I'd have to look for a job. In marketing, probably."

"And do you think that, with your INSEAD MBA, and your track record at Google and working in Silicon Valley, and so on, you would find it difficult to land what would probably be a high-paying job with a big tech company in Chile?"

The others around the table burst into laughter.

Point made.

We spent some time working out what I would do when I first landed in Santiago. How would I reinvent myself? What parts of my CV were most likely to appeal to Chilean businesspeople?

And they reminded me repeatedly that, despite my bitching and moaning that I often felt like an imposter, particularly in my new role as a coach, I was someone who had reinvented himself over and over again, had lived in eleven different countries, and that I had a great deal to contribute to a country like Chile, whose business leaders were in desperate need of the help and support and insight that coaching could give them.

I was a lucky guy to have a group like that to turn to. But what can you do if you don't start with that singular advantage? There's a range of options open to you.

First, identify people outside your circle of friends and family to whom you can turn for help and advice. It could be a high school principal you've kept in touch with, it could be your pastor, it could be the founder of your company, it could be fellow members of a service organization you already belong to, like Rotary or Lions.

Why should they help? Because people *love* to help. It's flattering to be asked for advice. It suggests that the person seeking help looks up to you, admires you, values your opinions. I've asked a lot of people in my life for help and, as far as I can recall, I've never been turned away.

It feels good to be needed. It makes us feel smart, helpful and important.

Second, surround yourself with the sort of people you aspire to be like. You'll learn from their example and you'll be inspired by their commitment and their achievements. I always look to build ties with entrepreneurs, because I know I can also ask them for help when I confront a problem or a crisis.

When I decided to get serious about cycling, I turned to Facebook and Instagram in search of cycling groups.

I joined one of these groups – athletes who were much better cyclists than me – and immediately started improving my own cycling. The members of Ciclo Club were always more than happy to help.

And, today, in our age of social media and web-based study, there are literally thousands of groups offering online learning and sharing new skills. Join one of these and you'll plug into a network of support that'll astonish you.

The key is to be active, get out there and raise your hand to ask for help. Also, be ready to help others along the way. As they say, what comes around goes around.

But the most spectacular example of asking for help, and getting it, in my life, followed my arrival in Santiago back in October 2018.

As my father had said, I knew just two and a half people in the city. Whatever network I'd managed to develop, 20 years before, had dissolved and dissipated. But, over nine months, I set out to generate a new network. This is how I went about it.

I called the few people I did know in the city and asked them to have a cup of coffee with me. I explained that I'd returned to the country, intended to work there, and needed their advice and wisdom.

We met. I gave them a short, informal presentation on my recent history, my aspirations as a coach, and asked them to help me get a fix on the Chilean business ecosystem. Which tech companies were flourishing, which were the most promising startups, and so on. In each case, my contact was both generous in sharing information and encouraging insofar as my own ambitions were concerned. Yes, they thought that, increasingly, executives in the tech sector were recognizing the value of coaching. They also gave me very specific advice on the business culture, which is more inward-looking than in the US, and more difficult to penetrate.

At the end of each meeting, I asked each of my advisors to suggest the names of two or three other people whom they thought would be able to shed further light on the tech sector.

I then contacted each of these, set up meetings, and had a conversation that roughly followed the arc of the one I've just described. At the end of each good meeting – and the overwhelming majority were positive – I asked for two or three names of *others* whom I could approach.

Do the math. After nine months of frantic networking, I had met half the movers and shakers in Santiago. I'd downloaded a massive amount of useful information, cultural cautions, and possible clients. I'd met many of the executives who later became clients, and I'd identified possible investors in my startup.

That network has made possible the business I founded here, and the growing success we have enjoyed.

Never be afraid to ask for help.

Later that day – Monday 6 December 2021, to be exact – the seven individuals who collectively make up LEAP, gathered to share their thoughts on how to make up the 77 percent deficit we faced.

"How about we offer clients who sign up by the end of December a discount?" said Valentin. Of course, it's the oldest sales trick in the world – but we hadn't used it, and perhaps now was the time to do so.

"Patrick," said Marta Morales, "we could offer, as a sweetener, a motivational talk by you to their staff. You charge $5000 USD for those talks. Sign up by the end of December, and Patrick Mork will motivate the hell out of your employees. That's quite an attractive freebie."

Not a bad idea at all. Why not?

"Patrick," Pablo, who had decided to attend the meeting as our resident Chilean "advisor", said, "I've been thinking about the role *you* play in the sales process."

"I support the team every step of the way," I said, a little defensively.

"Yes and, of course, I'm sure the team appreciates that. But maybe that sends the wrong message to the client. Perhaps we should keep you out of the process until we want the client to make a commitment. Then we roll you in, and the client will realize we've brought in the big guns for the signing ceremony."

There were plenty of other ideas, some of them a bit nuts, some practical and well worth trying. In an atmosphere of trust, *any* idea is worth listening to – and, sometimes, I've found that bad ideas can lead to good ideas.

I then relayed to them the wisdom Pablo had dropped on me.

It was time to get out there and start closing.

There's a marked contrast between asking your team for help in thinking of solutions to a problem, and telling your team what to do to solve the problem.

Most immediately, it's motivational. An individual who's told what to do, will do it – but has no skin in the game. If the solution doesn't work, they're likely to shrug and say, "Well, your idea didn't work."

But if the individual concerned has thought of the idea himself, or has been part of a group who brainstormed it together, then he or she's much more likely to feel responsible for making the solution work. This is kitchen psychology, after all, not rocket science.

But, perhaps, even more important than their commitment to making the idea work, is their accountability to the group, and to the leader of the group. I've thought of a solution to this intractable problem. What I'm doing, implicitly, is promising the boss that I *will* solve the problem.

So how did it go?

Right through December, we kept close track of the pipelines. Every Monday, we updated the team on how we were doing. In fact, so critical was success to our survival that, as we moved closer to Christmas, we started checking on progress at daily "close meetings".

By 19 December, we'd inched to within ten percent of our target, and Valentin and Marta each had a couple of big deals on the table that could do the trick.

Finally, at the end of year barbecue, arranged at Jeanine's house, Valentin arrived late with the news we'd all been hoping for.

"Not one deal," he told us. "Two deals. Signed, sealed and delivered."

We cheered. While Valentin filled our glasses with champagne, Sofia quickly did the calculations. We'd actually exceeded our target by twelve per cent.

You might have noticed a certain logic emerging from the experiences I've described so far in this book, and in the lessons it has taught me. I'll go back to this in the final chapter but, for the moment, let me spell out some of the implications I've noted.

Growth comes from stretching beyond your normal boundaries, reaching out of your comfort zone into the less predictable territories beyond them. To turn what could possibly be chaotic change into productive opportunities, you have to seek the help of people who've pioneered the route you'd like to take.

Asking for help does three things: it flatters the person you've asked for advice; it raises an expectation in their minds that you'll take their advice, or at least respond to it creatively – and therefore makes you accountable in some sense to them; and it helps you create a road map for your future growth.

In fact, I'd go even further and argue that *asking* for help, in itself, opens up new possibilities. It reveals fresh perspectives on things. It gives you new ideas. It shows you that the boundaries you previously thought impenetrable, are in fact knee-high and easily hurdled.

The more help you ask for, the more help you'll be given, and the more you'll be able to achieve. After all, haven't I read somewhere: ask and it shall be given you? Leaving your comfort zone will demonstrate to you that life beyond the pale is where the action is. Becoming accountable to others will help you achieve your goals. And you'll derive a deep sense of real satisfaction from knowing that your goals are in sync with your values.

Asking for help isn't always easy. Particularly in a work environment. Sometimes, when we ask for help, we might be afraid to be seen as ignorant, incompetent or vulnerable. The following exercises are designed to help you learn to ask for help from a place of safety and low risk. We hope you find them helpful.

EXERCISE #1
Small Asks

As we mentioned in previous chapters, particularly our chapter around goals, it's important to take small steps at times, so that we learn to "walk before we run".

With this goal in mind, set yourself a goal to ask for help in small increments and turn this into a habit. For example, you could decide that, twice a week, on Tuesdays and Fridays, at a particular meeting for the next six weeks, you might ask someone on your team to help you with something relatively minor and unimportant. Perhaps you're asking someone to help you out with gathering some data or putting together certain parts of a report. The goal here is to start asking for help in small, low-risk increments and to build a habit around doing it. If you want to speed up the process, try asking for small pieces of help every day for two weeks and see how it goes.

Keep in mind that we are more or less comfortable using certain communication channels, so some of you may prefer to ask for help using email, Slack or some other form of written communication, while people who are more extroverted may prefer to ask someone directly, over the water cooler or during a Zoom meeting. Pick a channel that works for you.

After each request, chronicle how it felt to ask for help and also what the outcome was. How did you actually feel after making the ask? How did the person respond? What was the end result? What are you noticing as you start to ask for help more often?

EXERCISE #2
How does it feel to be Superman / woman?

It's perfectly normal for us to feel silly or nervous sometimes when we ask for help. After all, we're admitting that we don't know everything and that can make us feel sheepish or vulnerable. One easy way to develop the habit of asking for help is to think of the last time someone asked us for help.

Take out your notebook or fire up Word or Google docs and answer that question. How did we feel the last time someone asked us for help? What was the context? What did they need? How did it feel to help that person and what was the outcome? What emotions did we feel when the person thanked us? How did it feel to be needed and serve someone else? In addition, what did we think of the person asking for help? Did it make us think any less of them? Did we find ourselves asking ourselves if they were incompetent or, did we see them as brave for asking for help?

If you're like most people, you'll notice something really cool. Helping others feels awesome. It generally makes us feel good. We feel helpful, knowledgeable, maybe even smart, and certainly needed.

The next time you have any doubt about asking for help, consider this: how would the person you're asking feel if they were able to really help you solve your problem? What feelings would they experience and how might that influence the relationship between you and that person?

How's that for a new perspective?

EXERCISE #3

What would my hero do?

Another way for us to find the courage to ask for help is to think of people we admire. The reality is that, one thing very successful people are all good at, is asking for help from others. They have networks of friends, advisors, mentors and colleagues, who are there to help them when they need it. As we'll discuss in chapter 7, they build teams and those teams are made up of people who complement their skill set and who, directly or indirectly, are in a position to help them.

The next time you're struggling to ask for help, ask yourself what your mentor would do? What would the person you most respect do? Then go out, make the ask and chronicle what happens.

Key #6

BUILD A TEAM

If you want to go fast, go alone. If you want to go far, go together.

—AFRICAN PROVERB

In August 2008, I received a call from the recruiting team of a venture capital company in London. Accel Partners is one of the world's leading venture capital firms with a string of great investments to feel smug about. They were early backers of Facebook, Spotify and Rovio, the developers of Angry Birds, as well as Atlassian, the company behind the popular project management software, called Jira.

Accel had recently invested in a small, six-man Lithuanian startup based in Vilnius. This little company, called GetJar, was doing something that I had dreamed about for the past few years: they were taking apps from developers and distributing them directly to consumers, bypassing mobile operators entirely. GetJar had essentially built the world's first app store. It had been launched back in 2005, three years ahead of Apple's App store, which wouldn't debut until July 2008.

Long story short, I joined the company. It seemed to me that GetJar was poised to be one of the leading players in the booming app ecosystem and I was absolutely determined to help get the company there.

GetJar was a business wholly dependent on downloads of apps from its app store. The more traffic it attracted, the more advertising it could sell. It was designed to operate on what were then called feature phones – basically, all those phones that weren't smart phones – think of your good old Nokia N95 or N72, and the like. I know it's hard to believe, but there were phones before the iPhone!

But we faced two huge problems.

On one side, there was Apple itself, which had introduced the iPhone in 2007.

And, on the other, Google. They'd bought a small company called Android, which had developed an operating system of its own. Google open-sourced Android to any phone manufacturers who wanted it. Built into every Android phone was what was called back then the Android Market, the equivalent of the iPhone's App Store. At first, the Android Market posed no real competition to Apple: it had lousy apps, it was buggy, and it was badly marketed. In addition, it only focused on apps and games and lacked music, books and movies.

Despite the fanfare behind the introduction of the iPhone, the market continued to be dominated by the feature phones of Nokia, Blackberry and Ericsson. While this was the case, GetJar enjoyed phenomenal growth. Within two years of my arrival, we had recorded over two billion downloads of apps from our store, opened offices in London and Silicon Valley and raised in excess of $40 million in venture funding.

But slowly, people began to realize all the many advantages of the smartphone and, as more and more mobile operators marketed the iPhone and other Android phones aggressively, and phone prices declined, feature phones began to take a dive.

Traffic to GetJar's apps started faltering and I realized we faced an existential threat. We were confined to feature phones – and feature phones were rapidly becoming the dinosaurs of the phone world. We couldn't get into Apple's App Store, because that was a closed shop. After all, why *would* Apple invite its competitors to sell their products in their store? And the new Android phones from Samsung, LG, Huawei and others all had the Android Market built into them, giving it a huge competitive advantage over us.

By the time the company was visibly starting to struggle (in late 2010), GetJar's founder, a serial entrepreneur called Ilja Laurs, had effectively handed over day-to-day control of the company to our COO, a guy called Chris Dury. Chris was an autocrat. He enjoyed making decisions, frequently after long and intense discussions with Ilja, and then instructing the various senior executives to execute them.

He traveled fast, and alone. He didn't enjoy being challenged. Chris was very bright, with a degree from Cornell, and believed he was best positioned to map the future of the company.

But I had my doubts.

I remember one conversation we had about that future. I'd pointed out to him our falling traffic numbers. Chris dismissed this. A blip, he said.

"We're the meat in the sandwich, Chris," I argued. "Google above, Android below. We're getting squeezed."

He shrugged. "It happens. We'll survive. Look at the Angry Birds story. It's just a matter of getting the right app developers on our side."

The Angry Birds story was one I knew very well. Under Google's nose, I'd managed to persuade Rovio, the developers of the best-selling iPhone sensation, to give us exclusive launch access to their game for a limited period ahead of the Android Market. The launch of the app had been so successful, our server architecture had been unable to handle the avalanche of downloads, and our systems had crashed. The snubbing of Android Market, and our subsequent system crash, had been all over Techcrunch and other media outlets and had infuriated Android's boss and founder, Andy Rubin.

But more recent numbers were difficult to ignore. Fewer app developers were knocking at our door. For reasons that were obvious to me, they preferred the opportunities Apple and Android offered them. Although we had done subsequent deals with other noted developers like Zynga and Zeptolabs, developers of Cut-The-Rope, the reality was that, with the exception of these games, we just didn't have the organic Android traffic necessary to make GetJar a viable platform for Android developers and, without traffic, they wouldn't buy ads on the store and without that, well… We didn't have a business.

But there was one huge opportunity I believed we could exploit. Android didn't operate in China. Google had made a decision not to work in China, given the Chinese government's insistence that their search results be censored. That left a wide-open market to provide Android apps to consumers in China.

"If we pivoted to China," I said to Chris, "we could own that entire market."

"China? I don't think so."

And he walked off.

But I didn't give up. At meetings of the executive team, I continued to argue that we should, at the very least, investigate the Chinese market.

Chris gave my proposals a frosty reception. "Our investors are Americans," he said. "They want to see us succeed in Silicon Valley."

But eventually, I managed to persuade him that an exploratory trip to China would be worth it. He went alone.

And returned a week later, his mind made up.

"I've looked at it, Patrick. The culture's so different, it'll be difficult breaking in there."

"So, no China?"

"Like I said before: our investors are American, they want to see us succeed in America."

How naive I obviously was. I'd thought, because our investors were American, they'd want to see us succeed. Anywhere. But he would have none of it. And, although I made a passionate plea to the board for them to reconsider this strategic decision, they preferred to listen to their COO. Who was I, after all, but GetJar's chief marketing officer? What did I know about strategy?

I gave up fighting for what I thought, at the time, and still do, was the obvious solution to our problems. Of course, China would be a difficult nut to crack, but then Apple and Google were *impossible* to crack.

Why didn't I fight harder? I blame myself for that failure to speak up loudly and more persuasively. But not altogether.

The fact is, although Chris Dury led our executive team, he wasn't particularly invested in yoking the team's collective and diverse insights, talents and skills. Like I said, he had an inviolable belief in his own instincts. And, while he had a brilliant and incisive mind – he and Ilja made a formidable pair – the culture the two of them created at GetJar was exclusive, rather than inclusive; it encouraged its execs to do what they were instructed to do, rather than take the initiative; and it didn't seek or value the opinions of its executives.

This chapter is about teams, and about how to infuse teams with a positive, can-do attitude. Books, of course, have been written on the subject, some of them brilliant. I will be relying on the good sense and advice of one of the best of them, Patrick M Lencioni's, *The Five Dysfunctions of a Team*.

Up to this point in this book, I've been concerned with what you might call self-management: how to establish your own purpose, values and goals; how making yourself accountable to others serves to boost your own performance; why putting your pride in your back pocket and asking for help can extend your reach and multiply your effectiveness.

So, why teams? Well, primarily because no man or woman is an island. In work situations, we are almost always either humble members of teams, or leaders of teams. And it's no coincidence that the strategies we've already described apply with as much force to teams as they do to individuals.

So, back to GetJar and its dysfunctional executive team…

GetJar's failure to take seriously my sense that we faced an existential threat points to the first of those five dysfunctions. Lencioni says the most important reason teams fail is that its members don't trust each other to treat their opinions and ideas and criticisms with respect.

My reluctance to engage Chris in a toe-to-toe battle sprang from my realization that my opinion was not welcome, and nor did it really matter. Chris and Ilja were the product guys, the tech guys. In the Valley, tech / product reigned supreme. Sales was headed by Bill Scott, an old friend and seasoned b2b sales guru – but even he was subjected to the philosophy that sales should be treated like mushrooms: keep 'em in the dark and feed them shit. The same was true of marketing at GetJar and is one of the not-so-endearing qualities of tech companies in Silicon Valley.

Contrast this with an incident that happened recently at my Chilean startup, LEAP. My co-founder, Jeanine, and I had held a workshop on how to improve feedback among the members of our team. At the end of the session, one of our team members stuck a Post-it on the board which said, simply:

"I feel that this is a hostile environment to work in."

This from a junior member of our staff, a normally reticent person, who rarely spoke. It was, perhaps, for that very reason her observation was so shattering. But even as I tried to work out what to say, I felt a stirring of satisfaction, even pride. She had felt secure enough in the environment we'd created to articulate a very powerful complaint.

Of course, we took it seriously but, what eventually emerged was that she was unduly sensitive to the sometimes-robust arguments and discussions that sprang up at LEAP – debates that we all felt often led to great ideas. The learning from that particular episode at the company was, first, that we needed to work much harder to encourage people to speak their minds and provide feedback. The second learning was that we needed to do a better job of recruiting people who really fit with LEAP's fast moving, outspoken and proactive culture. That person, sadly, was one of the first casualties of this realization and we agreed to part ways when we both grasped that LEAP's culture was really not a good fit for her.

Contrast my GetJar experience with my time at Google Play. Remember the complaints my team made about my communication failures? Feedback like that helps you identify your blind spots so you can start improving them. Google, in fact, after doing a great deal of original research into what makes effective teams, concluded, much like Lencioni, that the creation of a psychologically safe space makes possible the honest exchange of ideas, opinions and complaints, which can only enhance the functioning of the team.

In fact, Lencioni argues that lack of trust in a team makes it difficult, if not impossible, to manage constructive conflict.

Think about it. The process by which ideas are proposed, interrogated, amended and improved (or rejected) can be highly conflictual. Only if the members of the team feel comfortable to be engaged in this process, can the best ideas be forged and hammered out. (Which is why we encourage members of the LEAP to have robust arguments and really speak out when they disagree with something.)

At LEAP, I've tried to apply what I learned from my own failures in Silicon Valley. Chief among these was my failure, mainly at GetJar, to delegate authority to members of my team. This is clearly a trust issue. We fail to delegate when we don't trust our subordinates to execute tasks as effectively as we believe we could ourselves.

"If you want something done right, do it yourself," is the cry of the manager who doesn't trust his subordinates. This is something we come across frequently in our work in Chile and many other Latin American countries.

But, of course, if you don't delegate real authority to less experienced members of the team, how can you hope they'll ever *have* the experience to perform as you'd like them to?

So, when we recruited Valentin to the LEAP team, I was determined to overcome this reluctance. This, despite the fact that Valentin had no experience working in Chile, no experience selling in Spanish and no experience selling coaching services.

In the early days, I spent a ton of time mentoring and training Valentin. But he was a natural and it wasn't long before I started delegating more and more to him. In the beginning, I sat in on every sales call, I helped draft proposals, I headed the negotiation efforts.

But by April 2022, I had withdrawn almost entirely from the sales cycle and, today, I am no longer present in sales meetings with clients. I am no longer involved in writing proposals. I don't take part in sales negotiations. My only role, now, is to appear at the end of the sales process, to signal the fact that we expect the client to sign on the dotted line and to congratulate them on making a wise decision.

It's only when you trust your team to do the job that they'll step up and surprise you with their initiative and ingenuity. That's where the real magic happens.

Marriages are a different kind of team, and the health of a marriage relies absolutely on the existence of a safe space of trust as well as psychological safety. This is not least because it's only if that space exists that the difficult issues – those that invariably arise between life-long partners – can be handled.

My marriage to Laura broke down, in the end, precisely because we were unable to tackle the big and thorny issues of our relationship. I had not taken the time or devoted the effort necessary to help create that psychological safety. By the time I realized the nature and the scale of the problems afflicting our relationship, it was too late to fix them.

Ironically, it was in the apparent peace and serenity of our relationship – our friends praised us for never raising our voices at each other, for never having an argument – that the seeds of its collapse were buried. Conflict, particularly if it's uncomfortable, is necessary for a marriage, or any other team, to function.

Google's second ingredient for high-functioning teams is dependability. If team members can depend on their colleagues to do what they've agreed to do, to come clean with them if they fall short of their goals, and to help when their help is needed, then the team, as a whole, will shift into a higher gear.

Seems obvious, doesn't it?

At GetJar, my own marketing team suffered from an inbuilt defect, and it was a defect I have to acknowledge was entirely of my own making.

I was the seventh person to join GetJar, the first marketing guy. It was up to me to create my own marketing team. I snagged a great PR person.

Dianna Vincent-Galvan was high-energy, professional and a self-starter. But the others I hired were more junior. They followed orders reasonably well. I could sort-of depend on them to do what they were told. But I couldn't depend on them to initiate anything of significance.

It's a cardinal rule of leadership that, if possible, you should always employ people who are *better* than you are. After all, how else can you expect to raise the level of performance? At Amazon, they use the term "raise the bar". The idea is that each person you bring to the team makes the team better. That certainly wasn't the case when I was head of the marketing team at GetJar.

However, at Google Play, every member of my team was better than I was at what they were employed to do. At LEAP, Valentin and Marta are better at selling our products than I am. My co-founder, Jeanine, is better at devising programs than I am and a far more experienced coach. Jose is far savvier and more experienced at content editing and development and, also, much faster to pick up new things when it comes to digital marketing. One of the key questions we ask ourselves, when we're interviewing people to work at LEAP, is: "Does this person make us better, overall, as a team?"

The third reason teams fail, Lencioni argues, is that, lacking trust, and, therefore, the ability to manage constructive conflict, team members don't fully commit themselves to achieving the team's, or the company's, goals.

At GetJar, I'd become so frustrated with Chris and his authoritarianism that, at some point, I stopped bothering to object to a ludicrous solution he and Ilja suggested to the problem of falling traffic.

"Gold coins? Are you serious?" I remember asking somewhat incredulously.

"It's a great idea," Chris said firmly. "Every time someone downloads an app, they earn a virtual gold coin, which they can redeem for premium features of apps in the store."

It was a simple loyalty programme – GetJar Gold, they called it – but it overlooked the fact that, as our traffic had started falling, app developers were offering fewer and fewer premium applications on our store. Why would someone accumulate these coins if, in the end, there was nothing really to buy with them?

This seemed obvious to me, but I let it go and, in the few months before I resigned to join Google, I dutifully, but unenthusiastically, masterminded a marketing campaign for GetJar Gold.

It didn't work.

Something else happened, in my final months at GetJar, that illustrates another facet of dysfunctional teams. If there's no trust and if, consequently, there's no room for constructive dissent which, in turn, leads to reduced commitment, members of a team are more likely to focus on their own agendas and goals, as opposed to the company's overall results. The result is that they increasingly begin to operate in silos. When people are no longer committed, they don't feel they have any responsibility or ownership for the company's results so, as Lencioni says, they develop an "avoidance of accountability".

Let me illustrate how this works in practice, with this story from my GetJar days.

Sometime in July 2011, I walked into our executive boardroom one morning, where the team had assembled. I sensed immediately that something was really off.

"Somebody die, guys? Why the long faces?"

Tom Burke, our CFO, slid a piece of paper over the table to me.

"It's a disaster," he said.

My eyes scanned the letter. It was from a prominent legal firm.

The letter was written in the usual legal jargon on behalf of ... Apple Inc. It was, I realized, one of those "cease and desist" warnings that lawyers are so fond of issuing. And it concerned our use of the term, "App Store".

"They're claiming the words 'App Store' are exclusive to Apple, and that we're in violation of their copyright if we use those words," Tom said.

"In other words," Chris said bleakly from the head of the table, "we're fucked."

Telling people who run an app store that they can't use the term "App

Store" in their marketing is pretty much like telling Serena Williams she can't use a racket when she's playing tennis.

"This is crap," I said.

"It doesn't really matter whether they've got a point or not," Chris said. "They've got inexhaustible funds. They can afford to sue us up to the Supreme Court and back again if we don't do as they say."

I reread the letter and, somewhere in my memory, a bell rang.

"Can I hang on to this for a while?" I asked. "I have an idea that might work." In fact, if I was right, this letter, threatening as it was, presented us with a golden opportunity.

"What are you going to do?" Chris asked.

"I'm going to take care of this."

I think they were all so relieved to have someone else take the ball and run with it that no one said a word when I left the room a moment later. Of course, I wasn't as confident as I sounded – but what the hell. Better to exude false confidence than cower in a corner. And, besides, I'd already decided to leave GetJar. I reckoned it would be better to go out in style and continue to do my job to the best of my ability.

I spent the next few hours on the phone and trawling the internet and, by the end of the day, had confirmed my initial suspicion: Apple did not own the copyright on the term, "App Store". They had, indeed, tried to copyright it, but had been challenged by Microsoft in court and the issue was at that point in time in limbo.

My next task was to send copies of the letter to the New York Times, the Wall Street Journal, and a host of other prominent news outlets.

The next day, the story of a tech giant, Apple, bullying a feisty, small competitor was all over the airwaves and in the headlines.

Apple had made a classic PR mistake in attacking us. They'd assumed they could do what they did with most developers and most of their suppliers and partners: simply browbeat us into submission. They hadn't reckoned on the fact that GetJar had very little to lose.

The next few days proved to be a shitshow for Apple – and a barrel of laughs for us at GetJar. Virtually every news organization we'd alerted printed a story about Apple's outrageous demand. Many of them called and quoted me. "GetJar won't be subject to this kind of bullying," I said. "We're not going to 'Cease & Desist'."

To rub salt in their wound, we wrote a blog post on the subject with the title, "We're not going to take it," from the classic Twisted Sister anthem of the same name.

It seemed, at the end of the day, that the score was, Apple 0, GetJar 1.

But actually, it wasn't as simple as that. Because the truth of the matter is that, while it was a real blast, how I conducted the fight against Apple pointed directly at the heart of the problem at GetJar. Sure, we garnered a lot of sympathy for being the underdog, and held Apple at bay, but it didn't change the fundamental fact that we were screwed.

I was operating, not so much as GetJar's staunch defender, but more as Mad Mork; not as the leader of a marketing team, or a member of the executive team, coordinating a response to a potential threat from a much larger rival, but as a maverick loner, intent on proving a point and making myself look good in the process.

Who benefited most from the wave of publicity that followed my decision to blitz the press? I did. Was I responsible for helping GetJar fend off the attack? Maybe. But I wasn't responsible for helping to save the company from the wider threat that existed and I sure as hell wasn't committed to GetJar Gold. I was operating in a silo, as a maverick shooting from the hip, but I was hardly, as Lencion would say, "the ideal team player".

That's what happens in an organization in which, because there's little trust, the difficult issues aren't dealt with and there's no commitment: individuals within the company act in their own interests. Since they don't feel involved in many of the organization's bigger initiatives, they go off and do their own thing.

That's exactly what I did.

Google's third ingredient for highly effective teams is double-barreled. Great teams, their pioneering research suggested, are well structured and very clear about who's doing what.

At GetJar, the boundaries between responsibilities were vague and ill-defined. Nobody quite knew where their duties began and ended. Ilja and Chris took so much responsibility for steering the company, making decisions without reference to their executive team, that everyone on that team felt, with good reason, that the two seniors were capable of trespassing on their turf at any point. This led to a sense, among all the department heads, that they lacked true autonomy, that they were, in the final analysis, simply instruments in the hands of Ilja and Chris, to do as they were instructed to do.

Of course, this leads in turn to loss of confidence, poor morale and a lack of commitment to the company's goals.

At Google, by contrast, things couldn't be clearer. We were religious about measuring and tracking progress. Every person on the team had clear metrics and clear goals. Google used a framework of measurement called Objectives and Key Results – OKRs – to encourage transparency and accountability.

At GetJar, the marketing department held a lot of conferences, we prepared and issued endless press releases, we ran some ad campaigns and we sent out one hell of a lot of emails. But there wasn't much tracking and measurement.

In fact, the only proxy we had to assess whether our marketing efforts were making an impact was whether the company was visible in the press. That was our metric. And, because we focused so much on generating news that the press would pick up, just about all we got done was racking up column inches and mentions on TV and radio.

It wasn't a great metric for success for a company that should have been intent on attracting apps to its app store. We *should* have focused on how many apps the store was acquiring, on how many developers were attracted to our site, and on encouraging them to upload the latest versions of their apps…

It's worth spending a little time talking about that system, Objectives and Key Results. We adopted it here at LEAP – as have major companies around the world.

Objectives and Key Results is a way of implementing goals and tracking your success at achieving them. It was originally devised by Andy Grove, CEO of Intel, and popularized by a guy called John Doer who, having picked it up while he worked at Intel, went on to persuade Google's Larry Page and Sergey Brin to adopt it at Google, when he invested $12 million in the company on behalf of Kleiner Perkins, a venerable venture capital firm, where he had become a partner.

OKRs promote four key strategies.

First, they suggest that any organization pursue just one objective. Of course, this sounds crazy. And yet, the example of Google is a powerful one. When you focus relentlessly on just one thing, you're able to eliminate the noise, and say no to one hell of a lot of distracting and competing objectives.

Focus leads you to the second pillar of the methodology: alignment. When you're focused on just one thing, it's very easy to communicate that goal to every member of a team, and every team in the organization – and therefore to align everybody on the same axis, pointing at the same objective.

Imagine you're the commander of a platoon of soldiers. You've been given an objective: capture the tower on top of the hill. Don't worry about the fifteen other towers, or the castle in the distance, or the army in the valley beyond, just take the effing tower!

The platoon charges up the hill. They don't worry about anything else. They're totally in synch. They each know what the other members of their troop have to do. Communication between them is clear and un-ambiguous. Their responsibilities are clearly defined. Their target is clearly defined.

And they take the tower.

Third, OKRs are very clear about follow-through and accountability. If one member of a team doesn't hit his personal objectives, that can't be concealed. But, because the team works in an atmosphere of trust and psychological safety, when one person is not hitting their target, he won't be afraid of admitting it, and asking for help. The flip side is that someone else on the team might notice and offer to pitch in and help them out.

In an organization focused around OKRs, there are very high levels of transparency and accountability.

My task, recently, was to recruit a marketing manager at LEAP. I was struggling to find a suitable candidate, and shared my difficulties with my team. Valentin, who has a history of working in the recruiting industry, instantly offered to help. "Hey, Patrick, send me the job description and I'll see if I can help. I'll put in an hour a day, scroll through LinkedIn and compile a list of candidates."

Of course, I took him up on his offer and, within a week, he had secured a shortlist of two or three promising candidates.

And, finally, OKRs incorporate an idea called "Stretch". It concerns the target you set for yourself, or your team, or your organization as a whole. As the word suggests, it encourages you to set a goal that is unattainable – if all you do is apply your current business strategies. Business as usual will give you the usual results. If you want extraordinary results, then … stretch.

A goal that is beyond your current ability to achieve forces you to think of totally new strategies and tactics. It forces you to consider new ways of conquering the tower on the hill. It forces you, to use a well-worn but still powerful cliché, to think outside of the box.

The fourth reason teams fail, Lencioni argues, is that they're not accountable. This matches perfectly one of the key strengths of OKRs. A transparent working environment, in which goals are shared and, in which a high level of trust exists, will lead automatically to similarly high levels of accountability.

Individuals feel accountable to the team; teams feel accountable to each other; and, collectively, teams feel accountable to the organization they serve.

At GetJar, by contrast, there wasn't a high level of trust among the executive team. That meant it lacked the ability to deal constructively with conflict, which led to a consequent lack of commitment to company goals. And when there's no commitment, there's no accountability.

Various programs and services seemed to be regularly crammed down my throat, like the ludicrous GetJar Gold program. But, because I never really committed to them, I didn't feel responsible for their failure. Who cared? I didn't. In the end, I felt that, because Ilja and Chris had excluded the rest of us from every significant decision, the company deserved whatever fate awaited it.

At Google Play, my attitude and the attitude of every member of my team was completely different. Everybody felt committed to the goals of the team, everybody knew what their responsibility was, everyone got their stuff done – so the results were spectacular. We did, in two years, what it would have taken another company five. We completely rebuilt the App Store, launched books, movies, games, *multiplayer* games, and a sub-scription music service...

In two years, we took the business from $700 million to $2.5 *billion* in revenue (today Google Play does north of 25 billion) and, in the process, we built a fabulous brand. That level of execution is unheard of in most compa-nies because they don't have the team dynamics that make it possible.

Google's research revealed that, essential to the functioning of highly effective teams, is a conviction that the work they're doing is *meaningful*. People want to feel like they're doing something that goes beyond just earning a paycheck. Particularly today, in our post-Covid world, more and more people are waking up and asking themselves why they're grinding away at their jobs, traveling and working long hours. For what? To sell more toothpaste? To get another blockbuster M&A deal? A big reason for the "great resignation" is that people need to find meaning in what they do. The way I see it, we're moving to a world of purpose over profits.

This is precisely why people have joined us at LEAP. They love the fact that we're focused on helping organizations develop cultures of mean-ing and purpose. They love the fact that their work matters and that every person we help transform into a better leader, helps make their organiza-tion a more attractive and fun place to work. Put side by side, meaning will trump paycheck every time. It's just that simple.

And finally, at the peak of Lencioni's pyramid is the observation that dysfunctional teams don't care, one way or another, what the results of their work are.

Objectives and Key Results slot very neatly into this because, by definition, that's what OKRs are specifically designed for. They keep you focused on results. Not just your results or your teams' results, but the organization's results, and how your results contribute to these.

At LEAP, we hold meetings every two weeks, at which we review our OKRs. How are we doing in terms of sales? How are we doing in terms of impact? How well are individual members of the team handling their respective responsibilities? Where do people need help?

We're all explicitly committed to achieving the company's goals – and we each feel accountable for playing our part in that.

And how do you encourage commitment and accountability? By inviting the team, and the individuals in it, to set their own goals.

A few months ago, we met to set our goals for the next quarter. The sales team, Valentin and Marta, had excelled themselves in the previous quarter. Now it was up to them, in line with OKRs "stretch" philosophy, to set their sights on their next objective.

"What do you think, Valentin?" I asked. "Last quarter you exceeded the target by 12 per cent. What's your target for the coming quarter?"

"Give us a minute." He and Marta muttered to each other. We waited in silence for a minute. Clearly, they'd discussed this in advance because it didn't take long for them to settle on a response.

"Last quarter, our target was 4 000 UF. In this coming quarter, we think we'd easily be able to manage 5 000 UF – but because we like to stretch ourselves, we're going to go for 6 000 UF." Even though I had great faith in Valentin and Marta's capabilities, I admit I was a little doubtful. "You sure? That's a 50 per cent increase. You don't think that's a little steep, even for stretch goal?"

They were both shaking their heads even before I'd finished.

"We've got a great pipeline," Valentine said with conviction. "Of course, it'll be challenging, but we really think we can do it."

At our next quarterly review, they reported that they'd hit 5 500 UF.

When teams come up with their own targets, they're automatically committed to achieving them. Valentin couldn't turn around six weeks later and say, "We always told you the goal was too difficult." It was his and Marta's goal. Their pride was on the line. They were accountable, not only to themselves, but to all of us.

And, because we're all part of a team with a common goal, any one of us would be willing to pitch in and help them if ever they asked for support.

It almost goes without saying that, at GetJar, we didn't have this unrelenting focus on results. I didn't feel responsible for the results the company achieved because I was never really consulted. We were given numbers we didn't necessarily agree with, and so our commitment to achieving them was, at best, half-hearted.

Google's fifth ingredient for high performing teams is impact. If a team feels their contribution will make a real impact on the achievement of the company's goals, then they're likely to go all in. It's simple psychology. People want to understand how their hard work impacts the overall success of the company. Don't we all want that?

Google had cultivated a culture in which people were constantly stepping out of their comfort zones to do high impact stuff. That's a difficult environment to create. We're doing everything we can at LEAP to replicate that culture. It's not easy because human beings, by default, are fearful, and doing high impact stuff means you have to step out of your comfort zone and try something really hard. There's a good chance it's not going to work. People go, "Oh, my god, what if it doesn't work?"

But Valentin and Marta have put fear aside and set out to have maximum impact on our results.

What happened to GetJar? Well, the fact that I even have to ask the question suggests what the answer is.

Chris's commitment to taking the fight to Apple and Google in the US lasted for another year or so. But the company was fighting a losing battle. It had neither the resources nor the platforms to take on the two tech giants, and its failure was, as I'd suspected, predictable.

Three years after my departure, GetJar was sold to a Chinese tech company for $5.3 million in cash, and a block of shares. It was a pittance for a startup that had once been valued not far short of a quarter of a billion dollars. Once the world's leading independent app store, it went out with a whimper.

Ironically, its greatest legacy is the lessons we can learn from the mistakes it made.

In this chapter, we've taken a look at the importance of teams. The main takeaway here is that, if you really want to go places, go far and make a meaningful transformation in your life, you're going to need help. You're going to need a team of people to support you.

So how do you build this team? Team-building is complex and you could read multiple books on the topic so, to keep things simple, we've decided to include a few exercises that will help you build that vital first ingredient, which Google's Project Aristotle deemed so important for high-performing teams: psychological safety.

EXERCISE #1

Alice crosses the river

Get the members of your team together and have every member of the team read this story carefully and try to remember the names of its characters.

"Once upon a time there was a young girl named Alice who needed to cross a river filled with many fierce crocodiles. Alice was tremendously in love with James, who was standing on the other side of the river.

Alice had no means to cross the river and asked Carlos to take her in his boat to the other side. He told her he would do it as long as she slept with him. She didn't agree and turned to Daniel (who also had a boat) to help her cross to the river.

Daniel didn't want to help and told her to get lost.

Alice reluctantly turned back to Carlos and accepted the deal he'd offered. Carlos slept with her, welcomed her into his boat and rowed her across the river.

When Alice met up with her boyfriend, James, she told him what had happened. To her surprise, though, he declared that he never wanted to hear from her again. "It's over between us," he said angrily.

After James's abrupt departure, Alice found herself all alone – until Ernesto appeared. He was a good catch in every sense of the word: young, handsome, wealthy and single and seemed, on top of it all, to be morally sound. Sensing her distress, he asked her what the matter was. She told him her whole sorry tale.

Ernesto told her he considered her a young woman of extraordinary qualities and that, if she agreed to marry him, he would consider himself the luckiest guy in the world. She agreed and they got married."

Having now read the story, ask each member of your team to write next to the number 1 the name of the person they think behaved the best; next to the number 2, the person they think behaved the second best; next to the number 3, the person they think performed the worst; next to the number 4, the person they think performed the second worst; and next to the number 5, the name of the missing person.

1. _____   2. _____
3. _____   4. _____
5. _____

Now let's reverse the roles. Ask each team member to write down six reasons why the behavior of those they listed in points 3 and 4 was actually the best or correct behavior. They will also need to find six reasons why the behavior of those they quoted in points 1 and 2 was actually the worst.

Once you've completed this exercise, have an open discussión with the team to understand each of their perspectives and why they made the choices they did. The results should be eye-opening and help the team better understand one other.

1. ....
....
....
....
....
....
....

2. ....
....
....
....
....
....
....

3. ....
....
....
....
....
....
....

4. ....
....
....
....
....
....
....

Credit / Source: This exercise was provided by Jeanine Kenigstein.
Coach and co-founder at LEAP.cl.

EXERCISE 2

The walk of life

This exercise is designed to test the limits of your team's openness, and their ability to share and discuss difficult experiences with each other.

Get your team together in a space large enough to allow each member to take eight to ten evenly spaced steps from one end of the room to the other. You can also use an open space for this purpose, although we encourage you to choose a space that is private and where team members can feel comfortable sharing very personal information.

Next, one person should bring eight to ten pieces of paper or small objects and place them on the floor, spaced roughly six to twelve inches from each other.

The leader or appointed moderator should begin the session. At the first marker on their path, that person starts by telling the team their name and age. They should recount a very personal event in their lives which, they recall, had a deep and lasting impact on them. This should be told in the first person.

1. My name is X
2. The date (approximately)
3. What happened
4. How I felt
5. Why this event is important to me

For example,

"My name is Patrick Mork. It's November, 1980. I'm at the playground in my school. I'm in a fight with another kid who's been bullying me for the past few weeks. Kids are all around me, shouting and yelling, "Gringo! gringo!" I get hit across the face and collapse to my knees with blood trickling out of my nose. I feel ashamed and angry, but also proud for fighting back. It's the first time I ever fought back and this fight marks a turning point in my relationship with the other kids in my class. Despite having lost the fight, I finally earned some respect."

After this, the person takes a step towards the next marker and recalls another story, again in first person, from some point a bit later in their life.

The stories don't need to be long, but the important thing is for the person to share incidents or events in their lives which

are deep and personal. (Each person should take no more than ten to fifteen minutes to complete the entire exercise.)

The process continues until the person reaches the last marker. The final story they tell should be the most recent one.

At this point, each member of the team should acknowledge and thank the person for sharing such personal stories. Then the next member of the team volunteers and repeats the process. This continues until all parties have shared their "walk of life".

Stories should be a mix of positive and negative and designed to help team members get to know each other deeply and to promote a space of psychological safety where people feel they can share anything without fear or judgment.

Source / Credit: This exercise was originally shared by Alejandro Rivas-Micoud, an entrepreneur and INSEAD alumnus, who helped launch the INSEAD Personal Board of Directors initiative in San Francisco, California.

Key #7

ASK POWERFUL QUESTIONS

The wise man doesn't give the right answers, he poses the right questions.

—CLAUDE LEVI-STRAUSS

Guillermo is a go-getting entrepreneurial Venezuelan who, like so many of his compatriots, has fled his native country to seek his fortune elsewhere. He works as VP of operations for a bustling tech startup in Chile.

Guillermo enlisted me as a coach and immediately made a positive impression. He struck me as astute, thoughtful and highly motivated. His goal, he confessed to me, was to be the very best leader he could be. Early in our relationship, he also described the anguish he'd suffered a year before when his father died after a prolonged and agonizing battle with cancer.

In one of our sessions, Guillermo appeared to be bothered by something.

"What's up?" I asked. "Something you want to discuss?"

"Nothing that directly affects me. It's no big deal," he added, but I could tell that, actually, it was a big deal. He was restless and a little agitated. He was very different from his usual calm self. I pressed him for details and, finally, after a couple more denials, he came clean. "It's just a member of my team. Have I mentioned Natalie to you before? A real bright spark. Anyway, she came to me yesterday and asked if she could have time off to spend with her mother."

He paused. I wondered what the issue could be that would affect him so viscerally. When the silence stretched uncomfortably, I prompted him with another question.

"What was her issue?"

Guillermo sighed heavily. "Her mother's got cancer. Stage four cervical cancer. She's dying."

"I'm sorry to hear that."

"Of course, I said she should take as much time as she needs."

And, again, Guillermo hesitated. I couldn't help but think of his recent experience. I knew this was a very sensitive moment and I felt bad to bring it up again, but I saw an opportunity for him: "I know this is a difficult subject for you, Guillermo, but what do you think would be possible if you shared with her what happened with your father last year?"

He seemed to flinch and, at once, started shaking his head. He was clearly gripped by deep emotions.

"No, no, why would I do that?"

Guillermo got up and walked to the window, his back towards me. I hardly heard what he said next.

"It's just that I understand what she's going through – and what might lie ahead for her. It's not easy losing a parent."

He turned back towards me, took a deep breath, which seemed to steady him. "Cancer's a real bitch, y'know."

I felt as if I'd ripped away a scab from a half-healed wound, and decided to leave the subject be for the time being.

We went on to talk about other issues, but something was nagging at the back of my mind and, before our session ended, I returned to the topic of Natalie.

"Guillermo, would you mind me asking what sort of relationship you have with Natalie?"

I could see at once that he'd misinterpreted my question. He bridled visibly and I hastened to clarify things.

"I mean, do you get on with her? You say she's a bright spark. Do you acknowledge that to her personally? What does she think of you as a boss?"

"I'm not sure," he said, relaxing. "I'm not particularly close to her … but we get along. Why do you ask?"

"No, it just strikes me that, as you've said, you've already been down this really difficult path with your dad, and she's about to do the same with her mom… What do you imagine would be the effect on your relationship with Natalie if you were to share your experience with her?"

"My father's death was … difficult, Patrick."

He looked down at his shoes. I could see a glitter in his eyes.

"I realize that."

"Sharing something like that… It would be too painful for me. To have to relive that again—" His voice trailed off.

"What might sharing your experience with her do for your relationship with her?"

"I'm still grieving, Patrick, can't you see that? I wouldn't be able to hide that from her."

"What side of you might she see that she hasn't seen before?" I asked, as gently as I could.

"She'd see how vulnerable I am."

"And is that a sign of weakness, or of strength?"

He didn't answer me directly, just shook his head again.

"I can't do that, Patrick, I'm sorry. It's still much too raw."

This is a chapter about powerful questions – open-ended questions that dig below the superficialities to the core feelings and foundational motivations of people. The ability to ask them – and to listen, and I mean, really *listen* to the answers they provoke – will help you, as a leader, to improve your relationship with your team, develop trust and boost performance.

That phrase, "powerful questions", is borrowed from the world of coaching, but it is also widely used in the field of education and psychology.

I'm a huge fan of powerful questions for managers and leaders at every level because they can achieve three important effects, all of which are critical to building trust and relationships.

1. They can help identify what the person being questioned really wants – or what his organization really needs – and what's blocking them from achieving their goals.
2. Powerful questions can cause a person to become aware of a range of options previously overlooked. They can push them to look at an issue or challenge them from a completely different perspective.
3. And, most importantly, they serve as a catalyst for action since, without action, there simply is no change or result.

And they can do all these in such a way that the person being questioned takes ownership of, and responsibility for, the way forward.

In that session with Guillermo, I asked one powerful question: "What do you imagine," I said, "would be the effect on your relationship with Natalie if you were to share your experience with her?"

Note that I wasn't *telling* him to share his experience with her. All I was doing was alerting him to the possibility of a course of action that I didn't think he'd considered before. His immediate response was negative but, as we'll find out at the end of this chapter, it was a question that stayed with Guillermo over the next few days.

Let's take a look at another coaching assignment I had. I've referred to it before, but I want to focus now on the powerful questions I put to my client – questions that literally helped turn her life around.

You might remember Helen, the CEO of a large chain of Chilean cosmetics retail stores. She approached me to assess the team she'd assembled, and to suggest ways in which to strengthen it, as she prepared the company she headed for a possible sale.

Helen was a fiery French woman, short of stature, with a blazing personality.

As part of our assignment, she asked me to coach her on a one-on-one basis.

It wasn't long before it became clear to me that the board she reported to made her job much more difficult than it should have been.

"What sort of problems do you have with them?" I asked.

Helen snorted. "What sort of problems do I *not* have with them? They're incorrigible. They micromanage me. They go through every decision I make with a fine-tooth comb. They second-guess me on minor investments I make on behalf of the company—"

We were sitting in her office, where we met every two weeks. Helen had, for years, presided over the fortunes of the firm from the desk she currently occupied. The company had flourished under her direction. She had served the owners of the company – a family consortium – well.

"What do you think lies behind their attitude?"

"It's obvious, isn't it? They don't trust me. You'd think, after all these years, they'd have realized I'm not bad at what I do. They hired me, in part, I guess, because I have a Harvard MBA. And yet, month after month, they put me through the wringer."

As part of our assignment, we conducted a 360-degree diagnostic assessment of both her senior team – and, indeed, of Helen herself. It's part of the service we give our clients. It helps them get a handle on how well their leaders function and where they have room to improve. We ask their subordinates 72 questions across a range of subjects, including whether their manager listens to them, how much authority they're willing to delegate, how much their subordinates are involved in setting goals and devising strategies, how well they believe they communicate, whether they feel they can trust each other, and so on.

The findings of the diagnostic, when we revealed them to Helen a week or two later, stunned her.

"I can't believe this is what my team thinks of me."

She looked up at me from the report I'd just handed her, her expression one of complete astonishment.

"That's what our analysis suggests."

"On a scale of one to ten," she said, tracing her finger along one of the graphics in the report, "I score four point six when it comes to paying attention to them?"

"The point of the diagnostic, Helen is—"

"I know what the point of the diagnostic is. It's just that—"

She turned the page and read on for a minute or two.

"I don't listen?"

"Well," I said. "It's not that you don't listen, but—"

"I don't delegate?"

"I suggest you read the balance of the report before we discuss it. Can I make you a cup of coffee while you do that?"

"Make it a double shot, if you don't mind."

She'd come to our offices for this feedback session. I busied myself, for a few minutes, at the coffee machine while she paged through the balance of our report. I set her cup of coffee down on our board table just as she scanned the last page.

"I'm devastated, Patrick."

"However difficult these things are, they always help you move forward... But I have a really important question."

It was a question that had occurred to me when I first started running through Helen's diagnostic.

"You've seen the profile that we've assembled of you. You have your strengths and your weaknesses, areas that it would be worth working on. But overall, what does your profile remind you of?"

She frowned at the computer screen, thinking. And then her expression cleared and she slowly turned to me. Her hands went up to her face and she gasped: "Oh my god, I do to my team what I accuse my board of doing to me. It's exactly the same thing. I micromanage the hell out of them."

Who knows how these things work. Was Helen attracted to the company she now worked for because, at some level, she recognized and responded to a management style that felt familiar? Or was it simply that, over the years, she'd adopted the bad habits of the people managing *her*, when she was managing her subordinates?

The recognition that she was doing to her team what she so resented having done to her, was life-changing.

Two weeks later, at our next coaching session, Helen told me she'd resigned from the company.

I was totally taken by surprise, and wondered whether, at some deep level, I'd failed her as her coach.

"No, not at all," she said emphatically. "But, when you asked me that question, and I saw what the answer was, I realized I'd turned into someone I really didn't like. I'd become the micro-manager from hell. I'm no longer willing to work in an environment in which I'm managing people in a way that totally contradicts all the values I hold dear."

I put forward my hypothesis, that perhaps she'd unconsciously adopted the ways of the board, and she nodded her agreement at once.

"I'm sure that was a factor. But I take responsibility for my own management style. And I want to change that and I don't think I can do that here."

A single, simple question went to the heart of the dissatisfaction and resentment that had been years in the making – and prompted Helen to rethink the direction her career and her life had taken. That question helped her uncover a pattern of behavior in herself that she'd condemned in others, and gave her the motivation to reinvent herself along lines that she approved of.

The flip side of the coin of powerful questions, of course, is the attention they demand we pay to the answers. Behavioral scientists have identified at least three levels of listening. In the first, we're primarily concerned with what the other person says only insofar as it relates to our own problems and concerns. Sure, we're listening, but we're not paying attention.

At the second level of listening, you really are listening to the other person. You're hearing the words, you're making sense of them, but you're not listening with your inner ear. You're not paying attention to what the speaker's *not* saying, to the deeper subtext that lies between the lines of his dialogue, where meaning is to be found as much in the pauses as in the words. You're not necessarily observing their body language, gestures and emotions and you're not really curious about why they might be saying what they're saying.

That's what you're doing when you move into the third and deepest level of listening. Down here, you're constantly speculating about the meaning *behind* his words. This is where, for reasons you'd find difficult to name, you have a *hunch* that, what he's really getting at isn't his complaint about his colleague's ultra-competitiveness (say), but his own feelings of inadequacy.

I had a feeling that Helen hadn't realized she was mimicking the micro-managing behavior of the board she reported to but that, once she had, being an astute woman, she would take steps to adjust and reset. I didn't anticipate that she would decide to resign from her position. But, as she said to me later (we've remained friends, and I continued to give her life coaching as she set out on her new journey): "It was through coaching and the questions you asked me and the perspective it gave me on my own actions, that I realized the only real option I had was to move on and do something new."

Powerful questions can help people find their true purpose, identify (or re-identify) what they really want.

But, as I've already suggested, powerful questions can also open up the mind of the person to options he or she hadn't considered before. They can help them challenge assumptions they'd made and find the path to the best decision available.

Take the case of Pedro, for instance, an Argentinian running a startup in Buenos Aires. I'd learned, over a series of sessions with Pedro, that his company was doing pretty well in their field – they're involved in printing and publication. He was a novice at this business of running a company, but it seemed to me he was doing pretty well. He had some challenges with his co-founders, since they were also his friends, and negotiating hard decisions with good friends is always tricky.

But the problem he brought to me, at one of our online sessions, had nothing to do with his partners.

"It's my head of sales," he told me. "We keep missing our numbers and I'm not happy with him. I'm considering replacing him with somebody more effective."

Now, replacing the head of sales is always problematic. Sales teams are often tightly knit units where, if they're well-managed, the members of the team are fiercely loyal to their manager. So, with some experience under my belt, I asked Pedro a series of powerful questions.

"What exactly is going on, Pedro?"

Now, on the face of it, that's an innocent question, I think you'd agree. But it's powerful because it is so open-ended. It invites the person you're addressing to open up. It doesn't set any limits on his or her answers. It's non-threatening and the very opposite of confrontational. It's casual and easy going.

"It's quite simple," he said. "The numbers are down and I don't feel the sales team is fired up. I don't feel like we're stretching ourselves."

Okay, good answer. But it didn't establish a causal link between the poor sales and the head of sales. So, that's the angle I took then.

"How long has he worked for you?"

"Couple of years. Three, maybe four. I'd have to check."

"And, over that period, how well has he performed?"

"Not bad," Pedro admitted, stroking his chin. "But for three, four months now, like I said, sales have faltered. We're not hitting our targets. My partners are getting a little antsy."

"What's his relationship with his team?"

"Yeah, well, I have to admit, they like him. From what I can tell, he gets on really well with them… But that doesn't alter the fact that—" He trailed off. Pedro wasn't a happy man.

"Tell me, Pedro, what would the effect be if you did fire him? How do you think his team would respond?"

There was a short silence while he digested the question.

"They'd probably be upset."

"Worse than that? You know what that relationship is – you must have seen it a dozen times, sitting in at sales meetings?"

"Actually, it's been quite a long time since I sat in on a sales meeting—" That was an interesting piece of information that I made a note of. "But I pick up enough of the dynamic to know that firing him would stir up a bit of a hornets' nest."

"And what effect would that have on their productivity?"

I guess that was a rhetorical question because we both knew the answer: it would have a detrimental effect on sales. That's precisely why I say that firing the head of sales is so problematic. You frequently cause more problems than you solve.

But Pedro sighed and answered anyway: "Not good. Morale would suffer. The slump would probably deepen—"

"I'm interested in you saying you haven't sat in on a sales meeting for a while, Pedro. Do you mind telling me how often you interact with customers? I mean, how often do you accompany one of the salespeople on calls with customers?"

"Patrick, you know damn well that all my time's been consumed raising funds for the company and hiring people. I haven't spent much time in the field."

"So, you don't know what problems customers might have with your service or your products? Or what threats have arisen, in the last while, from competitors?"

"No, I don't."

"So, my next question might sound like a criticism, but I don't mean it to be. I know precisely how busy a CEO's life can become. I've been there, Pedro, believe me... But what I want to ask is: How wise would it be to fire the head of sales without really understanding why he's not hitting the numbers?"

Another pause, then his face broke into a grin. I couldn't help liking the guy. My questions had challenged his initial assumptions, had revealed a signal failure of his to keep in touch with market trends and, yet, his response was entirely positive.

"I'll make a point of sitting in on sales meetings for the next couple of weeks – and I'll arrange to keep one or two of the sales team company. In fact, I'll go further than that. I'll phone some of our best customers and check directly with them as well."

"In other words," I said, "you'll gather as much information as you can before you make your decision."

"You got it, Patrick."

"When's the next sales meeting?"

"Monday. Don't worry, I've already put it in my diary."

Two weeks later, at our next session, Pedro reported back.

"We've got a problem with our pricing. Our main competitors are underquoting us. It's not exactly a price war – but we've got to take account of this and act accordingly."

"Any ideas?"

"Sure. I've had words with our operations team and they think there's room for extra efficiencies in our printing works, so that'll give us wiggle room to bring our prices down, in line with the market. But I think we can outperform our competitors as far as our levels of service are concerned, so I'm implementing improvements there as well."

He paused for a moment, and then the words gushed out: "Jesus, Patrick, if I'd just fired Eduardo, I'd've been in real trouble. I'd've had a whole lot of issues with the sales team, who'd've been really pissed off – plus I wouldn't have solved the real problem."

He was right on both counts. Powerful questions help us get to the root cause of the issue and help us see perspectives that we hadn't considered, because we might have a pre-existing bias.

Before our initial session and a handful of powerful questions, Pedro had been committed to a course of action that would have been disastrous, not only for the company, but for the head of sales and members of the sales team.

But, sometimes, powerful questions can also clarify motives. My next and final story is about a man whose emotional drivers were complex and confusing and, only when he'd sorted them out, was he able to see clearly what path he needed to take. In other words, powerful questions can help sort out your priorities, separate the real reasons from the bullshit, and make your decisions much crisper.

Rodrigo, a former management consultant, was hired to run a startup financial services tech company, handling insurance products. They were competing in a highly regulated market, which demanded clever thinking and agile execution.

Rodrigo hired me as a coach because, having been a consultant, he had zero experience in senior management, running a company. "My big problem," he told me in our first session, "is that I don't know what I don't know."

Just as we did with Helen, we began by running a 360-degree diagnostic on him. The feedback we got was very positive. The most problematic profile you can get of a client is one in which the client rates himself much higher than his team does. That signals ego problems, and it's a tough nut to crack because people – men especially – find it very difficult to put their egos to one side.

But Rodrigo *undervalued* himself. His team consistently attributed higher levels of skill to him than he did himself.

So, I had high hopes that our time together would be productive.

The real challenge Rodrigo faced came not from government regulations, or his competition, but from the wealthy founder and owner of the company. And this guy, whom I never met, matched precisely the stereotype of an old-style Chilean top-down micro-manager from hell.

Rodrigo had been hired as CEO. But he was consistently second-guessed, countermanded and contradicted by the owner, who couldn't keep his hands off the levers of power and authority in his company. He threw himself into the work that the teams were doing. He fired off WhatsApp messages at people throughout the company at all hours of the day and night, and even on weekends.

"This guy is insufferable," Rodrigo said to me on a number of occasions. "He can't help poking his nose into all the operations. He's undermining my authority, he yells at me, he goes behind my back on things."

"And how sound is the quality of his decisions?" I asked, imagining that the owner, who sounded like an obsessive, micro-managing asshole, was highly experienced in the industry and might actually know what he was doing. Rodrigo sighed and leaned back in his chair.

He smiled in resignation. "That's half the trouble," he said, and confirmed my suspicions. "He really knows his stuff – I mean, he built his company practically single-handed. He knows the industry backwards and forwards. He's very astute. I really can't fault him on his decisions… But I do wish he'd also let me do the job he hired me to do."

For eighteen months, Rodrigo sang the same song, frequently beginning his litany of complaints with the words, "Oh, my god, I just can't handle the man any longer… Do you know what he did last week? He actually fired one of the people on my management team without even consulting me."

The thought that occurred to me, whenever Rodrigo began listing his grievances, was that, if life working for the founder was such hell, why not resign? What I said now was: "When we began this coaching, you told me you wanted to stay in your position for two and a half years. Why is it important for you to stick it out when you're obviously so unhappy?"

"Two reasons, I guess," he said slowly. "One, I want to prove to people that I can keep going in a job, despite Luis. And, secondly, I really wanted to build this company to demonstrate my abilities and talent. It's a reputation thing."

"What would be the consequences of leaving before that deadline?" It was, after all, a personally imposed deadline. He wouldn't be breaking any contract.

"Well, most importantly, I won't get the payout that I'm guaranteed after two and a half years."

"Is that a key issue for you?"

"It's not peanuts, Patrick. With that money in my pocket, I could take as much as a year to find my bearings and, perhaps, start a business of my own. At least I wouldn't have an investor breathing down my neck half the time."

"And why is starting a business of your own important to you?"

"Autonomy. Independence," he said, at once strong and confident. "The fact that I'd know that, whatever success the business enjoyed, was due to me."

And that's more or less when my spidey sense told me that, despite the results of the 360-degree diagnostic, Rodrigo had a very healthy ego – and that's where the bone of contention with his nemesis lay. But it seemed to me he'd boxed himself in. On the one hand, his ego couldn't take the beating it was getting from the founder but, on the other, his ambition to start his own company, be his own boss and give his ego free rein was dependent on his staying long enough to pick up the bonus he'd been promised.

"So, the problem you have currently," I said carefully, "is that you don't get to make the decisions you believe you, as CEO, should be making?"

"Damn right."

"What do you think this has to do with your ego?"

This question was followed by a long pause. Then Rodrigo laughed. "I'm the guy who said he wasn't ego-driven, right? But you're right. I've got to admit, it is an ego thing."

He smiled like a kid who's just been caught with his hand in the cookie jar.

"And do you think there are ways of making critical decisions that are *not* based on ego considerations?"

"Sure. It would be better to make decisions based on other considerations. Ego screws things up."

"So, putting ego aside, what options do you think are available to you now?"

"I could resign tomorrow. Find a job in a company that doesn't have a maniac in the driver's seat... Or, I could keep my ego in check and stick it out for another six months and pick up my big payout."

And, so it went on. We weighed the various options and their consequences. What he was now able to do – as a result of this conversation, and the powerful questions I'd fired at him – was keep in mind both his ego needs, and the vulnerabilities they created.

In the end, Rodrigo made a decision to stay for another three months. He gave up hope of picking up the big check, but neither did he leave in a storm of mutual recrimination. He left, knowing that his own arrogance and ego were in play – and probably always would be – and that he'd have to take account of these aspects of his personality in any future decisions he made.

This is a complicated story, I know that. It doesn't have a Hollywood ending. But it does demonstrate that powerful questions can identify and bring to the surface the deep motivations that drive us. And it has to be a good thing to know what our psychological needs are, if we're to make rational decisions about our careers.

A month, that is to say, two coaching sessions, after I'd nudged Guillermo to share his experience of being with his dying father, he said he'd like to start the session with a confession: he'd done precisely what he'd said so adamantly he wasn't prepared to.

"And how did that go?"

"It was tough. I told her to take a couple of months to spend with her mother."

"And you told her something about your own experience with your father?"

He nodded. "Like I said, that was difficult. Very emotional for me. Very emotional for both of us. The truth is, I cried."

The memory of that session threatened, for a moment, to overwhelm him, but he pulled himself together and went on. "I never thought I'd be able to share something so personal, so powerful, with a co-worker."

"Did you feel like you were exposing a weakness in yourself?"

"No, no, not at all. It actually felt like … like a strength in me."

"And what was the effect on Natalie?"

"Well, like I say, she was moved. I think she was deeply appreciative of it. I overheard her, later that day, saying something to a colleague about it. I immediately sensed a change in the atmosphere in the office."

"What kind of change?"

"A change for the better. People, all of a sudden, seem to be more transparent, a bit more open. They're starting to share things more freely."

Great leaders are not afraid to show their vulnerable sides to their subordinates. It's a sign of strength, as Guillermo discovered, and not of weakness. And it generates powerful and positive currents in the workplace.

Powerful leaders are also great listeners. They're able to empathize with their teams, and share the bad feelings along with the good. Powerful questions help lift the lid on those feelings, giving leaders insight into their team's motivations, needs and goals.

The key to using powerful questions is, first off, to really know what they are. We'll begin our exercises with a short list of some of the most common powerful questions we know. The second, more critical issue, is for you to start actually developing the habit of using them.

EXERCISE #1:
Sample powerful questions

The exercise is simple. Pick out three or four questions you think you can most commonly use in either a personal or professional setting. Then start by creating a habit of using them with others. Our suggestion is to pick the same day, time and place for you to use these questions, by adding them to your conversations.

For example, maybe you set Friday at 4 pm on Zoom as a time to have a one-on-one with someone on your team, and incorporate three or four powerful questions into your conversion. Next, observe how people react to your questions: what they say, how they move, their facial expressions. Try to compare this meeting with the way your meetings with these people went before you started to incorporate these questions. What do you see? What's different?

Powerful Questions

1. Tell me how things are going?
2. How are you feeling about this situation?
3. How would you characterize your relationship with X (who could be a friend, co-worker, boss, subordinate)?
4. What's the consequence of doing nothing (in relation to a certain situation)?
5. What do you really want out of this situation?
6. Why is this important to you?
7. How does this (did this) make you feel?
8. What would be possible if you did / said this?
9. Why does this matter? What's at stake?

10. What might be possible if you stopped doing X?
11. What does success look like?
12. What does failure look like?
13. What would the likely impact be on your team / family of *not* acting?
14. What other options have you not explored?
15. How do you think others might view your actions?
16. What is needed in order to move from this idea to reality?
17. What does this mean?
18. What might you be missing here?
19. If we asked someone you know, how might they look at this situation?
20. What are the next steps here?

EXERCISE #2
Dominoes

Powerful questions are even more powerful when you actually chain them together. Prior to your next important meeting or conversation, think of your first question and then consider what other powerful questions you might want to ask, to dig deeper into the situation at hand. Oftentimes, people want to avoid conflict, or are loath to reveal what's really going on. When you string several powerful questions together in succession, you force the other party to dig more deeply, which helps get to what is really going on. Make sure you give enough time for the person to answer, and be patient, but persistent.

EXERCISE #3
The Power of the Pause

If there's one thing we learn as coaches, mentors and parents, it's the power of the pause. Often, we miss things because, instead of listening, we're already preparing our response and mentally rehearsing what we're going to say once the other person finishes speaking. Instead, practice counting to five when the person finishes speaking and observe what happens. What you'll generally see is that "nature abhors a vacuum". People can't stand silence so, what typically happens when you say nothing, is that people keep talking and, often, end up saying either more than they have to, or revealing something they might not have intended to reveal. That's your chance to follow up with another powerful question and repeat the process.

Try to really listen, actively, to what the other person says, and take note. What is the person saying? What's changed? What's the underlying reason they said what they said?

Key #8

CELEBRATE FAILURE

Failure, is success in progress

—ALBERT EINSTEIN

I was halfway through my freshman year in Pace Academy, in Atlanta GA, when my father came home one night and announced over dinner that we were moving to Connecticut. At Pace, I hadn't taken my studies very seriously. I mean, I had decent grades – they were okay, but they consisted of a bunch of Bs and Cs (and worse), with the occasional A thrown in for classes I enjoyed, like history or geography.

Although unsurprising, the news of our move wasn't exactly music to my teenage ears. We'd relocated frequently through my school career, as my father climbed his way up the corporate ladder. Now, as I was entering the final years of high school and thinking about college, we were moving yet again. More to the point, I'd been coasting at the Academy, and a move meant I'd have to exert myself more than I wanted to, adjusting to a new school, making new friends, getting the measure of new teachers.

My father had very strong ideas on the topic of what sort of school I should attend in Connecticut. He drew me aside and told me, in no uncertain terms, what he expected of me. "I have to give you a wake-up call,

Patrick. If you think you're going to get into any of the top schools in the nation with your grades, you're just dreaming. You're completely deluding yourself if you think a string of Bs and Cs is good enough."

I was, as I remember it, not in a great spot. My dad is one of those people who doesn't discuss things. He issues commands, which he follows with an intense stare that seems to pierce right through you. To be fair, he was just calling attention to the obvious. But my predicament wasn't obvious to me. As far as I was concerned, things were generally fine. I didn't have a sense of urgency. The water had probably not reached boiling point, and I was happy just floating around.

"You're not going to get in with these grades," he said.

"In your opinion."

He instantly raised his voice. "It's not a matter of opinion, it's a matter of fact!"

But I stubbornly insisted that I would get into one of the top colleges of my choice. I knew how bright I was. Sure, maybe some of my grades were less than stellar, but so what? I could turn up the temperature and spew out a string of As any day I wanted to. I was convinced that, having lived all over the world, I could get into any school I chose. I based this on the constant changes of culture and schools I'd endured, together with my knack for languages (by then, I spoke four fluently).

Now, I don't want you to get the wrong idea about my father. He's a good person. Sure, he might be tough and blunt, but he was always willing to help me, particularly in terms of investing financial resources in helping me achieve what I wanted to achieve.

So, when we got to Connecticut, he hired a consultant, a man by the name of Dr Thomas Aquilla. Dr Aquilla was a college guidance counselor, basically an advisor who helps parents – well-off parents, particularly, as he was not cheap – to get their kids into the schools of their choice. Through a combination of consulting, advice on which high schools to attend, which elective courses to take and sports to play, he would map out a game plan for you.

Aquilla was himself a Yale alumnus – he had a PhD and insisted on being addressed as Dr Aquilla – and Yale, of course, was one of the schools I wanted to go to.

I went to meet him with my mom in his office. He looked at my grades and shook his head. "First up," he said, "your grades are not near good enough. If you want to even have a chance of getting accepted into any of the schools on your list, you're going to have to score nearly straight As for the next year and a half. Second, your best chance of getting those grades is to go to a really first-class school here in Connecticut. Third, you're going to have to work your butt off, seven days a week, for the next eighteen months. You up for that?"

Now, I was a smart kid, but I was not used to working hard. Actually, I worked at the courses I enjoyed – languages, history, geography, English – and had a good record there. But I had never really paid much attention to the subjects I didn't like, especially math and science. My record on those was just awful. I hated the subjects. I didn't invest time in them. And, naturally, my results reflected my indifference. I got Cs and Ds. Not good.

One of the first things we did under Dr Aquilla's direction was create a list of high schools that I might attend as a stepping stone to a college of my choice.

One of these was the Brunswick School, an all-boys prep school, highly regimented, with a uniform. Not a pretty school. It was located in downtown Greenwich. But it did have an excellent academic reputation. Going through the brochures, I got a sense that it took actual schoolwork very seriously. Not much of a place if your aim was having fun. To my mind, the place looked more like a prison than a school.

I was not a serious guy. I enjoyed having fun. I liked to relax.

My mother preferred a beautiful school by the lake called Greens Farms. *I* liked Greens Farms as well. It was much smaller, friendlier and more relaxed, it seemed to me. It didn't require a preppy, snotty uniform. and it was co-ed. Greens Farms was much more progressive than Brunswick. My kind of school.

"Look at the average class size, Eddie," she said over the dining room table. "It seems like a really nurturing environment."

"Looks cool to me," I chipped in.

My father frowned. "Looks more like a country club." He liked Brunswick.

Dr Aquilla said Brunswick was my best shot at getting into a top college.

"It'll give you the kind of bootcamp training that you need to get your grades up," Dr Aquilla said, over steepled hands.

"To be honest, Dr Aquilla, I'd prefer to go to Greens Farms."

"You could do that," he said equably, "and I'm sure you'd enjoy it, and you'd probably do okay academically. But it won't push you, it won't challenge you and, consequently, you won't have a shot at the colleges you really want to go to."

Resigned to my fate, I went to Brunswick.

In my second semester at 'Wick, my father gave me a present. It was a wall poster in a wooden frame. I hung it on the wall in my bedroom opposite my bed. It was the first thing I saw every morning, and the last thing I saw every night.

The poster featured a guy running down an endless road that disappears on the horizon. At the bottom of the picture ran a line adapted from Ecclesiastes: "The race is not to the swift – but to those who keep on running."

My father was not a great reader of the Bible, so I'm guessing he didn't realize the verse that began, "The race is not to the swift", ends up saying that, basically, we're all fucked.

But I looked at the poster every day for the next eighteen months and, who knows, perhaps it did inspire me in the way my father meant it to.

At Brunswick, I was surrounded by a group of very smart, very hard-working, upper-class prep school yuppies, whose entire aim in life, from the moment they entered kindergarten, was to crack Harvard or Princeton or whatever.

I had a year and a half to catch up.

My classmates, by and large, didn't have a funny bone in their bodies. They were serious about their work, they didn't play, and they certainly didn't seem to have much fun.

In my first week at Brunswick, I cracked a joke in class. It went down like a lead balloon. Everyone turned and looked at me like I was some kind of moron. Bear in mind that, at every other school I'd attended, I'd always earned the reputation as the class joker. People loved my jokes.

Long story short, I worked harder than I'd ever worked in school, except perhaps that year in Padres Irlandes, in Mexico. I worked deep into the evenings. I studied through weekends. Dad hired a math tutor to get me up to speed in my weakest subjects. I dove into science with a passion and even ended up really enjoying AP biology.

By my senior year, I ended up getting just about a perfect score: As in all my favorite subjects, and a B+ both in math and science. Hell, I even ended up on the Honor Roll.

But, more importantly, I proved to myself, to Dr Aquilla and my father, that I had been right all along: I'd never lost faith in my own capacity to step up to the plate when I needed to.

Of course, by the time I got these results, I'd already submitted my application for admission to all of the top colleges: Princeton, Yale, Dartmouth, Cornell, Duke, Brown. I didn't apply to Harvard, for some reason that I don't recall, but I made the best pitch possible to all the others.

My deep ambition, of course, was to get into an Ivy League school, but Dr Aquilla recommended that, just in case these colleges didn't recognize my potential, I should also apply to a few second-tier schools.

"Georgetown? Who goes to Georgetown?" I said dismissively.

"They're pretty damn good," Dad said. "Lyndon Johnson's an alumnus."

Yeah, well, Lyndon Johnson wasn't exactly one of my heroes.

"Georgetown is a great school," Aquila said. "Don't turn your nose up at it. Now, what I want you to do is apply to Georgetown's language school– "

"I don't want to study languages anymore, Dr Aquila. I've done it enough. I'm through with that," I said at once.

"That's beside the point. With your languages, you're bound to be accepted."

"But, Dr Aquilla– "

"And then," he ignored my interruption, "you can apply for an internal transfer into the School of Foreign Service."

That sounded more interesting. "So, why don't I just apply for the School of Foreign Service? Why duck and dive and go round the back?"

Dr Aquilla gave me one of his thin smiles, the sort of smile that says, you poor benighted kid, what do you know? And he said: "Because you'd never get accepted, on the basis of your grades. SFS is probably the best school in the country for studying history and diplomacy, short of the Kennedy School at Harvard."

"But I got a 3.6 GPA. That's really good."

"I doubt very much whether it's good enough to get you into the School of Foreign Affairs."

Crap, if Dr Aquilla didn't think my grades were good enough to get me into Georgetown, then what did he think of my chances of getting into his old alumnus, Yale? I decided not to ask him. I just *knew* I was going to make it into one of my first choices. I *had* to get in. It wasn't even a question.

But I was willing to humor both Dr Aquilla and my father. I agreed to apply, not only to Georgetown's School of Languages, but also to Emory and a couple of other schools that, although not among the Ivy league, were excellent choices nonetheless.

And then, together with tens of thousands of other hopefuls, I sat through the nail-biting tension of a spring and summer, waiting for a fat letter to drop into the mailbox, containing all the documents necessary to complete the application.

Truth be told, though, I wasn't as nervous as I think Dad was. Because I *knew* I'd get in. Maybe it would take a face-to-face interview to clinch the deal, but once the admissions people were exposed to my sparkling personality it would, as far as I was concerned, be a slam-dunk.

I think we all know where this is heading.

The first response came from Princeton. It wasn't a fat envelope. It was a very skinny one and it contained just a single sheet of paper that regretfully informed me that my application had been turned down.

The second, third and fourth arrived in a rush – and they were all skinny and full of fake regrets.

Then came the letter from Yale, on which I'd pinned my hopes. No go.

By July, there was just one Ivy League college that hadn't responded. Naturally, I assumed the delay was caused by the fact that I'd made it into the queue. Some admissions offices were simply not as efficient as others. My optimism was undented. After all, my academic performance over the past eighteen months had earned me my place on the Honors Roll.

But, when the last Ivy League response arrived – from Cornell, as it happened – it was as skinny and insubstantial as all the others, and I didn't even bother opening it.

The letter from Cornell proved too much for me. I think it was the eighth or ninth straight rejection in a row. In a fit of rage and despair, I tore the letter up and ran to my room. Slamming the door, I ripped down the poster of the runner and tore it into a million pieces.

After 30 minutes or so of yelling, crying and raging, I heard a soft knock at my door. It was my mother, who'd come up to see how I was doing. Whenever things were tough and I needed a gentle hand, it was my mother who was there.

She opened the door and entered, followed by our dog Sandro, a big, black Belgian shepherd who looked up at me with what, I swear, was concern in his kind, brown eyes.

"Patrick, the fact is, you've been accepted by Georgetown—"

Yeah, that bulging letter had arrived amidst all the others. I'd been happy to be accepted, but my hopes had still been to get into one of my top choices. The feeling of getting into Georgetown had been one of relief, as opposed to an "over-the-moon" celebration.

"Yeah, but Georgetown isn't what I want—"

"It's got a great reputation."

"I worked so hard, mom," I said woefully. "You'd think they'd take that into account."

"They had no idea how hard you worked. All they had to go on was your grades and your SATs. It's the system Patrick, it's not personal."

"Practically straight As," I pointed out.

At that moment, my father stepped into the room. He stopped as he stared at the hundreds of ripped pieces of poster, strewn across the room.

"Patrick, you made remarkable progress in the last eighteen months. You really did, and you showed what you were capable of. If you'd only taken high school seriously from the get-go, imagine what you could have achieved."

Now, the point of my tale is this: I didn't get into any of the schools I'd set my heart on. I was rejected by Yale, Duke, Brown, Princeton and the rest of them.

For the first time in my life, I had failed.

At the time I was devastated. I didn't enjoy failure. Nobody does. What I didn't realize, back then, was that failure has a reputation it doesn't deserve.

It took me decades to realize the importance of failure because, believe me, folks, I've failed more often than I've succeeded. My career is littered with failures. It's only later on that it became clear to me: there *is* no such thing as failure. Only learning.

I have a long list of failures, a very long list. But the reality is that, in each one of these, whether personal or professional, I learned an enormous amount about myself, business or life. Today, I look at each of them as a learning opportunity. As a treasure. As gold.

Unspoken Tales was such a nugget.

After I left Google in 2012, I didn't know what I wanted to do. I traveled to Peru. I went to Machu Picchu. I traversed the Atacama Desert in Chile. I was hoping to "discover myself"; find some clue about what I wanted to do.

After a few months, I was back in Silicon Valley, and within a few short weeks was introduced to a guy I still know quite well, a multi-millionaire, serial entrepreneur called Rick Thompson. Rick, together with his partners, runs a venture capital fund called Signia Venture Partners, based in Menlo Park, California.

Our first meeting in his office went very well. Rick invited me to work for his fund as an entrepreneur in residence (EIR). An EIR'S responsibility is to work either as part of the management team of one of the companies the fund has invested in, or to start their own company, which the fund will invest in. The EIR relationship is a symbiotic one. The fund gets the person's know-how, experience and help dealing with problems facing their portfolio companies, and the EIR is exposed to new business opportunities, gets to know the fund partners and potentially develops a business they will be interested in investing in. That's the theory, at least.

I spent the next year at Signia, looking at a bunch of startups, screening a lot of deals and thinking about what I wanted to do next. I sat in board meetings and I learned a lot about the inside of venture capital and how it works. The partners introduced me to a bunch of companies they'd invested in. The idea was that I would help realize the potential of these startups, and so give Signia a great return on their investment.

But the truth was that I was itching to start my own company. I'd left Google, in the final analysis because I'd wanted to be my own boss. That hunger hadn't deserted me. Looking at some of the budding young entrepreneurs Signia had invested in, I was even more committed to doing my own thing.

Because I'd worked in the video games industry and seen many great mobile games launch, both at GetJar and later at Google, I decided there was room to build better video games. I've always been in love with video games and I had a thing for games with these very deep, story-driven, richly immersive experiences. But, back in 2012-2013, I didn't feel that such games existed for mobile devices. I looked at the computer game or console game market and found there was no match for great games like Mass Effect or Diablo III on mobile devices. To me, the whole experience on mobile felt dry, repetitive and oriented towards squeezing as much money as possible out of gamers. There was no story. No depth.

Today it's a little bit better, but only marginally so.

Back in 2013, I decided to start a company to build this kind of rich, deeply immersive, mobile-gaming experiences, huge open worlds with fantasy characters and multiple levels of experience.

But, as I started to put together a business plan, I hit my first snag.

I couldn't hope to raise money without a team of experts on board. Venture capitalists invest in teams, not in entrepreneurs flying solo. That shouldn't be a problem, I thought. After all, I was Patrick Mork. I'd cut my teeth at, among other places, Google Play. I would just convince a bunch of the best people available to join me. And we would build this amazing company together.

I was, I have to say, very ambitious and very naive. I wanted to build something that nobody had seen before.

I networked relentlessly and, slowly, a team started coming together. I needed a great product manager, someone with a mind-blowing imagination and cutting-edge technical skills and experience, someone who could help write the script and design the game. I needed someone else to build the technology behind the concept; to build scalable infrastructure to support millions of players playing in real time. And, of course, no game is complete without eye-watering artwork, so I needed a third person, an artist, who'd create the look and feel of the game and life-like characters that populated it.

I wanted the game to dazzle gamers. Of course, there are games with horrible art, like Roblox or Minecraft, which have been fantastically successful. But I wanted my game to be a beautiful experience. I wanted something revolutionary. I wanted people to look at the characters and the horses and the axes and the dragons and say, "Oh my god, this is incredible."

Over the next couple of months, I met three people whom I charmed into becoming my co-founders. On paper, they were all fantastic. One had worked at Activision Blizzard – now an $8+billion a year revenue Fortune 500 company – for 10 years, running their art studio in China, which he built from scratch. He had an unparalleled resume, having worked on some of the biggest Xbox and PlayStation games to date. He, like me, was in love with the aesthetics of a great computer game.

No sooner had I recruited him than he, and a couple of freelancers, started generating the artwork for the game. At once I could see it was, in the currency of its intended market, awesome.

Then I found a product guy. He was a real oddball, brilliant, mercurial, and totally off the wall. It was his job to come up with the story and the mechanics of how the game would actually work. I could tell at once that he was inspired by the prospect of launching a great game and making a zillion dollars.

And, finally, I recruited a woman who'd been chief technology officer for several online gaming companies: very smart, very hard working and, like the others, with a dazzling track record. Her passion was technology: she was devoted to the dream of writing code that would take the gaming world by storm.

And then, of course, there was me – the marketing whizz kid from Google, who had the connections and who was going to raise the money to build the game, and then market it.

There was just one small problem, best expressed as a number. We estimated that we would need $10 million to design and code the game. The investors I approached took one look at the number and said: "You're fucking nuts."

Although I didn't realize it at the time, their point was painfully obvious. However good we were as individuals, we had never worked together on a project, much less something as ambitious as this. We had never actually built anything together.

At the time I was trying to launch my startup, I was still with Signia, working as their entrepreneur in residence. Rick Thompson, effectively my mentor, had a nose for potential unicorns – and for problems with startups.

"Look, Patrick," he said to me one day, "you're going to have difficulty getting this off the ground. What have you got to show investors?"

"Rick, the market for this is enormous. You've seen my research. There's simply nothing like this out there. We've developed pages and pages of story, rich characters and amazing artwork," I said. "This will be the game that'll dominate the mobile market."

"In other words, not very much," he shot back. Before I could protest, he pressed on with his argument. "Nobody's going to invest ten million bucks in an unproven concept being developed by an untested team in a highly competitive market."

"But look at the caliber of the people I've got on board, Rick."

"I agree, on paper they look great. But have they worked together as a team?"

"Soon as I've got some money in the bank, they'll *learn* to work together."

"And you're sure there's chemistry between them all? You can have the best people in the world, but if they don't jell, you've got a problem."

My mind spun back to a memory of a disastrous experiment once conducted by one of the world's best soccer teams, Real Madrid. With a bank account bulging with money, they'd decided to buy the best players on the planet – and did so. But the team never reached anything like its potential because they never learned to work together. It turned out to be one of the biggest fiascos in sports history.

And then Rick said something else about my pitch that I should have paid much more attention to. He said, "Your second big problem is, you haven't built anything. A brilliant promotional video – and it is brilliant, Patrick, congratulations – doesn't prove a thing. Investors want a prototype they can play with, however crude it is."

I shrugged off this advice and spent the next six months working my butt off trying to raise capital. But Silicon Valley investors are canny. They have to be. They're not playing with Monopoly money. Time after time, they asked me to tell them what our team had worked on before and, time after time, they told me it was a pity I didn't have a rough approximation of the game they could play.

"We love your story," more than one of them said. "Come back when you've actually built something we can play with."

In the meantime, while the artist on the team did some brilliant work, the other two, by and large, sat twiddling their thumbs waiting for me to come up with some money. It was a clear message that we didn't have the right team because, in an effective team, *everybody*'s building something...

Eight months in, I was so demoralized I decided to go for broke, booked a ticket to a big gaming conference in Beijing, followed by meetings at trade shows with Chinese venture capital investors, specializing in gaming. For two weeks, I pitched furiously at anyone I could persuade to stand still for 20 minutes. Every Chinese person I met on my rounds was very polite, very pleasant. Everyone smiled and invited me to dinner. One company even arranged a visit for me to the Great Wall.

But no one offered to invest a single fucking dollar in my company.

It was dawning on me by then that, as brilliant as I thought our ideas were, and as dazzling as I knew the artwork was, there was something fundamentally wrong about my offering.

I went back to Rick at Signia for advice. This time I swore I'd take it. But, instead of reminding me of what he'd said before, he took me entirely by surprise.

"Look," he said, "I like you. I admire your energy and your passion. You know about my reservations, but the fact is I still believe in you – so I'm willing to invest my own money in your project."

This from one of the most astute men in the business. Signia Venture Partners were early backers of a range of companies across the tech field. For Rick to offer funding for my gaming company was a signal vote of confidence. But he made it clear that he was backing me, and not the team that, as he'd suggested earlier, was untried.

I thanked him and asked for a couple of days to think about his offer.

You may well ask, what was there to think about? After all, this was precisely what I'd been seeking for months: an investor with deep pockets and a great instinct. But the reservations he, along with a bunch of other venture capital specialists, had voiced, together with the lukewarm reception I'd got in China, were enough to make me hesitate.

Plus, there was the fact that two of the four founders had essentially done little or nothing to promote or advance the business. Our tech prodigy, aside from whining about the unfairness of the cap table, that is, the distribution of equity between owners, hadn't written a single line of code. Not one.

Rick's offer wouldn't cover our financial needs, and although his endorsement of the project would probably unlock further investment, I couldn't see how I'd be able to raise the balance. All I *could* see was another six months, or six years, of beating my head against a brick wall, frustrated beyond endurance.

I remember standing in front of my bathroom mirror and asking myself whether I wanted to be spending the next five to seven years raising money for a startup based on a romantic idea, serving no greater purpose than providing gamers with yet another way to waste hours of their day on their phones, and surrounded by people who probably would never mesh together as a team.

The answer was obvious, so I went back to Rick and told him, regretfully, that, much as I valued it, I had to turn his offer down.

Was I crazy? Maybe. But one thing Silicon Valley had taught me was this: if you're gonna fail, then fail hard and fail fast – and start something else. The moment you realize a project, however promising, is *not* going to work, don't waste yet more time chasing it down, or pounding the pavements in search of investors. It's over. Accept it. Learn from your failures. Move on.

What did I learn from the manifest failures of Unspoken Tales? Three things, all of which I've applied consciously and deliberately at LEAP.

1. Start with your purpose: what do you want, deep down, to achieve? Design a great computer game for mobile apps? What if you fail? What do you do next? Set a purpose that is broader than a single product. Infuse your purpose with meaning. My own purpose, framed at those Coaching Training Institute sessions in 2018, is: "To be the magnetic energy that inspires people to find careers of meaning and purpose." At LEAP, our purpose is to give meaning and purpose to work. At Unspoken Tales, each of the founders had a different purpose than mine except maybe for our art director. It was a recipe for disaster. I remember thinking about how our product guy wouldn't stop talking about the zillions this game would gross when, what really drove me was the ambition of building something incredible and revolutionizing the mobile gaming industry.

2. Hire people based on their values. I started LEAP determined to hire people who were each better – much better – than I was in their field. But more importantly, I was adamant that we should

share the same purpose and the same values. Values were such a big deal for me that I identified our first eight values quickly and wrote them down in great detail. With my first hire, Jose, I had specific questions attached to each value to test whether Jose not only had the hunger and skills to do what I needed him to, but also the right values that aligned with the type of company I wanted LEAP to be. Today, we talk often about our values at LEAP and, every time we hire someone, we spend more time talking about the person's values than we do about their ability to do the job. Skills are a given. Values are much tougher to change. Looking back, the lack of common values was a major reason we hadn't worked as a team, and was a key reason Unspoken Tales failed.

3. Fail fast. I brought from my final days at Unspoken Tales the critical realization that, if something is irretrievably broken, don't spend precious time trying to fix it. At LEAP, we cultivate a nimble approach to product development: if the market doesn't like a new product, dump it and move on to the next. If our customers *do* warm to a new product, then improve it, iron out the glitches, and scale it up as quickly as possible. The important thing is to get something out to the market, get feedback on what's good and not good, improve and then start over.

Let me expand on a couple of these points. Let's go back to LEAP's early days, when it consisted simply of Jose and me. I spent a hell of a lot of time doing something that puzzled Jose.

"Isn't this a waste of time?" he asked at one point. "Shouldn't we be out there selling or something?"

What I was doing was defining our brand. I spent weeks, if not months, slowly compiling a presentation of just 20 slides. My objective was to spell out as clearly and unambiguously as possible what our purpose was, what our values were, what our brand personality was, and what we stood for in the marketplace.

I knew from both bitter and productive experience that I would attract the right people and build the best team if I was able to show them what our vision was. I wanted them to buy into that vision and those values. What was our "lofty purpose"? I had also learned from Unspoken Tales that people's values have to be aligned. If one person cares about helping people but another just cares about money, their values aren't aligned and sooner or later that's going to be a problem.

GetJar signally failed to articulate its lofty purpose and little to no time was spent hiring people based on values. Google, on the other hand, succeeded wildly on both counts – and that success accounts, in my view, for its dominance in the market today.

At Unspoken Tales, I was so taken with my dream of building the perfect computer game that I overlooked the need to fashion a more inclusive purpose.

At LEAP, I was determined not to make the same mistake.

If you go to our website, as applicants for jobs with us are encouraged to do, you'll find our clearly articulated vision – that is, our purpose – together with our values and mission. Again and again, applicants have expressed their enthusiasm for what they've read here. I remember what one applicant for a job in accounting – yes, accounting! – said:

"I just love a company that has this bigger purpose. You're trying to make the world a better place. That's important to me. I want to be part of that."

I think this is a universal truth: people are motivated best by something that goes way beyond financial reward. *They want to make a difference.* They want their work to mean something and to be something greater than just themselves.

So, if we can attract people who respond positively to our vision and our values, we have a much better chance of building teams that trust one another. Of course, you also have to build a climate of psychological safety in which trust is possible – and that's no easy thing.

But with trust, transparency is also possible, and transparency leads to mutual accountability. Mutual accountability leads to better performance: teams that perform above themselves, teams in which excellence is the norm.

It can be uncomfortable, believe me.

When I, as co-founder and CEO of LEAP, don't meet my own metrics, the first people to challenge me are members of the team, people junior to me, people a hell of a lot younger than me. They call me out or express questions and frustrations.

It's Monday. We're holding our regular Monday morning meeting at which we report informally on progress we've made in our separate areas of responsibility. Valentin, one of our sales guys, wants to know how I'm doing on the fundraising.

"Not so good," I tell him, and give him the figures.

"What are you doing about it?" he asks. "Is there anything we can do to help?"

I mumble an answer. Fundraising's difficult in the current climate ... global downturn ... post-Covid blues ... I have my excuses, but excuses don't wash on a Monday morning.

As I listen to another critic complaining at my failure to find a marketing manager, I think, don't these people know I'm the founder of the company that puts money in their pockets every month? Part of me just wants to say, "Listen, guys, won't you just trust me?"

But then I remind myself that, on the back of my many failures, this is *precisely* the climate I'd set out to build. Just as the members of the team are accountable to each other and to me, so I am to them. We've ended up with a group of people who are able to tell each other the tough things that sometimes need to be said to move the organization forward.

Of *course*, it can be uncomfortable – what the hell did you expect? But that's the price of excellence.

When I look back on my failure at Unspoken Tales, communications errors at Google, working in silos at GetJar, or other areas where I haven't lived up to my or others' expectations, I can now do it with a smile on my face because I know that those setbacks proved invaluable in becoming better. They helped make me the person I am today. Every mistake has helped me recruit the team we have today at LEAP and has helped our clients build better teams and leaders. Those stories are also great ammunition for keynotes and motivational talks, both of which I do a lot of in South America today.

Whenever you have a doubt about trying something hard, remember that, either way, you'll win. If it works out great, you'll be on a whole new level. If it tanks, you'll learn a great deal and you'll still be on a whole new level.

As I love to say: There's no such thing as failure. Only learning.

EXERCISE #1
Fear Setting

This very practical exercise is taken from the Tim Ferris Ted Talk on the subject of stoicism and is an exercise he developed for managing and over-coming his fears.

Start a document. This can be a Word Doc or a Google Doc, or it could even be an Excel or Google sheet. The title of the document should be: "What if I ... (insert what it is you want or need to do.)" Now create three columns headed, "Define", "Prevent" and "Repair".

Now think of your greatest fear. Start to list those fears in the first column. An example of the title could be, "What if I quit my job?" In the first column, you would start to list your greatest fears of things that "could" happen. The first fear might be, "I would run out of money". Another might be, "My partner would leave me".

In the second column, "Prevent", start to think of things you could do to prevent that outcome. In response to, "I would run out of money", you might place in this column, "Get a freelance job working a minimum of four hours a week", or you might say, "Get a loan from my parents". The idea here is to list ideas that could prevent or, at least, reduce the chance that your worst fears will materialize.

In the third column, "Repair", think of what you might do in case this fear did materialize. What actions could you take to repair the dam-age? Returning to our example, "What if I quit my job?" you might say in your repair column, "Withdraw money from my savings account". Or, you might say, "Move back in with my parents". The important thing is to proactively think of how you could minimize or undo the damage, in case your worst case fear came to pass.

But that's not all. Ferris also suggests working on a second document in his fear-setting exercise, which is very common in our world of coaching. It's a question I ask often of my coaches.

On a separate page, tab or document, ask yourself the question, "What is the cost of inaction?" In other words, what happens if I do nothing and just let the status quo run its course? Because, on occasion, we don't see an immediate impact in the short term, he suggests we answer this question with three time-horizons in mind:

- Over the next six months
- Over the next year
- Over the next three years

The key here is to really get detailed and consider the many ways in which inaction might negatively impact your life. What might it mean for me physically, financially, emotionally, spiritually, or in terms of the relationship with my partner or other loved ones. Tim suggests you do this exercise once a quarter but, in reality, you can do this exercise whenever you come across a particularly tough decision you need to make and where you feel stuck or afraid to move forward.

Ferris ends his Ted talk with a quote that really drives home the importance of facing our fears and making bold decisions:

"Easy choices. Hard life."

"Hard choices. Easy life." Jerzy Gregorek.

Credit: Tim Ferris Ted Talk

EXERCISE #2

Reframing

Fear inhibits many people from taking action because of the way they frame success or failure. For example, let's say you get a call from a recruiter for an amazing job. You're super excited, but quickly realize you might not have the experience necessary to secure an offer. The fear of failure in you whispers, "Maybe we shouldn't interview. They'll never hire me, given my lack of experience." Your success metric here is getting the job. What if you change your success metric? What if you decide the success metric might instead be, "Getting to the second round of interviews."

By changing the success metric, your goal, all of a sudden, becomes not only more achievable, but failure no longer seems to be as much of a risk. You might not get the offer but, by getting to the second round, you score a win for yourself and improve your own confidence for the next time you participate in a tough job interview.

In our work at LEAP, we also urge clients to reframe their definition of failure, and that's a big part of what we just discussed in chapter 9. Here, the trick is to reframe our definition of failure and to actually think of what we might learn from the process. Going back to our example of the job application, we would start to list all the things we might learn or gain from not getting the offer.

- We're going to meet new people.
- We'll get an understanding of our own value on the job market.
- We'll learn what we might be lacking in order to take our career in that direction.
- We'll feel great about the fact that they called us in the first place.

By reframing our definitions of "success" and "failure", we make success look more likely and are able to focus on the positive side of failure as a source of learning and improvement. Reframing turns problems into opportunities.

Another coach I spoke to had a client who didn't want to pass her fear of failure on to her kids so, every night for a week during family dinner, they would each share a win, a failure and a lesson. She said it got a little silly when they got competitive about who failed bigger that day but, ultimately, they got the message that most failures are not that bad … and some are even good. She said it was a fun exercise for everyone and that they really learned to embrace failure as an opportunity to improve.

EXERCISE #3

Collecting No's

One of the biggest fears many of us have is the rejection that comes with failure. For example, maybe we've been waiting for ages to ask for a raise but we dread the fact that our manager might say, "No." Fear of rejection or of getting a No is common, but there's a way around it. Learning to live with a No is about building the muscle of accepting and learning from that No. For example, I was recently out trying to raise money for LEAP. I got plenty of No's. Investors didn't get our market. They didn't value what we were selling. They thought the Latin American market was too small. They feared we didn't have a tech person on our team. It was easy for me to get discouraged or pissed about the outcome and to see my fund-raising efforts as a failure.

But, on the one hand, I reframed the process. I collected their input and feedback and built it into my pitch. I learned from it. On the other hand, I found that the more No's I got, the easier it was to push forward. We were able to get a few people to invest and, later, suspended our fund-raising for other reasons. But the experience was invaluable and we learned a lot from it.

Here's something you can do to help build that muscle.

For an entire week, every time you buy something, ask for a ten per cent discount. It might seem obvious, but the art of collecting No's makes us more resilient and stronger. You will probably collect a good deal of No's in the process, but you may have some surprises and you may also realize that getting a No is No big deal.

Likewise, you might also want to ask for help more often at work. Each time you get a No, get curious and write down why you think you didn't get a Yes, and see what you learned from the process. You'll find the No's become easier and easier to handle over time.

Happy hunting for No's!

Key #9

MANAGE YOUR ENERGY

"And what is a man without energy? Nothing – nothing at all."

—MARK TWAIN

Thinking about this final chapter of the book, I realized I could start it with a revolution … or with the day I bought Max, my French bulldog. Actually, I can't tell one story without telling the other. But let me begin with Max.

I hadn't been in Chile long when I realized I was lonely. Laura and the kids lived on the far side of the city and, although I spent regular weekends with the children, the days between seemed awfully long.

A dog seemed like a possible solution. When I raised the question with them, they were enthusiastic. So, despite my misgivings – it had been years since I'd had the responsibility of looking after a pet – I tracked down a breeder on the northern outskirts of the city and, one weekend, we picked up my new companion.

Max quickly became a fixture in my life, and a source of pleasure to both children whenever they slept over.

I hadn't realized what a commitment having an animal in the house was. I'd grown used to living alone but now I had to bear Max and his needs in mind from the moment I woke up – or rather, from the moment Max woke me up – to the moment I fell asleep.

I fell into the habit of bouncing ideas off him.

"What do you think of Jose?" I once asked him, soon after I'd hired my first employee. Max cocked an ear and looked up at me with his big, brown eyes. It was the confirmation I'd been seeking.

A couple of months after Max became my brainstorming partner, I started to become vaguely aware of stirrings in the city. A news bulletin reported that students had been jumping the turnstiles in Santiago's metro system, to avoid paying recently increased subway fares.

"That's not cool, Max," I told him on one of our walks. "But they must be pretty pissed off."

The issue didn't affect me. I'd bought myself an electric scooter and whizzed around the city without having to go underground. So, I had no idea just how pissed they were.

A few days later, I scootered to a business appointment with a client some blocks away from our offices on a street called Hendaya. After a session dealing with their purpose and their values, I descended to the lobby of their building and prepared to return to my offices. As I emerged onto the street from the lobby, I heard a roar from the Avenida Apoquindo, a six-lane boulevard that pierces the heart of the city. Curious, I zipped up the half block or so to Apoquindo. There, to my left, marching toward me, was an enormous crowd of people holding posters and banners aloft, vigorously banging pots and pans and chanting.

The mass of people had taken over the entire six lanes of the avenue.

It's difficult to describe my reaction to the sight. I was at once shocked – there seemed to be tens of *thousands* of people in the procession – but also, in some sense, thrilled. One poster read CHILE, WAKE UP! another, WE ARE NOT AT WAR – WE EDUCATE FOR PEACE. Others declared that 30 PESOS IS 30 PESOS TOO MUCH.

I remembered the students jumping the turnstiles. But this

demonstration was about much more than a 30-peso increase in subway tickets.

This looked like a revolution in the making.

I decided to follow the crowd and see what gave. They were taking the route I would anyway have followed to get back to my offices and my final meeting of the day with Jose.

I kept to the sidewalk. Attracted by the cacophony, shop keepers had emerged from their shops along the avenue to gawk at the demonstrators. Some were alarmed, but others made their support clear.

We headed up Apoquindo towards the intersection with another major arterial, Americo Vespucio. Just beyond the junction stands the Escuela Militar, the military academy where the country's army officers are trained. It's hallowed ground, the fountainhead of Chile's conservative values. I couldn't believe the demonstrators had the Escuela in mind as a target – it would be suicide. But further north on Vespucio were the high-end residential neighborhoods of the city.

I'd studied history in Georgetown and, if I'd learned one thing, it's that, with the right motivation, the oppressed masses will make a beeline for the rich and privileged to take out their frustrations and demand a fair shake.

The question was, was this crowd sufficiently frustrated to want to express their resentment against Chile's upper classes? I didn't know. What I did know is that inequality is a South American disease, and that Chile is not immune to it. An awful lot of the country's wealth is in the hands of a small minority of rich families.

As the crowd flooded into the junction with Vespucio, I decided to race ahead of them to join Jose on the eleventh floor of our office building. It would be an ideal vantage point from which to observe events, since our building overlooked Vespucio.

I dumped my scooter in the lobby and bolted into the elevator. A minute later, I dashed out onto the eleventh floor. Jose was busy at his computer.

"Come on, compadre, you've got to watch this," I said, heading for one of the floor-to-ceiling windows on the west side of the building.

"What's going on?"

"I'm not sure. But it's big. Look, down there." I pointed back down Apoquindo. The crowds were surging down the block towards us.

"Patrick," Jose said. "Look."

Jose was pointing in the opposite direction. At the end of the block, three armored personnel carriers had appeared, the machine guns in their gun turrets ominously turned in the direction of the demonstrators.

"Oh my god," I breathed.

By now, we'd been joined at the window by our fellow WeWorkers. Orianna, Jose's girlfriend and Matt's assistant, said, "I've just heard that they've shut down the metro."

"This could get very bad very quickly," I said. "I think we should get out of here. I've got my scooter but, with the metro down, you guys should grab an Uber and go home."

The elevator was crowded on our way down to the lobby. Clearly, we weren't the only occupants of the WeWork building who'd decided to head for the hills. The Uber Jose had summoned appeared a minute after we hit the street.

"Get home safely, Jose," I said.

"You too, Patrick."

I wheeled my scooter up to Apoquindo. The demonstrators had come to an uneasy stop, waving their placards and shouting at the APCs. Ranks of police armed with riot shields and batons were taking up position behind the armored vehicles. A moment later, tear gas canisters arced through the air to land among the vanguard of the protestors.

Yells sounded and the crowd started breaking up as the tear gas took effect. But individual protestors advanced and lobbed what looked like stones at the police. Time to get the hell out of Dodge, I thought, as I hopped on my scooter.

On my way home – not very far from the site of the confrontation – I was passed by a truckload of armed soldiers in full combat gear. I thought back to the days of Pinochet and what had happened way back then. If one of these young soldiers lost their cool, things were going to get ugly real fast.

◆   ◆   ◆

Revolution or no revolution, I still owed my French bulldog his daily walk.

Later that evening, I dutifully leashed Max up and led him – or, more accurately, was led by him – down our elevator to the lobby, where our concierge, another Jose, gave me a strange look and said, *"Señor, no debe salir. ¿No sabe que existe toque de queda?"*

Now, I knew what the first part of his question meant: "Sir, you shouldn't go out. Don't you know there's a—" But I hadn't come across the expression that ended his sentence: *"toque de queda"*.

My Spanish was fluent, but I was still familiarizing myself with a range of vernacular expressions in Chile that I didn't quite get.

Max was in a hurry, though, and I knew better than to delay him. I didn't want to be apologizing for a puddle in the lobby of my building.

"I'll be fine, thanks, Jose."

I closed the gate that led out onto Americo Vespucio,

"Bit strange, huh, Max?" I muttered.

It was early evening. The streetlights had come on. Usually, at this time of the day the boulevard – a busy four-lane artery serving our corner of the city – would be full of traffic, the pavements awash with pedestrians. Today there was nothing. Not a car on the street. Not a walker in sight.

We walked along to the intersection with Apoquindo.

"Feels like a sci-fi movie, Max, doesn't it?"

And then I thought back to Jose's counsel: "You shouldn't go out—" What was the phrase he used? *Toque de queda?* "Better check on this, Maxie pants." I hauled out my phone and Googled the phrase.

"Holy shit. They've declared martial law!"

I pocketed the phone and tugged on Max's leash.

"Let's get the hell out of here before we get arrested, Max."

"But I haven't done my business, Patrick." Well, that's what he would have said if he could have. But I paid no attention to his protests and hauled ass back the way we'd come. I caught a glimpse of the reflection of an armored personnel carrier in a plate glass window as we swung into Americo Vespucio, but made it to our building where Jose, who must have caught sight of us, was holding the gate open for us.

Over the days that followed, my worst fears started coming true.

Frustrated by the strong-arm attempts of the government to suppress the protests, the demonstrators turned to violence – and arson.

Seventeen metro stations were burned to the ground.

Supermarkets were looted and torched.

Twenty people were killed, and over 2 500 injured.

Cop cars were mobbed by crowds of people, who then set about trying to yank out the terrified policemen. Fortunately, they failed.

And, of course, the army was let loose on the city.

These were echoes of the dark days of Pinochet's suppression of the country a generation earlier. I still remembered my ex telling me how calm and peaceful it was back in 2018. Now it looked like I was living in a warzone.

The curfew didn't last long, thank god. But for a number of days Max and I risked arrest, or worse, whenever we ventured out for short dashes to the nearest park. What concerned me more than the state of his bowels, though, was the state of my business.

I'd come from one of the most prosperous corners of the world – Silicon Valley – to the small capital of a small country. And it now seemed to be engulfed in the flames of social repression and violent protest. What the hell had I gotten myself into?

When the violence was at its height, with pictures of looters running out of department stores grasping flat screen TVs in their arms, I met with Laura to discuss our options.

"I worry about us, sure," I told her. "But I worry about the kids, especially."

"I know," she said. "So, what do you think we should do?"

For fuck's sake, I'd only arrived in the country four months before. To leave now would be humiliating. But to stay might be dangerous if things continued to deteriorate.

"If it gets any worse, we'll have to leave."

"Oh, my god, Patrick."

"It's not just the immediate danger. It's the kids' future we should be thinking about."

We went on talking for a while, but came to no definitive decision although, when I left, I did so with the understanding that, if the protests did move any further north, we would meet again to discuss the practical details of fleeing the country.

On 25 October, an estimated million people took to the streets. Miraculously, peace prevailed. The pressure brought to bear on the president by what was quickly called "the biggest march", caused him to fire his cabinet and promise the people of Chile a new constitution.

The danger, and the need to consider fleeing for our lives and our children's futures, receded.

Slowly, Jose and I, back in business in our WeWork office space, continued doggedly to breathe life into LEAP. We recruited our first customers, continued to pump out great content and I started coaching some exciting entrepreneurs.

The new year opened full of promise.

And then Covid-19 struck.

Obviously, I didn't for a moment believe that the greatest pandemic the world had experienced in a hundred years was directly aimed at frustrating my ambitions, but sometimes it felt that way.

When Chile imposed a very strict lockdown on its citizens, we all became prisoners in our own homes. Yes, it was still possible for me to see Rafi and Natasha, or for Laura to bring them to spend weekends with me, but the bureaucratic hoops we had to jump through to apply for permission to do so were time-consuming and annoying.

I could no longer take bike rides out into the hills of La Dehesa whenever I liked. I could no longer take the kids out on our regular monthly road trips. I could no longer have my daily walks through Parque Araucano in the city center with Jose – during which I'd teach him the basics of marketing, and together we'd strategize our next moves to snag customers.

Within months of launching LEAP, not only our business, but Chilean business in general, had been hit with two major disruptions: massive social unrest on a scale nobody who knew anything about Chile had ever witnessed before and now, a global pandemic that that threatened to gut what was left of Chile's fragile economy.

There were days when I wondered if I was ever going to get LEAP off the ground. Here I was, 48 years old, alone, single, living in a foreign country, facing one massive crisis after another. I realized something crucial during all this time. If I was going to have any chance at succeeding, my state of mind and my energy levels were going to have to be at their best every single day.

If ever I needed to stay positive and maintain peak levels of energy, it was now.

Effective personal energy management is possibly the most critical of all personal management skills. In the final analysis, it doesn't matter what your values are, whether you've identified your purpose or not, or whether you've established ambitious goals – if you can't get out of bed in the mornings, you might as well throw in the towel.

I was at rock bottom at the start of lockdown in April 2020.

What I'm going to tell you now is how I dug myself out of that pit of depression, managed to keep my energy levels high and went on to build LEAP into the small but vibrant coaching business it is today.

The tactics I used to fight off depression and re-energize myself every morning can, I believe, be applied, regardless of who you are. *You* can use them, not just on those rare occasions when revolutions break out on your doorstep, or global pandemics trigger economic collapse, but in any circumstances.

So let me dial back a bit to the start of lockdown.

It takes time for the implications of a catastrophe to sink in. It's like getting home after a pleasant evening out to discover you've been burgled. You see that the door's open – but for a moment, it doesn't dawn on you what that means. You think, oh great, I forgot to lock the door.

You go in. Something's wrong in the living room. There's a broken lamp on the floor. There's a *smell* in the house that feels wrong.

But you still don't get it. Even when you see that there's something missing on the wall…

And then you do get it. What's missing is the TV screen. Your eyes skip to the music center in the corner of the room. The stereo's not there. And the laptop you'd left open on the dining room table.

Only then does it sink in that your place has been broken into and that, most likely, anything that was portable and valuable is gone.

The start of the pandemic was a bit like that.

Lockdown? What did that really mean? Well, we thought at the time that we could imagine some of the effects of lockdown would be. It meant working from home. No big deal. Fiber means you can do most things remotely.

It meant that you and the kids were going to have to get used to amusing yourselves in the apartment. Buy a ping-pong table, clear out the living room. No problem.

It meant buying a stand for your road bike so that you could work up a sweat in the mornings on your balcony instead of cruising the streets of Santiago in the early morning light. It might not be as much fun, but it gives you a workout.

But then some of the consequences you *hadn't* anticipated start hitting the fan.

In February, I'd been booked by a government ministry to give a series of motivational talks at a conference promoting Chile as an investment destination. Not only did they pay well, but the exposure was important to the growth of our fledgling company.

I was scheduled to share the platform with some very well-known Chileans. It would have put me, and LEAP, on the map.

And then, a week before the event, an email hit my screen, announcing that the ministry was "regrettably freezing its budgets and canceling the conference".

That was ten grand down the toilet.

It wasn't the only speaking engagement that fell victim to the growing pandemic.

And given that these talks generated most of our income at that stage in our development, these cancellations felt like a series of body blows.

And I hadn't thought of the fact that businesses throughout the world would react to the pandemic by cutting their expenses. Between March and August of 2020, Jose and I failed to sell a single coaching program.

I remember riding my balcony bike and screaming at the top of my lungs, "Why the fuck is this happening to me?"

Max's whimper brought me back to my senses.

"Sorry, Max. Sometimes you just gotta vent."

Of course, venting didn't solve the problem of my looming depression – and my steadily ebbing energy levels.

And that's when I reminded myself that I had the power and, more importantly, the techniques, to manage those energy levels, restore my sense of equilibrium and continue to pursue my goals.

And that's what I want to spell out for you now. It's not rocket science and, in fact, many of the positive habits I'm going to share have popped up in previous chapters.

But in the aftermath of Chile's social and political unrest and, in the opening months of the pandemic, those positive habits were to be stress-tested more severely than ever before.

Managing your energy resources is a matter of building habits on top of habits. Think of your personal energy levels like the gas tank of your car. When the tank is dry, so are you. You just can't keep going without any gas in the tank. Staying motivated and positive requires you to get up each morning with a full tank of energy and find an effective way, when you feel your tank is running dry, to top it back up again. I have developed a series of habits over the years – early morning cycling, meditation and so on – which have been essential whenever I needed to refocus and remind myself that, not only was life worth living, but I could overcome any challenges in order to reach my goals.

During lockdown, I threw myself into these routines with the sure knowledge that they would see me through, that they would charge my batteries, not just for the day or the week, but for however long it would be.

Here's what a typical day looked like.

I woke up at 5.30 am and settled down cross-legged on my bed to meditate for 20 minutes. I'd started meditating in Silicon Valley, shortly after Laura and I divorced, my startup had failed and I was fired ignominiously by the asshole at Singular. By phone.

Laura herself had meditated for some years, as had her parents. And I was in search of a practice that would help slow me down. What the hell, I thought, I didn't have much to lose.

I started by listening to three- or five-minute meditation videos I'd discovered on YouTube and found it instantly effective. Over time, I've built up to a regular daily session of 20 minutes. It's dead simple, consisting of deep and steady breathing: breathe in for four beats through your nose and count those breaths as you do them. Hold it for a second, then exhale for six beats through your mouth.

Try to not think about anything but your breathing. You find yourself becoming acutely aware of your immediate environment, the play of air on your skin, the temperature of the air, the feel of the floor or the carpet you're sitting on, the fabric of the clothes you're wearing, or the individual notes of the music you're listening to.

I listen to a video of Tibetan gongs to keep my mind focused on my breathing, block out any other distractions and let go of any negative emotions.

Meditation slows you down, and it also makes you more aware of yourself and your motivations.

During high stress moments at the office, I'll sometimes excuse myself, go to the bathroom, and practice a little meditation to calm down and get centered. The simple act of putting on headphones and listening to relaxing music, while breathing deeply releases stress, helps me identify the feelings I'm experiencing, and gives me control over my emotions during difficult times. It gives me pause – and enables me to calibrate my responses in tough situations.

It lies at the heart of my energy management regime. The benefits of mindfulness meditation, as this type of meditation is called, aren't new and have been well documented. According to a 2016 article in Forbes, meditation has been proven to improve cognition, reduce anxiety and stress, increase concentration levels and even body satisfaction, among many other benefits. For me, it's been a lifesaver and really helped me keep my cool in the toughest of times.

Next, exercise. Pre-lockdown, I'd cycle through the streets of my new city around 6 am just to wake up my body, work up a sweat and get focused. Now, I'd snap on a pair of headphones and cycle through the streets of my imagination on my balcony, on a bike mounted on a stand. Or, with Max gazing at me reproachfully, I'd do yoga stretches in my living room while watching Yoga with Adriene on YouTube.

"Your turn, Max. Downward dog?" I'd jokingly ask him.

Rafi and I went to the park a couple of weeks ago to do a little yoga together. He'd not tried it before. To start off with, he was a little scornful but, as he copied the moves I made and the poses I adopted, he began to appreciate just how testing a routine it can be. By the end of our session, he was elated.

"It's a lot harder than I thought," he said as we walked back to the apartment. "You're not bad, Dad. You're actually a LOT more flexible than I thought." Did I catch a glint of admiration in his eye? I hope so.

Back in lockdown, though, there was no yoga in the park, of course. But I was able to take Max for walks. I'd get the leash out and we'd prepare for our morning walk. Bear in mind, though, there were strict rules about venturing out into the streets. Dog owners were granted permits, which they had to apply for every day by phone, to take their pets for a walk. One walk a day was allowed.

I figured, however, that both Max and I needed more than one walk a day. He obviously needed to do his business, and I needed to avoid the inevitable cabin fever that we all suffered from during those dark days.

So, I cheated.

I would prepare my request for permission to take Max for a walk on my cellphone. I knew that if I sent it, an automatic response would bounce back within seconds. So, I *didn't* send it. Instead, I'd walk round the block, or to the park, with my phone in one hand and Max's leash in the other.

My plan was, if I saw the police, I would instantly transmit my request.

By the time they asked to see official authorization for me to be breaking curfew, permission would have been given.

And so, for the months of lockdown, Max and I settled into a routine in which we took a walk at breakfast, lunch and supper.

I was, in fact, never challenged by the authorities. But I rarely ventured out without having prepared myself for that possibility.

"A man's gotta do what a man's gotta do, right, Max?" Particularly if he's single, trapped far from his family, and really, really doesn't want to go freaking insane.

Exercise has become an absolutely essential part of who I am. It is, for instance, inconceivable that I would get up and *not* do a workout. I'm sure I don't have to state the obvious but, since I'm in the business of coaching and helping people, let's just say there is a ton of research that regular exercise provides enormous benefits, from improving your mood and boosting your energy levels, to increasing your blood flow and circulation and improving the quality of your sleep. As if all this weren't enough, research published back in January 2022, in the Journal of the American Medical Association, showed that as little as ten minutes a day of vigorous exercise could save as many as 110 000 lives a year in the US alone. All you need is ten minutes!

After working out, I'd take a cold shower. Now, a great deal has been written about the health benefits of cold showers, so I won't go into all the details or the science behind the Wim Hof method, or the benefits of ice-cold showers. But an article published on WebMD summarized it nicely when it acknowledged that cold showers boosted people's energy, improved their blood circulation, mental health and even their immune system. What they do for me, though, is wake me up, clear my head and infuse me with energy.

Another trick I use is to accompany those cold showers with positive affirmations. "I am healthy. I am successful. I am debt-free. I am a best-selling author. My children are happy and healthy."

Much has been written about the power of negative self-thought and the same is true for positive self-talk and affirmations. The more we reaffirm what we want in life and the more we accompany that with actions that help us make those thoughts a reality, the more likely we are to get what we want and to be happy.

In the mornings, I take a cold shower – and in the evenings a warm one. The logic is simple: cold wakes you up, warm prepares you for sleep. And sleep, of course, is the great equalizer. I need seven to eight hours a night. If I don't get them, I'll be irritable, slow and unfocused, which has a massive impact on my ability to get things done during the day.

But my warm shower routine is a perfect set-up for a good night's sleep. I sleep exceptionally well. Whatever's happening at work, I will sleep like a baby for seven or eight hours. The science is extremely clear and compelling: if you get fewer than seven hours of sleep a night, it will impact on your ability to focus and to think clearly. Insufficient sleep affects your digestion – and it leads to premature aging.

In his TED talk and ground-breaking book, *Why We Sleep*, sleep expert Matthew Walker, a neuroscientist at the University of California at Berkeley, explained how our society is facing another pandemic: a massive lack of sleep. According to Walker, sleep is the bedrock of our entire system. Not enough sleep impacts our ability to concentrate and retain information, our sex life and even increases our chances of developing serious or even fatal diseases, like cancer.

I'll never forget a chapter in his book in which he shared research showing that people who'd slept four hours or less, and who got behind the wheel of a car, were eleven times more likely to have a crash than people who'd had a good night's sleep. Walker's book totally changed the way I viewed sleep after leaving the sleep-deprived mecca of Silicon Valley and today, no matter what time I go to bed, I tell Google to "wake me up in seven and a half hours".

Then breakfast. A good nutritious breakfast. You don't eat well, you'll run out of energy. Not a complex argument, but you'd be surprised – or maybe you wouldn't – by the number of wannabe high-achievers who believe a cup of strong coffee in the morning is the only fuel they need.

It's no secret, after all, that a balanced diet, not too many processed foods, not too much red meat, and great hydration, is essential for someone hoping to remain in good shape for as long as possible. Remember Michael Pollen's wise advice: "Eat food. Not too much. Mostly plants."

We're talking about energy management here, remember. The reason most people run out of energy at some time during the day is that they haven't eaten enough of the right sorts of food, or they simply haven't slept enough the night before. Sugary, processed foods might give you a sugar spike and an instant rush of energy – but it never lasts long, and leaves you hungry for more sugar.

I've found that I function best when I build snacks into those long stretches between meals, and limit my intake during meals.

Plus, plenty of water.

And finally, I would devote ten minutes or so to writing my morning pages. This gave me the opportunity to spell out for myself the positive things in my life: the fact that I and my children were healthy. The fact that, despite the pervasive economic gloom, I had every hope that my fledgling company would survive and thrive. The fact I had a faithful companion in Max.

And then I'd have the first of a couple of stand-up Zoom meetings with Jose and the rest of the team.

Rinse and repeat.

I told you there was no rocket science involved in my response to lockdown. Just one good habit followed by another. It's one of the pieces of advice that James Clear gives in his best-selling book, *Atomic Habits*. He calls it Habit Stacking.

Of course, one dimension of my life that didn't form part of my daily routine was Natasha and Rafi. I could no longer rely on Uber to take me across the city to Laura's house. Uber didn't operate during lockdown. I had to rely on Laura to bring the kids to me which, of course, she did. But since every visit required authorization, we spent less time together than we had in the months preceding the pandemic.

But, boy, were they important to my mental health. A weekend in the apartment with them was enough to top up the charge in my batteries. A steely ping pong tournament between ultra-competitive alphas: Rafi and me. A hectic game of Exploding Kittens with Natasha. I even found myself baking cookies – me, Patrick Mork, serial entrepreneur! – with Natasha.

And the three of us would do a kind of manic exercise routine in front of the television.

I'd never worked out more strenuously before in my life.

Or felt as energized.

Energy is there for the taking. The key is to recognize when your batteries are running low – that's more difficult than you think; it takes a degree of self-awareness – and then to identify the routines which will help you restore your energy.

What works for me might not work for you. I know that ice-cold showers in the depths of winter might not necessarily be your thing. I do know that enough sleep makes a definitive difference to your energy levels; that a balanced diet is essential; that exercise of some sort or other keeps your metabolism humming; and that friendships and family are critical ingredients for a life filled with joy.

A dog helps too.

Finally, in September 2020, six months after Covid hit the country, the lockdown was lifted and it was possible, once again, to stretch our wings. The beaches of Valparaiso, a one-and-a-half-hour car trip to the coast, beckoned.

Natasha cuddled Max all the way, singing to him. He joined in the chorus.

We were heading for Playa las Salinas, a stretch of beach just north of the city.

"Pity we can't get a chocolate volcano here," Rafi said.

Our life back in California seemed a million miles away.

The sea was terrific, though, cold and refreshing.

Max loved being outdoors. Well, so would anyone after six months trapped in an apartment. The illegal walks we'd taken had been brief and limited escapes. Here, on the beach, he could run to his heart's content.

"Why does he run in circles like that?" Rafi asked.

Max was hurtling round the beach in crazy loops, crashing through the shallows, then spiraling and repeating the move. Natasha was running after him, but she couldn't keep up. And then he plowed into the sand at our feet, panting. Natasha flopped down beside him and fondled his ears.

"He's a great dog, isn't he?" Rafi said, joining her.

My mind returned involuntarily to an episode that had happened months before, not long after Max had taken up residence in the apartment. I'd never told the kids about it.

I'd just taken a shower. I was in the bedroom, drying my hair, when something alerted me in the living area. I walked through. On the floor at the couch lay my most prized cashmere sweater, a relic of the days when I could afford cashmere. Max looked up gleefully at me, his mouth full of shredded wool.

"What the fuck! What have you done, you miserable dog?"

It wasn't the first time Max had had a go at one or other article of my clothing. He'd ruined a couple of trainers already. This, though, was his worst crime.

"I can't take this anymore, Max, I'm sorry."

Max sensed my anger and released the sweater.

A couple of hours later, I placed an ad on an online forum: "French bulldog, six months old, pedigree stretching back to Louis XVI, had all his shots. No charge." I stuck a picture of him on the site.

I went to bed that night cursing myself for thinking that I could ever give a dog the sort of uncritical affection it deserved. I had no doubt, though, that someone else could. It had been a mistake from the get-go.

Next morning, I got a text message from a widow who lived alone and would welcome the company of a beautiful dog like Max. I replied that she could come by that evening, if she liked, and pick him up. We settled on 6 pm.

During the course of the day, Laura called about some detail of Natasha's schedule, and I mentioned that I'd given Max away. I told her about the cashmere sweater. "I just can't take the stress anymore."

"You can't give him away, Patrick," she said, in a shocked voice.

"Why not?"

"Have you thought about the kids? They love Max – Rafi especially. They'll be heart-broken."

Rafi was going through a really bad patch at the time, trying desperately to adjust to life in a strange country, relying on his not very firm grasp of a new language. Shit. I hadn't really thought this through.

Long story short, I messaged the old lady and apologized to her. Then I apologized to Max and, of course, never mentioned a word of any of this to the kids.

Looking out over the ocean and watching the kids sprint around, with Max following them at full throttle, I was deeply grateful to Laura for having nudged me into not getting rid of the dog. He'd been a life saver right through both the social upheaval in Chile and the pandemic. More than a life saver – an antidote to depression and a spur to optimism.

"Come on, Dad, let's run with Max," Natasha held out her hand to me where I was sitting on a towel.

"I'm exhausted, honey," I began, but then realized what I was saying. Exhausted? I was spending the day at the beach with my family, whom I loved, and with my dog, whom I adored. I wasn't exhausted. I was exhilarated. I leapt to my feet and ran along the beach. Natasha whooped and urged Max to run faster.

A wave broke on the sand to our right and icy surf washed up over our bare feet. Sunlight glanced off the surface of the sea. Max, barking madly, shot into another loop-de-loop.

"This is great," Rafi said, at my side.

"It's perfect," Natasha yelled. "Perfect!"

ends

We hope that you enjoyed this book. If you found it in any way interesting, powerful and helpful please consider leaving a review in your preferred book-related site. It helps readers find the book and helps us help more people.
Thanks! Patrick and Richard.